PUSHING THROUGH THE CRACKS

CW01629336

Trigger warning:

This publication contains reference to subjects that some readers may find distressing including: self-harm, suicidal thoughts, alcoholism, gambling, anxiety, depression, OCD and eating disorders. Reader discretion is advised.

Copyright © 2021 Emily J. Johnson

All rights reserved

This is a work of creative nonfiction. The events are portrayed to the best of the author's memory. While all the stories in this book are true, some names and identifying details have been changed to protect the privacy of the people involved.

Cover design: Clare Baggaley

ISBN (ebook): 9781739834708

ISBN (paperback): 9781739834715

No part of this book may be reproduced in any form or by any electronic or mechanical means, including information storage and retrieval systems, without written permission from the author, except for the use of brief quotations in a book review.

Created with Vellum

PUSHING THROUGH THE CRACKS

EMILY J. JOHNSON

For my husband & sons... You have taught me things about myself I couldn't have learned without being a part of your difficult journeys. May you each find your own dandelion.

PROLOGUE

Four years ago, my world was rather ordinary by most people's standards. I was happily married to my second husband and my two sons were settled and enjoying a new, more stable life after much upheaval from moving schools, homes, countries – and a divorce.

Our newly blended family of six – including four teenage sons – shared weekends together in an average suburban house and life seemed, for the most part, happy. It was filled with love, laughter and it was emotionally rewarding. But then the rumblings of addiction and mental illness that had subtly threatened us in the past, slowly crept in, permeating all our lives.

Crushed by the weight of caring for my two teenage sons, both struggling with mental-health disorders, and my alcoholic husband, nearly destroyed me. I still had all the usual pressures of working, shopping, cooking, and cleaning, but in between, I was up all night dealing with one son's endless compulsions caused by his severe obsessive-compulsive disorder; mopping up the aftermath of my husband's drinking relapses and devastating self-harm; all whilst trying to protect my other son from his gambling addiction.

The responsibility I felt to heal them, protect them, and deal with every aspect of their constant fragility made me want to run away from all of them, to escape. But I couldn't allow myself to leave; I was tethered to these men by invisible emotional restraints. I'd bound myself in them, in a warped attempt to feel worthy, to feel loved.

I found refuge in stolen moments of writing. My journal was my escape, my release; a way of leaving my pain somewhere else, to give me space to carry on. It gave me hope, until even that was taken from me.

The Covid pandemic was the worst public-health crisis the world had experienced in just over a century. For more than twelve months, people were isolated from their families and friends for weeks at a time, unable to see or embrace them, or share social gatherings. The physical disconnection many experienced was very damaging, and the effects far-reaching. The day-to-day glue that bound humanity together became unstuck.

Although these measures were necessary at the time, they have undoubtedly resulted in a whole range of mental-health consequences, including anxiety, depression, and substantial fear of an uncertain future for our world, especially for young people. We are yet to see the full extent of the pandemic's effects on world mental health, but what is clear to me, right now, is the impact it had on my family. It turned my world, and everyone else's, upside down ... yet in some ways, it was as much a blessing as it was a curse.

My sons, husband and I have lived through addiction, mental illness, separation, isolation, despair, and neglect by the mental-healthcare system.

We are still weathering a mental-health storm, but we are surviving.

This is our story.

DANDELION

MAY 2021

"No... No... *No, I cannot take any more of this!*" I roared.

Anger, frustration and desperation bubble up in my chest, overwhelming me; threatening to suffocate me.

I am finally broken. It has taken me four excruciatingly difficult years of propping up three other human beings to reach my snapping point.

My husband, Paul, relapsed yesterday, spiralling back into self-harm with drink, prescription pills and a razor blade, from his place of isolation and deep depression. My son Jack's obsessive-compulsive disorder has gone into overdrive over me touching raw meat and *'it'* has had the audacity to forbid me from entering my own room, suggesting I sleep on the kitchen floor to prevent the outbreak of deadly food poisoning. (An imaginary risk of course, but OCD is a cunning parasite squatting in my son's mind, and it's very convincing.)

I grab my keys from the little hook in the hallway and run outside to the sanctuary of the communal lane, slamming the door behind me with enough gusto to rattle the entire block of flats.

Bursting into hot, angry tears, I run, sobbing, as far up the lane as my legs will carry me, oblivious to whomever may be watching. I am way past caring. *"Fuck you all, and your struggles!"* I cry.

But no one is listening.

At the back of our communal lane is a strip of no man's land that the neighbouring flats sit adjacent to. The back of a large building sits on the other side, so no one overlooks it, making it the perfect dumping ground for discarded mattresses or fridges, left there to disintegrate.

It is also the perfect place for me to collapse on the ground; to sob unseen, defeated and broken.

Mental illness is invisible in many ways, especially to the outside world. People outside immediate family and friends can't see it, especially if, like me, you hide it. Yet it is the biggest and ugliest of unseen beasts at times and it has permeated our home, filling every inch of our place with its heavy, sombre presence. None of us invited it in, but it didn't care to wait for an invitation. It has shamed me into hiding away, covering its tracks, and making excuses for it, carefully treading on thousands of eggshells around it each day. I hate it, resent it, in fact, and I despise what it has done to my whole family. But for now, the beast I am running from cannot find me here, I am safe from its relentless taunting.

It is the end of May 2021, a warm, sunny Sunday afternoon, and the first holiday weekend since the third lockdown has eased. People have flocked to the seaside for their staycations. I can hear life all around me: people laughing in nearby flats, cooking BBQs in the warm sunshine; traffic bustling past and the faint hum of jet skis at the beach nearby. I despise their normality. The last thing I want to hear right now is people enjoying their lives whilst mine lies shattered in pieces.

I pick up my phone and call a crisis support line – twice – but it rings out both times. I desperately want someone to listen to me, to ease my pain; to hear my stories of Jack taking a knife to his throat during lockdown, and of his overwhelming OCD compulsions that are consuming both of our lives around the clock; to listen to my tales of Paul's self-harm, his depression and alcohol relapses and of Thomas' gambling and depression.

I long for someone to verbally soothe me.

What I really want, though, is a stranger on the phone to tell me it is okay to run away, even just for one night; something I seem unable to permit myself to do. But nobody is on the end of this phone. No one is listening.

Their absence sparks a flicker of fire in my belly. In all honesty, I've finally gone beyond the point of asking for anything.

Why the hell do I need to ask anyone's permission to start living? This is my life, and it is about time I claimed it back.

I search my phone frantically for a local hotel room to escape to, but I can only find one room in the entire town. Everywhere is completely sold out, apart from one extortionate penthouse suite and there is no way my budget can stretch that far. Finally, after twelve long months, I've actually summoned the gumption to escape and there is not a single place left to run away to.

I throw my phone across the path in frustration and pick up a small stone, scraping at the concrete, angrily scratching crisscross patterns across it. Something catches my eye: a beautiful yellow dandelion is growing through a crack in the concrete. Its golden yellow petals cut through the greyness of the broken path, and it overshadows the filth and discarded cigarette butts around it. It may be just a weed, but I see it in all its beauty. In this moment, it is the most beautiful living thing I have ever seen. Despite its surroundings, it has found its way to push up through that crack, to have life. It is not complaining or giving up; it's surviving, and it will go on to finish flowering. One day soon, the wind will carry its dainty seeds somewhere else to carry on the cycle of its life.

Just like that dandelion, I have pushed through adversity and survived. The only difference is I have fought it the whole way, kicking and screaming and complaining, constantly trying to control outcomes when all that was needed was to grow with life, not fight against it.

I close my eyes and raise my face to the sunshine, bathing in its gentle warmth. I find myself smiling. Even in the midst of all this chaos, this darkness, there is warmth and light.

There is hope.

SUNSHINE

I WAS BORN in London in the 1970s and grew up in a happy, average family. My mother, born in Northern Ireland, had moved to England in the late 1960s after marrying my father. We led an unremarkable life in a terrace house in Teddington, long before the suburb became fashionable. My father worked away a lot of the time, so my mother took on the role of both parents, caring for me and my older brother.

As a little girl, I loved my own company and would spend hours in the garden brewing make-believe perfumes out of flower petals and water. My nickname was Sunshine, so named by my mother because apparently I was always smiling.

I was a happy-go-lucky kid, quite the chatterbox – I had 'the gift of the gab' as my mother would often tell me – but rarely got into any trouble, and that carried right through into my teens. I'd spend all my time barefoot, wearing homemade crowns of daisies in my long, golden curls. It drove my mother to distraction, and she was always scolding me: *"Jesus, Mary and Joseph, Emily, would you put some shoes on? You'll catch your death of cold."*

I carried a pocket-sized sketch pad everywhere and would spend hours meticulously drawing with a fine ink pen; I drew shells, flowers and other objects I would find during my garden adventures. My mother always maintained I was born in the wrong decade and should have been a free-loving, flower-in-the-hair, hippie, living in a 1970s commune. (It's an ideal that has always appealed to me, much to my family's dismay.)

Our family moved to England's south coast when I was ten, and I settled into my new life and school, though I was painfully shy in my new environment. My parents divorced when I was eleven, and I was sent away for six weeks to stay with my family in Ireland whilst my parents sold our home. It was a strange and unsettling time – lots of hushed family conversations and quiet tears from my mother. My parents had been married for twenty-three years. It was a significant upheaval for us all.

After my return from Ireland, we moved into a new house, and I lived with my mother and brother. Within a couple of years, my mother remarried, and to begin with, she seemed happy. Life was a little more settled for us all, but my new stepfather's external charm soon wore off to reveal a gambler with an explosive temper.

My father emigrated to Australia shortly after. I think my father may have been running away from his own pain and disappointment at the time. He still loved my mother dearly, but in reality, he was also running to the other side of the world and leaving his two teenage children behind.

In the mid-1980s, we had no internet, no mobile phones or video-calling. My only means of contacting my already emotionally distant father was to call him from the home phone, which was very expensive, or send him an airmail letter. I rarely did either. Australia was a long way away, and he may as well have moved to the moon for the amount of contact we had.

Just after my seventeenth birthday, I moved in with John, my first boyfriend. My grandparent's health had deteriorated, so my mother moved back home to Ireland with my stepfather to care for them. She wanted me to go with her, but I was young and head-over-heels in love with John and had no intention of moving away.

Instead, I moved in with my brother and John, jumping feet first into the role of a young housewife. I found myself alone in England, and I clung on to John for dear life, fulfilling his every need. I enjoyed looking after him and other people; mothering them, feeding them up. It gave me pleasure to please people and I never really questioned it or the reasons why I did it. I simply adjusted to my new role and habits formed then were to last many years.

My aspirations of attending art college disintegrated and I shelved my dreams, swapping them for the conformity of a secure but frightening government job and a suffocating domestic life. I withdrew from my friends completely and my life centred entirely around John, and his hobbies and friends.

At the age of twenty-two, my father, who had been living in Australia for several years at that point, gifted me a plane ticket to visit him. We had become even more estranged through time and distance, but Australia seemed exotic and enticing, and I accepted the offer willingly. It had been several years since I'd seen him and, he felt like a stranger. I hoped the trip would allow me to get to know my father once again.

John and I spent three wonderful sun-filled weeks in Australia and became intrigued by the different way of life the country offered. We married the following year and decided to give it a go there. I was twenty-three and my whole life ahead of me. That new life was on the sun-drenched shores of Western Australia.

I was twenty-eight and overjoyed when I fell pregnant with Thomas. I was living in Australia at the time with my first husband, John. I had followed my father there in 1995, just over a decade after he had emigrated, following his divorce from my mother. It was my second pregnancy, as my first ended suddenly with a miscarriage at eleven weeks. That loss was my first real experience with grief, made more painful because my body would not let go of the little human life that didn't make it. I went into hospital for my baby to be taken away and when I awoke from surgery, the realisation of my loss hit me abruptly. I'd been placed at the very end of the maternity ward in a room alone. I lay crying for my lost baby, forced to listen to the sounds of newborns crying at the other end of the corridor.

Although I'd been anxious during the first three months, when I got past the twelve-week stage, I started to relax, determined to enjoy the remainder of a trouble-free pregnancy. But when I was eight months' pregnant, my father was diagnosed with kidney cancer. He was convinced it was caused by his fondness for beer, though the consultant dismissed that idea and deemed it treatable. My father underwent surgery to remove his kidney and I returned to enjoying the last couple of weeks of pregnancy, optimistic for the future with my new baby and my father's recovery.

The hospital induced me at a full fifteen days' overdue. I remember the midwife commenting that my baby would need to be dragged into this world. Thomas was more than happy where he was and had no notion of arriving of his own accord. Despite having a long and complex delivery that kept me hospitalised for almost a week, Thomas was born the most placid, peaceful baby any new parent could hope for, with a mop of dark-brown wispy curls and huge dark eyes.

The day I brought Thomas home from hospital was bittersweet. In fact, that day turned my entire world upside down. My father came round to visit us. He held his grandson for the first time and began to weep. Whilst I had been in hospital, tests had revealed his cancer had already spread, undetected, prior to his kidney surgery. My father's cancer was terminal. What should have been a wonderful and exciting homecoming with a new baby, soon turned into a day of devastation and disbelief.

My father's illness overshadowed many of Thomas' milestones. In fact, the first two years of Thomas' life were spent accompanying me to my father's hospital appointments, caring for him when he became bed-bound, and finally visiting him in a hospice. I would sit Thomas in his pushchair in front of the TV in the hospice lounge for hours at a time, whilst I spent precious time with my dying father.

Despite my father being in a hospice, I remained in total denial. His impending death was too much for me to face, to comprehend. I was only twenty-nine years old. It could not be real; it could not be happening. My father was finally back in my life after a lifetime of absenteeism and now cancer was going to steal him away from me. The reality was too painful, so I locked it away tightly in a little box of denial and threw away the key.

Despite further surgery and radiotherapy, it was too late to slow the spread of the disease. The cancer spread to my father's spine, slowly paralysing him, then finally to his brain. It was a long and painful death. Thomas was just twenty-two months old when my father passed away. He died unexpectedly in the middle of the night, denying me the opportunity of saying goodbye. He was fifty-nine years old.

Unlike my pregnancy with Thomas, during Jack's, I was fraught with worry the entire time. Jack was an assisted-fertility baby. Complications from Thomas' birth had left me unable to conceive naturally and it had been a long and difficult journey to conceive another baby. My days consisted of daily progesterone injections into my stomach to help sustain the pregnancy, and hospital appointments every two days for blood tests to monitor my hormones.

In 2004, at seventeen weeks pregnant, I started to bleed heavily. My placenta was struggling to sustain the pregnancy, and miscarriage was a real risk. My consultant was gentle but realistic, and not overly optimistic that my baby would survive. He sent me home to get complete bed rest for two weeks. That's no mean feat when you have an active toddler and no immediate family to help out, but we muddled through. After resting as much as

Thomas would allow me to, miraculously, the bleeding subsided.

A subsequent scan showed the baby was still growing, and the placenta had stabilised. The blood tests continued three times a week, with weekly scans and trips to the fertility clinic for reassurance. It was a fraught time, filled with uncertainty and sorrow from my father's sudden death just a few months earlier.

At thirty weeks pregnant, the bleeding returned. By this stage, the pregnancy was past the critical point, so I knew that if the baby came early, it had a good chance of surviving. Sent home from hospital once more for bed rest, I managed to incubate my baby boy for another four weeks until he arrived unexpectedly at thirty-four weeks.

My waters broke with dramatic force at 5.30am one morning. Due to Jack's breech position, an emergency caesarean was hastily scrambled. I was relieved to see the familiar kind eyes of my fertility consultant peeking from behind his mask and scrubs. Apparently, he had heard I was in labour and wanted to deliver this baby himself. He had been an important part of my quest to have Jack, and it was only fitting that he was there to bring this bundle of marvellous creation safely into the world.

Jack was born at 8.36am the same morning; a scrawny 5lb with the frame of a fragile bird and a delicate dusting of fine, dark hair. He may have been premature, but even then, Jack's will to survive was strong. After a brief few hours in an incubator, he was back in my arms.

It still makes me smile that Jack defied all the odds to even be here on this Earth, despite his decidedly shaky start to life. He had jumped into the world feet first and just under six weeks early in perfect health, albeit a little small.

Jack truly was my miracle baby.

THE GUILT MONSTER

"ONCE YOU'RE married or a mother, you'll always feel guilty about something," my mother informed me once, with a sharp Irish tongue that hinted of her own painful experiences.

I felt guilty for leaving my mother and only brother behind to pursue my new life in Australia in 1995. They were both heartbroken. Australia was a long, long way away from England and it took considerable time for them both to adjust to life without me.

Those feelings of guilt from leaving my family lay dormant, undetected, while I had the distractions of my new home, work, and life in a foreign land. But as time went on, after I'd given birth to my first son, Thomas, they reawakened. The Guilt Monster was born whilst I was juggling my dying father's needs and those of my young child, my husband, and my role as a part-time worker in a respected government position. It didn't matter which house I lived in, or which continent for that matter, the Guilt Monster would find me and permeate my head, filling it with nonsense:

"Look what you did Emily.
It's all your fault.
You're a bad mother.
You're a bad daughter.
You're a bad wife.
This is all your fault."

I've cohabited with the Guilt Monster for about twenty-five years now. It's an unwelcome partner that has reared its head to taunt me mercilessly at some of my most vulnerable moments.

It's been a very one-sided relationship. It takes, takes, takes and I've sat listening to it many a time, accepting its verbal abuse and punishment. And I give, give, give, believing its criticism and fuelling its fire in doing so. It's been really rather convincing at times.

I cannot recall my father being around that much in my childhood. I have a vivid recollection of my past, yet no matter how much I search, I still can't recall many memories of him.

My father worked overseas for weeks at a time, and I have vague recollections of my mother buying my brother and me a world map. We plotted his location with pins in far-flung places on the map, counting down the days until he returned.

The trouble is, I cannot really remember his homecomings either, other than him bringing me back a stuffed lion from a trip to South Africa. I was around seven at the time. I was old enough to be able to remember a lot more about him, but sadly that only goes to demonstrate his absence in my childhood. Even when he was home for brief spells, he would often withdraw into his work at home, or a nearby bar.

I've no doubt my father loved my brother and me deeply, and was immensely proud of us both, but he didn't really know how to be a father or show affection. It was always very awkward and a little staged. He just never seemed particularly comfortable with that role. It's fair to say that I lacked a healthy connection with my father as a child and as a result probably developed what one would call 'attachment issues'.

As soon as I entered the world of dating, marrying or birthing males, I needed to know that I was loved by them all. I was worried that they might leave me, so I overcompensated by giving them all I had to offer to ensure they stayed. I needed constant reminders of their love and that neediness would push men away, leaving me in the very place I was trying to avoid – alone.

When I emigrated to Australia, I had to get to know my father all over again, from scratch: his likes, dislikes and his quirks. My father had lived alone for well over a decade, but he had been alone in his own head for a lot longer, so he found it difficult at times sharing his life with a grown-up daughter he barely knew.

But my father had a kindness in his eyes that said everything he had been unable to say for years. I felt his love and admiration for the woman I'd grown into. Behind the kindness, there was regret too. I caught that sadness in his eyes many times. We never spoke of our past. We were never able to bring it all out in the open to be healed. Something sat stuck between us like a giant elephant in the room.

I could not call him Dad or call him anything in fact. It was as if the word 'Dad' were stuck at the back of my throat,

I simply couldn't form the sounds. It stung, him, more than me. I could write it in a birthday card, but never verbalise the word to him or ever address him in any way, so I didn't, and he remained nameless to me.

How was it possible that warm, caring, chatterbox Emily could not say one simple word, a word whose absence caused my own father obvious pain and deep rejection? I cannot explain it, neither can I resolve it now and make peace with my father for my apparent mountain-sized emotional block. All I do know is, I never once uttered the word 'Dad' to my father, not even on his final day on this Earth and that big old bag of regret sat with me for an exceptionally long time.

As a child, if I were sad or unwell, my mother would often bring me hot buttery toast in bed, or other culinary delights, so it's hardly surprising that I have grown to see food both as a symbol of comfort and love for most of my adult life. My mother was a fantastic baker, so my childhood was filled with homemade bread, cakes and rice puddings. Golden Haystacks were my favourite: a deliciously sticky concoction of cornflakes and so much golden syrup, my teeth would stick together. They are warm, very comforting memories of my mother's love, and it is a habit I unconsciously carried on with my own children.

After my father's sudden death, I buried myself in the role of the quintessential mother.

Home-baked sweet treats would be waiting for my children when they returned from school each day. I was being the best version of a mother I could be, but I did not consciously try; I was simply emulating my mother's behaviour. I was following a strong female role model who'd unknowingly shaped both my beliefs and behaviour.

My mother spent a lifetime in servitude to others and she seemed to take great pride in that role. She cared for my father, my brother and me with every fibre of her soul. I cannot remember her ever doing anything for herself, not once. She never went out with friends or bought herself new clothes or took holidays. Of course, I wasn't aware of it at the time, but perhaps that's another reason I threw myself to the bottom of the priority pile in life – I didn't know any better.

After her divorce from my father, my mother continued in that role of service by looking after her new husband's every need, despite his poor behaviour and gambling habit. And then she returned to Ireland to care for her elderly parents. For twenty years, until their deaths, she catered to their every need with little help – she sacrificed her life entirely. She suffered two strokes with the strain, but she refused to have it any other way. They were her parents, and this was her duty, and she was fiercely protective of that role.

Throwing myself into projects to distract myself from the grief of my father's death, I volunteered at my son's school and hosted kids' parties, branching into small charity events and catering for John's football team every weekend throughout the season.

For two years, I spent my entire weekend preparing homemade feasts for over forty people and enjoying every single minute of it, almost as much as the football team enjoyed devouring my home-cooked spreads. I was feeding people and I revelled in their contentment. I loved to make them happy and found that food was the perfect route to pleasing them. Somewhere inside was a lost little girl, a version of me who craved her father's attention and love, and I found that love through pleasing others.

SHAKING THE FOUNDATIONS

2010

THOMAS AND JACK had been happy, active young boys growing up in Australia. They'd enjoyed a wonderful outdoor life with lots of friends, and the children seemed secure and settled in their environment. Our home was constantly filled with neighbours' children and school friends swimming in the backyard pool and I adored the hustle, bustle and energy a houseful of exuberant children brought with them.

John and I were the epitome of domestic bliss to the outside world, but behind the façade, it wasn't so happy. I felt disconnected from John. He was my husband, the father of my two sons and a wonderful provider for our family, but I felt a little numb about him and I didn't understand why.

I'd never known anything outside of a life as John's sidekick and was content for most of the time to tick on in my pleasant but mundane life. Whatever John said, I believed and whatever John wanted, I went along with. I was a passive partner and I accepted that role. I continued for five years this way; going through the necessary motions every day, with a forced smile on my face.

Eventually, my unresolved grief over my father's death gave way to what I now recognise as depression. After much persuasion, John reluctantly agreed with my pleas to pack up our life in Australia and relocate back to the UK to be nearer our families. I thought that was the answer and that back at home, nearer my family, I would feel more alive.

Things happened very quickly; the house sold the first weekend it was listed, and we were back living in the UK within six months. The boys were six and nine at the time.

In July 2010, we bought a cottage in the English countryside and settled the children into a local school. I found part-time work at a popular restaurant within days and enjoyed being around the upbeat energy of the youthful team I worked with.

I should have been happy. After all, we had moved countries, just as I had wanted, and bought a beautiful home in an idyllic village location. Once again, I was surrounded by everything I needed materialistically, but life was no rosier in England. The same emptiness filled me, and I continued to go through my days a little indifferent and emotionally distanced, only this time in a different country.

My shifts spent working with the young staff in the restaurant were filled with raucous innuendo and much laughter. Their fun and slightly risqué humour made me feel alive and I enjoyed flirting with life for the first time ever.

Some of the staff had planned to go out for drinks after our shift one night. They invited me and I jumped at the chance. I mentioned it to John, and he asked to join us, but I gently declined, wanting to keep this little escape from the mundane just for myself. John was visibly hurt by my rejection and that simple incident poked at the green-eyed monster that had been surfacing from time to time over my newfound enthusiasm for my young work colleagues.

I snuck out my best dress and some new heels, and after a swift change in the staff toilets, I joined the others at a local bar, feeling confident and feminine. I felt like a woman; not a frumpy mother or housewife, just Emily, and that was something I'd not felt in years. Maybe not ever.

Once home, I silently slipped into bed in the darkness. John was still awake; I could sense it. He had waited up for my return, sulking. I fell asleep without acknowledging him. I couldn't face the Spanish Inquisition at 12.30am.

The next morning, John was moody and sullen, and sat on the edge of the bed with his back towards me. I could sense the tension and wanted him to speak, to break the ice, so I tiptoed around him coyly, trying to coax him out of his sulk.

"Are you having an affair?" he blurted out.

"*What?!* What are you talking about? Me? No, of course not, John. Why would you even say that?" I countered indignantly.

I had never even looked at another man, let alone flirted with one or even considered straying. John was the only man I had ever known, both emotionally and sexually. Other men were just not on my radar. They never had been.

I had an Irish Catholic upbringing. We never spoke about boyfriends or sex. So, like so many young girls of my era, before the age of the internet, I gleaned my sexual enlightenment from the pages of women's magazines. Even so, I didn't really understand sexual intimacy and never thought that men or sex was something that I could enjoy, or benefit from.

John turned to face me. "No, no, I know, Emily. I am sorry. I should never have said that. I just hate it when you go out." He spoke softly, hanging his head. He leant over the bed and reached for my hand, but I pulled it away.

And that was that; the switch had been flicked off. In that very moment, something that had been festering subconsciously for a long time – years probably – came to a head.

"I don't know how I feel anymore, John ... about us," I blurted out of nowhere.

The words hung in the room between us, heavy and unexpected. They were probably the hardest words I'd ever uttered. And probably the most bewildering. John stared at me, his dark eyes filled with desperation and pain.

We tried hard for three weeks to act normally, as if nothing had been said, but for me, all feelings were gone. I couldn't feel anything – just numb.

We sought counsel from our families who were devastated. My mother questioned if I'd been having an affair, as if this were the only plausible reason for our marriage apparently imploding, suddenly and without warning. She suggested we seek counselling, but I never even tried. I knew that deep down, nobody could counsel romantic love back into my heart.

A week later John packed a bag and left to stay with a friend, utterly heartbroken. He didn't tell me where he was going, or make any contact, leaving me to lie to the boys about him working away.

The following six months were extremely painful for us both. We cried rivers, together at times, grieving for the end of our marriage, as if we had lost someone very dear. We not only grieved the present version of us, but the future us too. The dream of watching our boys grow up, welcoming our grandchildren and spending the rest of our lives together; all those dreams died along with the marriage, and we mourned them too.

Our separation, although unexpected, was amicable, but the effect on the children was heartbreaking. It's hard enough to process your own feelings during separation and divorce, but it was harder still to witness our sons' confusion and sadness at their safe little world being blown apart. They were still young and couldn't understand why we didn't love each other enough to live together anymore.

No one was at fault really. We had been together for twenty-three years, from the young ages of fifteen and seventeen. We had grown up together. But we had also grown apart during that time.

Once the children were born, we became immersed in our roles as a mother and father, roles we both relished and willingly poured every ounce of energy into, to the detriment of our marriage. We lost ourselves in our little family. We never went out on dates or spent any time alone throughout ten years of parenting our sons, so we forgot what drew us together and bound us as a couple in the first place.

After our sons were born, my focus shifted entirely to nurturing them and John was swiftly pushed to the back of the family pecking order, with me and any scraps of a sex life firmly behind him. My body was not for pleasure; well, not my pleasure at least. It was for procreation, and it had served its purpose twice, with much pain and difficulty.

I still loved John dearly, but over the years that love became more platonic; it was not the way a wife should love her husband. Cracks had formed in our relationship without either of us noticing, and they gradually grew into caverns, until all we had left in common were two children.

With the benefit of hindsight and after all that has happened since, would I have stayed in that marriage to spare my children's subsequent pain and suffering? Perhaps, but it would have been at my own personal cost. I was not flourishing in the marriage anymore. I'd lost all my fire, my drive for life and sacrificed myself entirely to the role of devoted wife and mother.

I know many women do stay in their empty marriages. Two of them approached me after my separation, curious as to how my newly single life was unfolding. Both women confessed to feeling trapped in long, loveless marriages but were too scared of what lay beyond the safe and familiar to attempt to leave. The loss of financial security, their children's happiness, and loneliness were the things they both feared. Both women still remain in their financially comfortable, but unfulfilling marriages despite their children being adults now. Loneliness is a much-feared place, though you can feel equally alone whilst lying next to the wrong person.

I remained in the cottage with my sons, and we got on with life. The boys adjusted to seeing their father every weekend and once during the week. The children settled into life in England and our home became filled once more with noisy children, chaos and after-school playdates.

I'd never been alone, ever, so I found myself looking forward to little gaps in time where I could do whatever I pleased without being accountable to anyone. To begin with, it was wonderful, though over time, the novelty wore off.

In time, John moved on and met Sarah, a woman ten years my junior. Despite not wanting to be married to him anymore, I still found it painful. We had been separated for two years but the announcement of their new relationship brought all the recently settled pain up to the surface once more, rather like a pond being disturbed. John asked me for a divorce. I had been replaced by another woman and it stung.

When John announced Sarah was pregnant, I smiled and hugged him warmly. I was genuinely happy he had found someone to give him something I was unable to. John had always wanted more children, but my fertility struggles and Jack's stressful pregnancy had ended that notion entirely. I refused to go through pregnancy again. In fact, I felt so strongly about it, I booked my own sterilisation after John refused to have a vasectomy.

The same fertility consultant performed the procedure. He had patched me up from the birth of my first son, helped me conceive the second, delivered him and repaired the subsequent damage and now he was ensuring it would never, ever happen again. How is that for a holistic service? I am sure he was just as glad to see the back of me and my gynaecology as I was.

A few months later, John needed somewhere more permanent to live, having been staying in temporary accommodation. John moved back into our family home with Sarah, who was by then heavily pregnant, and I rented a lovely furnished flat not far from the beach for me and the boys.

A couple of months later, my sons welcomed their new baby brother with open arms, despite the significant upheaval in the family dynamics. However, things weren't quite so settled as I believed them to be.

Sarah had taken my place in what had been our family home. A new baby had taken my sons' place in their father's life. What was our furniture, became hers, and she took control over the family lounge we used to sit in. There were no more cartoons for the boys to watch after school or friends over to play. She claimed ownership of the remote control, the television, and the lounge, along with everything else in the home.

Jack's bedroom became hers because it was the biggest and she wanted it. Thomas' bedroom became the new baby's, meaning my boys were forced into sharing a small spare room. Everything had been turned upside down once again, and these changes played a significant part in both boys' new model of instability.

DIVORCED, LOST ... AND FOUND

2011-2013

FOLLOWING MY DIVORCE FROM JOHN, I slid slowly back into depression. I'd been with the same man since I was fifteen years old, and when my marriage ended, I found myself alone at thirty-eight, inexperienced at independent life and unsure who this woman was. Suddenly I had time to myself and weekends alone – it was unfamiliar ground for me and I wasn't sure how to fill that time.

I'd launched into a partnered life at seventeen years old, and from then on, rarely ventured anywhere on my own. When I separated from John, I'd only been to a nightclub once, but never drunk a drop of alcohol or partied with my girlfriends. I'd led a quiet life. After the divorce, when my children stayed with John, I did some foolish, out-of-character things.

Like a bird being freed from her gilded cage for the first time, I was eager to experience all the things I'd never done, including visiting pubs and nightclubs and staying out until 5am dancing – often alone and always sober. It was a confusing and lonely time. I wanted the excitement and thrills after a very secluded life, but it never really felt like me doing those things. It was as if I was an observer, watching someone else dabble in new and risky experiences from afar. I am not sure I really enjoyed half of it, and most nights would end up with me back at home, staring at the four walls, crying, wondering why I'd left the security of marriage for that emptiness.

I'd just relocated back to my hometown after fifteen years away, and my old school friendships had scattered many years before. As with most separations, our friends distanced themselves from me for fear of being seen to take sides. Ours was a very amicable situation, but separation can often shake your longest friendships, and so it left me with very few friends.

I'd often get dressed up and sit in a busy pub alone, watching people mingle. I'd observe friends laughing and smoking together with carefree boozy abandon, enjoying life. I wanted that but didn't know how to get it. It sounds strange, but I didn't know how to drink, had never smoked, and had no idea how to socialise as a single woman. I sat watching, wishing it were me being flattered by a man, or giggling with a group of girlfriends.

Sometimes I'd sit in restaurants alone and eat, as if somehow stamping my foot in a show of independence. I'd watch couples dining together and wonder what it would feel like for someone to look at me like that across a table, to hold my hand. I wanted to feel love again instead of feeling alone. I foolishly thought that someone else could give me that feeling of completeness, that my happiness depended on a new man. But I was naïve – the only new love I needed in my life back then was self-love and I was not about to find that in a pub or nightclub.

I eventually made new friends through my son's school and went on my first overseas holiday with girlfriends at the age of thirty-nine, still feeling like an outsider – the sensible, boring one. Whilst they sipped cocktails, giggling, I sipped orange juice and tried my best to fit in.

For some excitement, I secretly crept into the unfamiliar world of dating, wanting to be noticed by someone … anyone. I didn't feel good about myself, so I sought flattery from men, which is such a damaging thing to do. After all, dancing alone, smiling innocently at those around me in a nightclub was like waving the *'I'm available'* flag. In my naïvety, I thought it was harmless fun, but when I refused to join them in bed, they would throw a few choice words at me for being a tease, and I'd head home alone and confused at this new version of adult life I'd found myself in.

I reluctantly tried alcohol for the first time aged thirty-nine in a vain attempt to fit in. Partying, alcohol and emotionally unavailable men became a cocktail of disastrous elements for someone with low self-esteem and no clear direction in life.

On one such night out alone, I bumped into a six-foot giant in a local pub. He seemed different to the others: gentle and softly spoken and he shared the same interests as me. I was still raw and vulnerable from my divorce and seeking that elusive something from a man. He paid me attention and I fell hook, line and sinker for his quiet charm.

Mr Emotionally Unavailable was damaged goods, though, and although he never divulged why, when prodded about his dating history, his eyes would fill with a visible distance. He never married his long-term partner and clearly wasn't over his most recent ex-girlfriend – or rather what she had done to him – so between my low self-esteem and his inability to open up or commit, we were a relationship disaster waiting to happen.

To begin with it was enticing, full of fun and secret

adventures. But the closer I got to him emotionally, the more he panicked and distanced himself. As the months rolled on, he stopped acknowledging me in public and ghosted me regularly, ignoring my texts for hours on end and declining my invitations at the eleventh hour because he was 'busy'. I spent many a Saturday night alone, let down and rejected at the last minute, yet still I'd chase after him, his rejection picking at the scabs of old wounds and stoking my fear of being left yet again.

Mr Unavailable had a disproportionate amount of female friends. His best friend was also a woman who was older than him, not unlike his mother in looks. We danced a strange and painful tango, all three of us, at times. It often felt as though I was the mistress in their twisted marriage, competing for his attention. My only advantage over her was sex.

Mr Unavailable never really told anyone about me; I was his dirty little secret, his plaything when it suited him. Sex is a powerful weapon, especially for a woman with low self-esteem, and I'd wield that weapon regularly in front of him, soon learning it was the only thing that got his attention and kept him coming back to me. Well, that and my showering him with generous gifts and weekends away. I tried to prevent this man from leaving me with the two means I had at the time: money and sex.

If I was privileged enough to be invited out with him in company, I was only ever introduced to other women as a friend, yet he trophied me on his arm to male friends like some sort of sexual prize from a neanderthal hunt. I was guilty of polishing that trophy myself at times; I enjoyed being displayed as his 'catch'. It made me feel attractive and desirable sometimes, but for the most part, his treatment left me feeling hollow and cheap.

He seemed to revel in women's attention, often surrounding himself with them, and I tolerated being invisible, pawning myself in a toxic relationship in silent secrecy for nearly two years. I foolishly believed he was the last man standing, the only one who'd ever want me. Under the misguided belief that men are scarce and no one else would come along, I hung onto this one, despite his abysmal behaviour.

Eventually Mr Unavailable got spooked by my neediness for a 'normal' relationship and bolted into the arms of another woman without so much as a goodbye. It took every ounce of self-restraint to not slide into her DMs and let her know that the man who was probably sharing her bed now had been keeping mine warm just two weeks earlier. Utterly heartbroken, but with my dignity intact, I had no choice but to let him go, but his departure emotionally destroyed me.

If I could go back now, well I'd probably have a few choice words to say to him and the women who draped themselves off him. I'd also have a few words to say to that old version of me. What the hell was I thinking?

But it wasn't all bad. My Mr Emotionally Unavailable taught me a couple of things. He was my very own personal Christian Grey. He gave me a long-overdue sex education and despite our torturous acquaintance, I dusted off the cobwebs of a Catholic upbringing and years of sexual repression through him.

More importantly though, his sudden exit caused those banked-up feelings of grief and rejection over my father's absence, John's departure, and a couple of other short-lived flings who did a runner, to surge up and out with primal force. All the men I had shared my life with in one form or another had upped and left; every single male I had encountered. It cut deeply, and I blamed their departures on my clinginess and unlovableness. All the painful emotions I had stored away in an emotional repository for many years, came flooding out.

Although physically present for my children, I pushed them away during that time, keeping them at arm's length whilst going through the necessary motions. I still did the school run, cooked their dinners, washed their clothes – always with a smile – but I was more than a little emotionally absent.

Jack would chat eagerly to me about his day at school and I'd respond at appropriate intervals with a customary acknowledgment but without really paying attention, or lifting my head from my phone.

Of all people, I should have known better. Children crave their parents' love and attention – I know I did – yet here I was doing the very same thing my father did to me: ignoring my child.

I started to slip into a place of deep depression and was an emotional mess. I cried constantly, but always in secret. After dropping my children at school, I'd go back to the flat, close the curtains and climb back into my bed to wallow in a tearful, black abyss until it was time to get back up again and start my shift.

I searched for help online and stumbled across a man in America who offered a self-healing course that stood out as entirely different. I was on my knees at that point, and unable to shake the overwhelming grief I felt from Mr Unavailable's swift exit. His departure had cruelly ripped open old wounds of abandonment and I felt bereft.

I signed up for the foundation Ptsen-Nuh energy-mapping course with its creator, Steve Gunn. It's difficult to encapsulate the course in a few words – it's something you *do* and its unlike anything else out there. I learnt a set of skills that helped me begin to release my old emotional wounds, giving me freedom from some of the triggers, and therefore more emotional independence. It's incredibly powerful and probably one of the most beneficial skill sets I have ever learned. It changed everything. I was a new woman afterwards, empowered and strong, with a voice at long last. Quite literally, I felt ready to take on the world.

After completing the course in late 2013, I felt a renewed sense of self and independence. I'd found a thirst for life, for adventure. It was what a fire in the belly really feels like – a hot and blazing energy. You feel *alive*, and it makes you jump out of bed in the morning and exclaim, "*Yes!* I want this!" It was a desire, passion and lust for everything I'd never felt before.

I had been toying with taking a trip to India with Mr Unavailable, but he'd been non-committal to most things, not just me. He pulled out of the trip, before swiftly pulling himself out of my life too.

"*Well, fuck him then,*" I thought, and I went ahead and booked a two-week trip to India alone to learn Yoga. The country had fascinated me for years, but I never thought I'd get the chance to go, let alone on my own.

Before this solo adventure, not even my closest family knew I was travelling alone. I told everyone I was going with a guided tour group, but I wanted no such restrictions. I was seeking solace in my solitude and craved the space to lick my wounds from my divorce and the abrupt ending of my secret affair with Mr Unavailable. The secrecy was freeing and prevented my mother from talking me out of the trip, which she most certainly would have done, had she known the truth.

I flew to Delhi in early December and then took a long train trip to Haridwar in northern India before making my way to Rishikesh, a little town nestled in the foothills of the Himalayas. The Beatles had made the town famous in the late 1960s and it was now the unofficial capital of Yoga in India; a mecca for pilgrims, tourists, wannabe Yoga teachers and women just like me – women on a journey of self-discovery.

It may be a cliché: woman runs away to India to learn Yoga and find herself, but believe me, there is something utterly beguiling about India. I'm not ashamed to say I became that cliché to a tee. I learned about Yoga, but more importantly I learned about me.

It was terrifying travelling alone in India. It's really not a country for the faint-hearted, but it was exhilarating and liberating too. For the first time in many, many years, I was just Emily – no one's mother and no one's wife. I didn't have to consider anyone else or cater to anyone's needs but my own. It was the first real time I'd tasted complete and unadulterated freedom in my entire life.

Sure, I had my weekends when the children were with John, but they were often wasted sitting in bars alone feeling sorry for myself or in dalliances with the wrong kind of man.

This was different. I could buy anything I wanted, and no one was counting my pennies or scrutinising my purchases. I could eat anything and everything, whenever I wanted. I could wear my colourful clothes or flowers in my hair, and no one would tease me for my appearance. I could rise at the crack of dawn and practice Yoga or sleep until lunchtime, and no one would care.

I found myself taking a ride on the back of local's motorbike, riding pillion without a helmet. I hung on to his waist for dear life, my long unkempt hair flowing behind me, tangling with my colourful scarf as we dodged all manner of monkeys, cows, pigs, rickshaws, and locals on the winding foothill roads. I'd never been so reckless in fortysomething years. I'd never been so free either. There were no rules, no restrictions. My goodness, I felt *alive!*

One early morning, around 7.30am, I had taken a trek into the foothills and stopped for some respite from the steep climb. Sitting by the edge of some farmland, vibrant green ginger fields fell away beneath me. I watched as the sun rose over the hills and bathed the horizon in a wintry, lemon glow. The chilly overnight temperatures birthed a morning mist that sat across the hilltops and hid the snowy peaks in the distance.

There was not a soul around. The world was silent. Sitting on the edge of the gravel road, I wept quietly. If there is a god, then that is the closest I have ever felt to their presence in every living thing around me. I have never seen such beauty nor felt more at peace, in utter awe of nature.

I'd found peace within too, at long last. I finally loved and accepted that woman whose reflection I saw in the mirror later – she was beautiful and smart. She was fearless and strong, unapologetically so and would *never* compromise herself for a man again.

BLENDING FAMILIES

2014

I MET Paul on a dating site in early January. He was a breath of fresh air after my divorce from John almost three years earlier and the stint of dating disasters that followed. We clicked quickly and shared many things in common.

Paul had lost both his parents within three years of each other by the age of thirty, and it was clear from our long chats that their deaths had a profound effect on him. It seemed he'd never allowed himself to grieve properly for either of them. At the time of their deaths, he'd been married to his first wife and was a new father, so life was hectic and he'd pushed his grieving aside.

Paul was very caring and thoughtful; an old romantic too. After a long day at work, I'd return to my flat and he would have a bath ready for me, petals floating on top and candles everywhere. Dinner would be in the oven, waiting. I lapped up his attention; he made me feel loved and cared for. Paul never criticised me or dismissed me. He was always on time and he never let me down.

We had remarkably similar beliefs and shared a love of

music and would talk for hours, reminiscing and playing old records. Paul was a musician and had spent years fronting a band in his younger years, along with writing songs and playing the guitar. He reminded me of my father in many ways. Paul was easy to love, and I fell for him quickly. We only saw each other a couple of times a week at that stage. It took me a long time to introduce my sons to the idea that mum had a boyfriend, let alone one that might stay over.

After dating for ten months, we decided to rent a place together as we were both paying separate rents and between us, paying a small fortune. Paul's two sons, who were a similar age to mine, joined us at weekends.

My sons embraced Paul and his boys, and our relationship appeared to give them some stability after several years of constant change. I didn't think it was possible to fall in love with someone else's children the way I fell in love with Paul's sons, but I did, and I loved them as much as my own two sons.

Life was wonderful, to begin with. All our boys were together on weekends, playing and having fun, and we rattled about in a beautiful old Victorian house in a noisy boy-filled chaos. We were deeply in love and incredibly happy.

After twelve months, Paul asked me to marry him. I never *ever* envisaged marrying again after my divorce from John, but it somehow felt right. Over the following year, we enjoyed some wonderful times together with all the children, with family dinners, movie nights and short holidays, but it was not always a bed of roses, especially as the boys entered their teenage years.

Blended families are a challenge at the best of times. Throw into the mix four teenage boys and it's a cauldron of raging hormones, adolescent angst, often with blurred parental boundaries. At times it felt like we were literally feeling our way along and surviving the weekends together.

"HELP ME, MUM. PLEASE..."

FEBRUARY 2015

"*I'M GOING to fucking kill myself!* Watch me do it. You can watch me die, and then I won't be a burden to you anymore!" Jack screamed at me, pushing a sharp kitchen knife into his neck.

"Oh Jack, put the knife down... Please, put the knife down... *Jack, please...* " Tears were streaming down my face as I pleaded hysterically.

Thomas stood behind me, holding my arm tightly, desperately trying to protect me and help his brother, but at thirteen years old, he had no idea how to cope with the situation any more than I did.

Jack dropped the knife and slid down the wall. "Help me, Mum. *Please* get me help. I can't go on like this. I don't want to feel this way," he begged, cradling his head in his shaking hands as his body convulsed with sobs.

Once Jack turned eleven, things began deteriorating with his moods. An increasing inability to cope with his emotions started to manifest in angry outbursts; full-blown rages, in fact. Items would get thrown around his room, followed by frantic attempts to climb out of the second-storey window of our house to escape me if I was endeavouring to contain the outburst to his bedroom. These were a child's tantrums in a young man's body, and they would start over the most minor, seemingly insignificant things.

The first time it happened, tears stung my face, mortified that my child, *my child,* could behave this way. The words he spat at me with such venom stung. They were insulting and disrespectful, and I couldn't fail to take them personally. Naturally, as a mother, I wanted to run to him to calm him down, ease the situation and return our blended house to normality as quickly as possible. Equally, I wanted to run after him and throttle him for behaving that way and shaming me in front of Paul and his sons.

During those meltdowns, it appeared that Jack had no regard for whomever may be spectating. Paul would stand in the house, bewildered, wanting to help me but not knowing quite how to get involved. It's far harder to manage a child's behavioural outbursts when they are not your own children – especially the first time – and these situations would stir up complex feelings between Paul and me.

Paul would step in and try to calm Jack down during the heat of the moment but to no avail. When Paul's children went home on a Sunday night, I would feel relieved if we had survived another weekend without incident. Ashamed and humiliated, I somehow felt I was failing as a mother. My children had always been so well-behaved and well-mannered. It was shocking to witness these outbursts.

When the dust settled after each episode, and it always did, Jack would be extremely remorseful and often couldn't remember the extent of what he'd said during the heat of the outburst. I think he subconsciously chose to shut it all out as if it was too painful to recollect. Now, with the benefit of several years of dealing with mental illness, I know Jack didn't mean those awful things, but at the time, only an armour of objective steeliness could prevent me from being wounded by his hurtful words. Nothing, and I mean *nothing* in the prenatal classes or parenting books ever prepares you for these kinds of situations.

After the particularly distressing episode involving the knife, I took Jack to the family doctor, who was very understanding. He spoke gently to Jack about his feelings, the outbursts and how they were affecting the whole family. He suggested a referral to CAMHS: the Child and Adolescent Mental Health Services. The doctor warned me there could be a substantial wait, but at the time, I was just grateful to be offered some help.

By this time, Thomas had moved to his secondary school and seemed to transition smoothly. But during his second year, he began to get bullied. A small group of students had decided it was fun to mock him on social media as well as spreading childish rumours at school. They taunted him regularly and began to call his phone persistently.

One evening, he passed the phone to me. "Mum, it's them again – they're on the phone. *They're driving me crazy!*"

I answered and made it very clear that I'd be involving the school and their parents over their bullying if they didn't back off. I was incensed, and my protective mothering instinct well and truly kicked in. It seemed to do the trick, and they left him alone after that. However, mud sticks and the public comments they made about him on social media subsequently haunted him. Thomas removed his profile picture online and he has remained faceless ever since, without ever posting a single thing again. Thomas was a quiet sensitive kid, and this simple incident really impacted him.

The versions of Jack and Thomas that were beginning to emerge in their teenage years were so very different to the young carefree boys of their early childhood. Both had gone through an enormous amount of change in a short period of time. The instability they experienced as a result of my decision to move us all home to England, coupled with the dissolution of our tight little family unit when my marriage to John ended, was having a slow but profoundly detrimental effect on them both.

TROUBLE AT THE DOOR

MARCH 2015

ABOUT A MONTH LATER, there was a knock at the door one evening. I answered and a large, slightly menacing man stood there. He introduced himself as a bailiff, there to collect goods to the value of just over £500 in place of unpaid council tax.

"There must be some ... mistake?" I said, somewhat bemused, my foot wedging the door, determined not to let this giant into my home. We were registered and paying council tax at our property each month. It made no sense.

The bailiff explained that it was for the flat that Paul had previously been renting from a private landlady and gave us some paperwork, suggesting Paul contact the council the next day. But as far as Paul knew, all payments he'd made to the landlady were up to date. It transpired that she had not paid any council tax after all and left Paul liable for over five months' arrears.

We drove to her house when our attempts to call her failed. A neighbour told us she had sold up a few months prior and had moved to Spain. Despite searching online, we couldn't track her down. Paul had no choice but to pay the debt in instalments.

A couple of months after the bailiff's visit, court paperwork arrived for Paul. It was regarding an unresolved traffic infringement. He'd been ignoring the notification letters and the consequence was court proceedings or paying a hefty lump sum to settle the matter.

"For goodness' sake, Paul, why did you let it get to this stage?" I barked. He looked down sheepishly.

Having always been someone who just got on with things, it was hard to understand Paul's avoidance. He must have been hiding the letters, and perhaps the bailiff's too, until I intercepted this one quite by accident. Paul looked broken. First the bailiffs, now the court paperwork. Life was becoming a series of old debts, unpaid bills and a trail of financial destruction that was following him about from his life before me.

I loved Paul deeply, but he was often disorganised and chaotic. He was still wading through years of unresolved grief from losing his parents and, he said, losing his children and a happy family life when his first marriage broke down. But wrapped up in that package of a broken man was a sweet, loving and kind soul who made me feel special, and it blinkered me to the warning signs.

GET OFF MY BACK

SEPTEMBER 2015

PUBERTY ARRIVED, with all its hormonal guns a-blazing and it seemed to amplify everything for Jack. As we waited for the first CAMHS appointment, incidents of his anxiety increased, especially relating to school. Jack would start to panic en route; small, insignificant things would trigger him.

Tuesday was sports day.

"What if I need my rugby top, Mum? What if it's football? I don't have my boots!" Jack would question, panic rising in his voice.

The only way to appease him would be to turn the car around and grab the entire sports kit to cover all possible sports scenarios. The mad kit scramble would inevitably make us late for school, bringing about a whole new wave of anxiety. I swiftly learned to pack every item of his sports kit every week.

Once at school, although a little on the shy side, Jack never showed any signs of his inner turmoil to his teachers. He was a popular boy who tended to gravitate towards the kids who needed support. He was and still is, a compassionate, empathetic boy who wanted everyone to be included. If one of his friends was experiencing anything distressing, Jack felt their pain along with them. He would tell me their stories and often pause in silent contemplation before telling me it made him feel sad and that he wished he could help in some way. It touched me to see that gentle side of Jack surfacing.

During a conversation with the support worker at his primary school, I explained how we experienced these horrendous meltdowns at home. She reassured me that this was very common. Children become skilled at controlling their anxiety and anger, and some contain it whilst at school, but come hometime, they unleash all their emotions on the unsuspecting parents. Jack was one of those kids.

Jack finished primary school, and as we continued to wait on the CAMHS waiting list, the incidents continued over the summer holidays, though less frequently as school was no longer in the equation.

John and I had a shared-care arrangement for our boys and they would visit him every other weekend and on Wednesday evenings. Jack's relationship with John was very heated at times and somewhat strained.

At the time, John was sadly in the centre of another relationship storm with Sarah. The tense atmosphere was fuelling Jack's resistance to seeing his father. There were many occasions when Jack would refuse to go to John's place. Arguments would often ensue with me, John or both of us. The refusal always led to heated, angry episodes.

John and Sarah went on to separate shortly after and I felt incredibly sad. I genuinely wanted him to be settled and this was not the happy-ever-after I'd wanted for him. John slowly slipped into depression himself and I think his instability, as much as he thought he was guarding the children from it, was affecting both of the boys.

After an eight-week wait, Jack had his initial assessment with CAMHS. It coincided with him starting at his new secondary school in September. Jack was assessed as having mild depression with moderate anxiety. The nurse practitioner agreed that he would have a series of CBT (cognitive brain therapy) sessions and be offered some techniques to help him work with his anger. The sessions were conducted at his school once a week.

Jack did not gel with the nurse who worked with him – and nor did I, to be honest – but he attended the sessions, practised the techniques, and was discharged back to the GP, having demonstrated he had improved.

A couple of years later, Jack confessed that he hated the sessions and told the therapist what she wanted to hear so they would finish quicker. He may have only been eleven, but he was astute enough to manipulate the system to get them off his back.

ALCOHOL – THE PAST AND PRESENT

I MADE a conscious choice to never drink alcohol myself whilst growing up. I felt quite the odd-one-out as a non-drinker in both the UK and Australia. Both countries have a reputation for their strong drinking culture and I was often teased for it – it was tiresome having to explain my non-drinking status to others. I think it was partly because I feared being drunk – I'd seen enough drunken behaviour during my late teens to deter me from ever losing control of myself like that. But I also had a real aversion to the smell of alcohol, especially spirits, and whisky in particular...

When I was a young child, my mother had an extension built on the back of our home during one long warm summer. My father was working away at the time. A local builder, Glen, and his small team of labourers came in most weekdays. One of my pastimes was to sit on our staircase and look through a porthole window out onto the street, watching the world pass by.

One day, a labourer employed by Glen came into the house under the guise of using the downstairs toilet, which was hidden under the stairs. Instead, he headed towards me, grinning. His teeth were yellowed and his skin aged and weathered brown. He took a small glass bottle from his back jeans pocket and took a large slug of honey-coloured liquid, before smiling at me.

I can still remember his lined face, his long greasy black hair and the faint smell of cement that lingered about him.

He pinned me down against the stairs and forced his rough tongue into my mouth as I stiffened, paralysed with fright. I remember the leathery texture of his tongue and the sour, pungent taste of whisky from it.

Interrupted by the sound of my mother returning to the kitchen from hanging out washing in the back garden, the drunken monster climbed off me and put his grubby fingers to his lips, smiling. "Shhhhh...' he whispered clumsily, before heading out to the back garden.

I didn't understand what he had just done to me, but I knew I didn't like how it felt and I ran to my mother. "Mummy, I don't like the man with the black hair," I whispered shyly, my arms wrapped around her waist. I wouldn't say anything more when quizzed.

Alarm bells started ringing for my mother. A couple of days earlier, he'd made an unusual comment to her in passing that had left her feeling uneasy. She had made him a mug of tea and as she passed it to him, he stared at her.

"Are you not worried about being here all alone at night with your kids, you know, with the back of the house open like this? Anyone could get in..." He'd questioned her with an unsettling tone and grin that was more of a sinister taunt than concern.

My mother told Glen about his comment and of my

sudden dislike for the long-haired labourer. Glen gave him his marching orders, and just as well – sometime later, Glen discovered he had recently come out of prison for manslaughter.

It was 1979 and I was seven years old, but the taste of his whisky has never left my memory. I still detest the smell. It took me until I was nearly fourteen years old before I summoned the courage to confess to my mum what he did to me that day.

When I was seventeen years old, I got myself a very grown-up job, one that introduced me to the darker side of alcoholism, drug addiction and mental illness. It was 1989 and England was heading towards a recession – that's how I found myself recruited by the Department of Social Security.

My job was to sit behind shatterproof glass and metal grills, interviewing benefit claimants, many of whom were desperate for money. Day after day, I experienced people at their lowest ebb: alcoholics, drug addicts, homeless, victims of domestic abuse and people suffering with extreme mental illness, left to fend for themselves in a community that didn't know how to care for them.

I stayed in that job for six years, until I emigrated to Australia and in that time, I witnessed some of the most shocking aspects of human behaviour, the perpetrators often under the influence of one illicit substance or another. I witnessed a stabbing, public defecation, public sex acts, and at aged eighteen, my first addict overdosing on heroin. It happened in my booth, right in front of me, because I couldn't give him any more money.

I had chairs thrown at me more than once, daily verbal abuse, personal threats and even a stalker who became obsessed with me. It was one hell of an introduction to the very worst humanity had to offer and left me absolutely terrified of the frightening effects that alcohol and drugs had on society.

As a child, I was oblivious to the fact that my father drank more than he should have. He was never around often enough for me to witness it.

My father was a session musician and would often be overseas, touring with various artists. When he returned, if he were not in his makeshift studio writing or playing, he would spend his lunchtimes in the pub drinking pints and paying for his popularity by buying half the patrons pints too. My father refrained from eating during the day to avoid gaining weight from his liquid diet – especially before a tour – and would often return to the pub in the evening for a second drinking session.

My father was a shy man and I believe alcohol gave him a little confidence, an edge, which in turn may have been a route to feeling more accepted by people for the man he was. My grandmother had never approved of his career choice, or his musician friends, nor his long hair and casual clothes and she would tell him so, often.

Boozing all night, long hair and fast women went with the territory of being a session musician in the 1970s and my father was no exception. My mother hid all this from my brother and I, protecting us from the seedy reality most of our lives, well into adulthood and long after my father had died. Like me, she spent most of her life covering up unpleasant situations in order to protect the ones she loved.

When I moved to Australia, I thought nothing of my father sinking six to eight large bottles of beer a day during the long hot seasons. After all, he never appeared drunk. Nor did I ever question his reasons for asking me to bring him several bottles of gin to the hospice each week. I just believed I was helping to ease his pain as he lay there dying.

I never thought of my father as an alcoholic, yet alcoholism comes in many guises. I, like many others, used to believe that an alcoholic was the proverbial lost soul, sat on a park bench, destitute and drinking from a bottle hidden in a crumpled brown bag. But that's not the case. People can function daily, hold down jobs, lead outwardly respectable lives and yet still be an alcoholic behind the scenes. I believe that my father was one of those people.

My brother was a heavy drinker too, binge-drinking at weekends. He was quite the comedian after a skinful and always the life and soul of every party. Throughout my late teens and into my early twenties, whilst I lived with my brother, he would often stagger back home in the early hours of the morning, often incoherent, and I would put him to bed most Saturday nights in an intoxicated stupor, mopping up the aftermath of his drunken antics in my mother's absence.

Shortly before Christmas in 2015, I came down to the kitchen to make breakfast one wintry Sunday morning and caught Paul finishing off a bottle of wine that had been in the cupboard. He was drinking it straight from the bottle. It was 9.30am.

"What are you doing, Paul?" I demanded.

"There was only a tiny bit left. I was just finishing it off before I threw it out," Paul said convincingly. I didn't think too much of it at the time and brushed the incident aside.

A few days later, I remembered that bottle of wine had been given as a gift and I had put it in the cupboard myself. It was unopened the night before he drank it. Unless I was mistaken, Paul had polished off an entire bottle of wine at 9.30am on a Sunday morning in a matter of minutes.

I'd never really paid attention to Paul drinking. He'd have the occasional can of beer but always kept it by the side of his chair and would never drink in front of his children.

On one occasion, his youngest son, who was about ten at the time, caught Paul swigging from a can and blew up at him in a fit of anger and tears. "Don't drink, Dad! You told me you didn't drink," he sobbed.

I sat on the stairs with my arm around his son, soothing him, unable to understand his disproportionate reaction to a can of beer. His son calmed, and I reassured him that Paul rarely drank alcohol.

After the children had gone home, I asked Paul why his son would have reacted so strongly to seeing him with a can of beer. Paul explained that he used to drink regularly before meeting me and sometimes when he had the children; but never to the extent that he was out of control or drunk, just merry. But of course, this was Paul's way of denying he had a drinking problem and not wanting to accept that his sons were aware of it.

In my naïvety, I assumed this was an old issue that my love had helped to resolve. Paul had *me* now, after all; I looked after him and his sons and loved them all, so he didn't need drink because all his problems were now fixed.

Paul would wait for his sons to go home, then nip out and buy a four-pack of beers. The first one would be drunk in one or two huge gulps, and the others sipped slowly. I rarely saw him drink them. That was the problem, Paul was drinking in secret.

Paul was a functioning alcoholic. He worked hard and held a job down and to the outside world, was an altogether happy man. But his exterior was paper-thin, and inside, Paul was slowly sinking, and his life was spiralling. The more he tried to cover up the lies, the more Paul panicked and drank. The more anxious he'd become about being rumbled for drinking, the more he drank, and so he was caught on a perpetuating merry-go-round that he never seemed able to step off. I was oblivious because he hid it so well.

Sometime later, I discovered that Paul was drinking heavily in secret before we met and hiding the empty bottles behind the bath panel in his shared house. That was alcoholism, and he was in denial.

A WORLD OF ADDICTION

DECEMBER 2015–JANUARY 2016

One evening just after Christmas, Jack complained of feeling hot and nauseous. He was taking a bath when he suddenly felt like he was going to throw up. He quickly got out of the water, dressed and went to his room. I settled him into bed, gently reassuring him he was okay.

Jack had never been a sickly child. At most, he had thrown up maybe three or four times in his lifetime. Within minutes of leaving him, I heard a frantic call followed by the uncomfortable sounds of him retching. Jack had projectile-vomited all through his bed, across the carpet, the landing, stairs and over himself. He was a tearful, vomit-soaked mess.

From then on, Jack associated the bath with the discomfort of the vomiting episode. For the entire time we remained living in that house, he never stepped foot back in the en-suite bathroom. In his brain, the association between the vomiting and the preceding bath was so strong, it prevented him from having a bath again.

Sadly, this simple but unpleasant vomiting incident slowly manifested into a full-blown, larger-than-life phobia known as emetophobia. This surprisingly common phobia was to have a life-altering impact on every aspect of his life.

Later that week, on the Friday night, I was feeling unwell and was dozing on the sofa. It seemed I had gone down with the same bug Jack had earlier that week.

Paul arrived home late, and a vague smell of drink followed him into the room.

"Where were you? I'm not feeling well. Have you been drinking? "I questioned.

"It's just a stomach bug. You'll be fine," he snapped.

Hoping for comfort, I winced at his sharpness, and a lump rose in my throat. Paul was uncharacteristically dismissive.

"I'm sorry, I can't do this," he declared, and he grabbed his keys and left the house, driving away before I could pull myself up off the sofa to chase after him.

I'd never seen Paul behave this way, and his indifference shocked me. I tried to call him immediately, but his phone went straight to voicemail.

After the umpteenth attempt and hearing his irritating voicemail recording once again, I was enraged and threw my phone across the room. *How dare he*, I thought.

Lying in bed that night with the curtains open, I kept jumping up at every headlight that lit up the room, hoping it was him, preparing for a showdown. But he didn't come back, and he still hadn't returned the following morning. His phone was still turned off. My anger had subsided, but worry had set in.

I knew Paul wasn't coping, but I didn't realise how unbalanced he was. He'd had months of old debts finding him, bailiffs, and court threats, along with me discovering his drinking. It had been simmering under his surface for a long time. Paul had been acting most days – pretending to cope with work, kids, and everything else, smiling through gritted teeth – yet slowly falling apart on the inside with fear and crippling anxiety. Paul had finally reached overload.

Unable to reach him by the following evening, I called the police and reported him missing. This behaviour was out of character and concerning, given his recent state of mind. But somehow, I managed to keep up a happy-go-lucky facade with my children. They had no idea what was unfolding, but inside, I was beside myself with worry and couldn't eat a bite or sleep a wink. I was convinced Paul would do something to harm himself.

A few hours later, the police called me to say Paul's vehicle had been spotted driving through the centre of town. The police used the cameras on traffic lights to trace number plates, so they were watching. Relieved he was still alive at least, a little anger crept back in. I was astounded at his selfishness and found it difficult to remember that this was the behaviour of an unbalanced man.

Another night passed, and still no contact – and another night of no sleep. I felt weak and exhausted, both by the virus and the immense stress of the uncertainty. I sat at the lounge window all day on the Sunday, watching for a sign of him, waiting. Suddenly Paul appeared, pulling up outside the house.

Leaping from the chair, I ran to the front door, but by the time I reached the garden path, he had spotted me. Paul looked stricken, terrified to have been seen and clearly wasn't ready to face me, so he quickly sped off, with me chasing behind as far as my bare feet would take me on the rough bitumen.

A mix of exhaustion and frustration at being almost able

to reach Paul, but not quite, overwhelmed me. His phone was still turned off. I burst into tears.

Returning to the sofa, I sat there staring, waiting for hours. Finally, Paul returned around 10:30pm. He was dishevelled from sleeping in his small van. He reeked of stale drink and cheap food, a disgusting souvenir from a weekend of drunken disarray. The smell of alcohol oozed from his pores and filled the room around us. Paul was apologetic but didn't want to discuss anything, however, I wasn't willing to let it go.

"I don't want to talk about it, okay?" he muttered under his breath.

"No, no... That's not fair. You don't get to walk in here after disappearing for the whole weekend. Where the hell have you been? I've had the police out looking for you!" I shouted in between angry tears. All compassion had long since gone.

"I'm going to bed. I've not slept properly for two days," Paul replied, before attempting to leave the lounge.

"I've not slept for two days either, worrying about you!" I shrieked, slamming the lounge door behind me, blocking his exit. A fiery rage was rising from my belly and threatening to unleash on him.

"I'm tired, I don't feel well, and I *don't* want to talk about it, " Paul offered defensively.

"*How dare you.* Who do you think you are, disappearing like that? Do you have any idea how much I worried about you...?"

But before I could finish, Paul thumped both fists down on the coffee table angrily. "I'm going to bed, and I'm *not* going to talk about it tonight," he said, walking past me.

I let him go. I'd never seen this side of him, and I was taken aback.

If there had been a spare room, I'd have slept in it. I was seething inside. As it was, I barely slept lying next to him, overwhelmed with anger and hurt. Paul stunk and the odious smell of strong alcohol permeated the room.

Just for a moment, I was seven years old again – the familiar foul smell of strong alcohol took me back to a place I'd long since forgotten about. It was an uncomfortable and unpleasant reminder of the nightmare I'd found myself in all weekend. It was new and unfamiliar territory to me, and I wasn't sure of my next move.

The following morning, Paul was extremely remorseful and feeling very unwell. Not only was he feeling ill from the concoction of drink and cheap food he'd consumed all weekend, but he was also very scattered and anxious.

I marched him to the doctor, without giving him a say in the matter, and he confessed how he'd been feeling and that he'd been secretly binge-drinking large amounts of alcohol. The doctor recommended he contact Alcoholics Anonymous (AA) to get some support and prescribed some antidepressants.

In amongst the chaos of the night before, I had forgotten to inform the police that Paul had returned home. As a matter of protocol, they had to come round and confirm he was safely home.

Paul was agitated and anxious when the police arrived. Their tone was a little scolding and they gently reprimanded him for worrying me. Paul became defensive, but it was hardly surprising. He was well aware he'd caused an enormous amount of worry to me, and no one wants to be called out for their poor behaviour, least of all with a monster of a hangover and overwhelming anxiety.

When the police left, I asked Paul to call AA. He complied reluctantly. No one who has an unhealthy relationship with drink wants to admit to themselves or anyone else, for that matter, that they may have a problem.

Later that evening, two men turned up from the AA's fellowship to meet Paul. Listening to him open up about drinking made me realise the seriousness of his addiction. It was unchartered water for me; I didn't like it at all. I felt embarrassed and humiliated sitting there, listening to his sorry admission of how drink had got the better of him. I wanted my world to be perfect, and it wasn't. This was messy and ugly, and it made me feel very uncomfortable.

The men arranged to collect and accompany Paul to an AA meeting the following evening and suggested I contact Al-Anon, which was a support group for families of alcoholics. But I refused to accept the existence of this dirty little situation. This wasn't really a problem, I reasoned, and I certainly wouldn't be needing any help; it was just a blip. Paul would get over it, and I'd get my loving, kind, sensitive partner back and everything would be rosy once again.

PLACE YOUR BETS!

FEBRUARY 2016

AT FOURTEEN, Thomas was like any other typical teenage boy, interested in games and an avid fan of streamers and YouTubers. He had seen a few live-stream events where people he followed online had won money gambling, and in his young naïvety, he thought he could make a small fortune.

It began with some of his Christmas or birthday money being spent buying 'skins' for fictional weapons in his games. Skins are virtual enhancements that can be won or purchased within certain video games to decorate and customise weapons. They rarely affect gameplay and are mainly aesthetic, but a marketplace has developed to trade skins due to their popularity.

If he wanted, Thomas could trade his skins with other gamers on the in-house marketplace. However, it wasn't long before third-party sites would pop up on the side of the screen, enticing him to trade his skins for a coin flip, a roll of the dice or a spin of the wheel, landing on black or red for the big win. Only the big win rarely came, and Thomas would end up losing all his money, time and time again.

If you've never experienced the hook of addiction, it's very easy to say, well, just don't gamble, but it isn't that easy. It's about as effective as telling an alcoholic not to drink. It takes strict discipline and abstinence, just as with any other addiction.

Thomas is not alone with his online addiction. Skin gambling has only recently become recognised as an issue, but it is a genuine problem without any proper regulation. Only a few third-party gambling sites use age verification and do not operate under any gambling licensing or regulatory bodies. It allows teenagers to log in through third-party sites and gamble. Most teenage boys who game online are aware of skin gambling.

The thought of Thomas getting caught up in gambling and where it could eventually lead terrified me. My mind ran wild at times, conjuring up the worst possible scenarios of financial loss, but with good reason. I had terrible memories of my stepfather's gambling and the effect his addictive behaviours had on all our lives.

After my mother returned to live in Ireland, my stepfather's increasingly abusive behaviour and spiralling gambling debts led my mother to run away into hiding, safely away from him and his loaded-shotgun threats. He was nasty piece of work at times. He was a bully.

When he couldn't find my mother's whereabouts, he returned to the UK. At the time, John, my brother and I were living in a flat owned by my stepfather and we would pay him rent money every month. Each month he would arrive to collect our rent money for his mortgaged flat with obvious resentment towards us for being his now-untouchable wife's offspring. However, instead of heading to the bank to pay the mortgage, he would head straight to the bookies and blow the lot on horse-racing.

Several months later, he arrived one morning and barked at us to leave, giving us a couple of weeks' notice. He was unapologetic and I'm sure, deriving a vindictive kick out of displacing us and therefore upsetting our mother in the process. My stepfather had successfully gambled his flat, *our* home, into repossession from the bank, leaving all three of us homeless.

My brother stayed with a friend, and John and I were forced to live in his parents' dining room for three months whilst we found a new home. Gambling had turned my life upside down as a young woman and it was in danger of doing so again, this time through my own son's addiction.

Watching television at night, it angered me when multiple gambling commercials appeared, enticing would-be gamblers with colourful, clever marketing, offering free spins and bonus money to spend. Every advert was rounded up with some snappy slogan disclaimer about knowing and managing your own limits. The gaming company websites had multiple options for restricting amounts spent, self-restriction, and site-blocking, but let's face it, television is a powerful medium. Try telling a gambling addict to quit when they're ahead or to stop when it's no longer fun. The companies were making a fortune off the back of a highly addictive and very destructive pastime.

"Just one more spin. Just one more bet. Just one more hand and I'll get my money back or double my money. If only I could get that lucky break, that big win!"

I'd heard Thomas say the '*if only*' mantra many a time after his losses, so to see it in my face night after night on TV incensed me. I was grateful Thomas rarely watched TV with me, so he didn't have to see the relentless gambling advertising.

By the age of fifteen and after multiple episodes of losing money, I approached an advice line. Unfortunately, Thomas couldn't access counselling due to his age as he was deemed too young. Skin gambling was, at that point, still relatively new and not widely known. But eventually, I found someone willing to see him. However, Thomas denied he had a problem and refused to go to counselling. I had far too much going on with Jack and Paul to fight another battle at the time.

It saddened me more than anything. Gambling is such a crippling addiction, and for someone of his age to be afflicted, well, it broke my heart. I had moments of anger with him too – his gambling triggered old resentments towards my stepfather and the destruction his addiction had brought into my life, and my mother's. It would often highlight Paul's addiction too and I would sometimes unleash all that old built-up anger on poor Thomas.

DROWNING HIS SORROWS

APRIL 2016

Paul regularly attended AA meetings and remained sober for several months. Things seemed to settle back to normality, but within a few months, we were forced to move into more affordable accommodation as rental prices were soaring. It was a significant change for us all. We'd gone from a large three-bedroom, two-reception room house to a two-bedroom flat. Not only was it a great deal smaller, but, as we were no longer able to afford the leafy luxury of safe suburbia, our new home was smack bang in the town centre. It sat amongst the shops, restaurants, and bars – all just a five-minute walk from the beach. Its location seemed appealing at the time, and in all honesty, it was all we could afford. The monthly cost was less than half that of the old rental, allowing us to breathe again financially.

Acutely aware that my children had been ripped from their home in Australia, then had their new family home taken over by their father's new partner, I wanted to compensate them somehow, and from a place of misplaced guilt, gave them a bedroom each and opted for a sofa bed in the lounge myself. It was unconventional, but Paul went along with it and didn't seem particularly bothered.

Initially, Paul's sons shared bedrooms with my boys at weekends, but it was very cramped as the bedrooms were small. Paul eventually boarded the loft space and created a temporary room for his sons. At last, we all had a little space to call home.

We set about planning our wedding for later that year, not a large affair but a simple one, and the prospect excited me. But a couple of months after moving, Paul began secretly drinking again. More disturbingly, he began self-harming. Of course, drinking is a form of self-harm; it's poisoning the body: self-medicating to alter how you feel, to escape feelings of pain, and relieve anxiety or depression. But Paul had moved into a different realm of self-destruction. He began to use blades from his toolbox to nick minor cuts on his arms. They were tiny, inconspicuous scratches at first, cuts that he could easily hide under his T-shirt, and I was unaware he was hurting himself. But he soon progressed to deeper cuts, until one day, he sliced a deep gash on his forearm about 6-cm long. That one he couldn't hide, and I was distraught when I saw it. I'd never been exposed to someone who cut themselves before, so I had no idea how to react, or help him. When I asked Paul why he'd done it, he said it was like a release, and the sight and feel of the warm blood somehow eased his internal torment.

We had a joint bank account, and I started to notice a pattern. Paul would go out, and then money would disappear from the bank account: ten pounds here, twenty pounds there. Sometimes I wouldn't notice until a text came through from the bank saying we'd gone overdrawn. Paul always gave a plausible reason: petrol, food or something else, but the money was never spent on those things. He was secretly drinking, sometimes considerable amounts. Paul denied it, of course, and it was to be sometime before he revealed the extent of his drinking.

However, I wasn't that naïve. Paul's erratic behaviour created an anxious, snooping monster within me – I was constantly checking the bank account for withdrawals and living on the edge of my nerves every day. It was also obvious when he'd been drinking, especially spirits or cheap cider. They changed Paul's personality, and I hated that version of him; it was like an alter ego: either defensive or over-the-top nice. I didn't recognise him and never knew which version I would get. I tiptoed around him, trying to ensure my children didn't see him drunk.

Life became like a twisted relay race for me, running from one stressful event to the next, with just enough time to breathe in between each frantic sprint. Paul wasn't drinking every day, maybe once or twice a week, but when he did, he would binge-drink a large amount which was just as destructive both physically and financially. After too many drunken episodes to recall, I'd had enough. Paul surrendered his bank card for our joint account. He felt it was better if he didn't have access to money, and I was relieved and felt back in control, safe in the knowledge there would be no more nasty bank texts telling me we were overdrawn.

In between the drinking episodes, he was my lovely Paul, albeit remorseful and unbalanced. He'd cry a lot, and he recognised that he had a problem. Paul would venture back into AA from time to time, but never stick at it for more than a few weeks at a time. As soon as he had an emotional trigger, or felt overwhelmed by stress, he would turn to drink to mask his emotions.

It's difficult to remember alcoholism is a symptom of something, without losing your patience with an alcoholic. I often wanted to scream at Paul to just stop drinking, as if it was that easy. People don't lapse into alcoholism without reason; there is always an underlying cause, a trigger, whether that be a traumatic experience or an untreated underlying mental-health disorder. Many people are intolerant of alcoholics and their behaviours. I am also guilty of judging people in the past for problematic drinking. My government job had gifted me that.

My uncle had died in his early forties through his alcoholism. He killed himself in a car accident, whilst drink-driving. I was only young woman at the time, but remember thinking how irresponsible he was, and I questioned why he couldn't just stop, why he continued to hurt his family that way. But alcoholism and responsible behaviour don't go hand in hand; quite the opposite in fact – careless and impulsive behaviour is unfortunately the norm. Alcoholics don't want to hurt their loved ones deliberately; they are self-harming in a slow and destructive way, in the grip of a massively addictive drug, and their actions unintentionally shatter the lives of their loved ones. Not until alcoholism permeated every aspect of my life, did I learn to understand it a little more. Only then and after many relapses and episodes of reckless behaviour, did I slowly gather the tolerance and patience needed to continue loving an alcoholic.

By then, I knew it was my choice. I could have walked away, I could have thrown in the towel and declared it all too much. But my exposure to my family's mental illness softened my judgements and allowed me to see past the alcoholism, to understand the reasons why and to recognise

Paul never meant to hurt me or upset me. In fact, when his actions indirectly caused me pain, it broke him up so much that he turned that self-loathing inward into more painful self-harming in one form or another.

I knew the man underneath the alcohol, and I loved that man deeply. It took an exceptionally long time, several years in fact, to recognise and understand his anxiety and torment and to forgive him for his actions. I tried my best to comfort him and help, and he loved me dearly for it, but neither of us realised I couldn't mend the broken pieces of him. It wasn't my job to, but I was killing myself trying. It was to take me three more years to realise I couldn't fix him or anyone else for that matter.

At times I felt like I was being punished by some unseen force. I must have really wronged someone in a previous life to deserve all that misery. But addiction had thrust its way into my life through both Paul's alcoholism and Thomas' gambling, with its brutal and unwelcome consequences. I was in way over my head and floundering in the darkness.

REHAB AND REVELATIONS

JULY 2016

By summer, Paul had wasted hundreds of pounds of his savings on alcohol, and he recognised that he needed professional help. He researched private rehabilitation centres and found one he could join the following day. Using the last of his savings, he booked himself into rehab for a week. Along with the train fare and loss of wages, the week cost a small fortune.

Realistically speaking, and with the benefit of hindsight, a week was never going to be enough time to get to the root of Paul's addiction, but that was all we could afford. Funded rehabilitation is very difficult to acquire, and if Paul had been lucky enough to qualify for a place, he would have most certainly had to sit on a lengthy waiting list, several months long.

We told all the children Paul was working away, and he left the following day for a six-hour train ride to Blackpool. For most people, this would have been a pleasant journey where they could sit back and relax, but for Paul, his anxiety was at an all-time high and his confidence at an all-time low, so it was an uncomfortably long and anxiety-filled journey.

Whilst Paul was travelling, I received a call from the rehabilitation centre: "We're just preparing things for your partner's arrival. Can you tell me how long Paul has been smoking crack cocaine?"

"Wait... what... What did you say? There must be some mistake. Paul's an alcoholic – he doesn't take drugs?" I replied, incredulously. My heart began racing.

"Um, I'm sorry if you didn't know that... We understand he's been using cocaine and smoking it," the care worker offered, somewhat bemused.

"No... no... *no*." I couldn't take it in. My legs felt like they would buckle underneath me.

Smoking cocaine. My experience of crack cocaine was watching local addicts sucking crack rocks from dirty pipes in the phone box. Not my Paul. I believed that after one rock, you were hooked into a lifetime of hopeless addiction. My head spun, conjuring up images of Paul laying in a filthy crack den, high as a kite, surrounded by semi-comatose drug addicts.

Paul had dabbled in party drugs at festivals during the 1990s. Many people of my generation had, and some continued using cocaine and amphetamines as part of their weekend socialising. But I'd not been around drugs since my early twenties and was naïve to the current reality of street drugs, and even more naïve to my partner's apparent drug habit. It transpired he'd smoked crack cocaine twice, alone, but had been snorting grams of cocaine regularly, along with drinking.

This accidental revelation brought a whole new sordid world to my doorstep, and I *hated* Paul for dragging me into it.

I considered carefully what to say to him. After many deleted text drafts, I settled on something simple: *"I'm sorry you couldn't tell me about the drug-taking. The rehab centre just told me. I don't know what else to say. Take care x"*

That was the most objective text I'd ever sent. What I really wanted to type was, "*YOU FUCKING BASTARD, HOW COULD YOU?*" in capital letters for full shouting effect and it took every ounce of self-restraint not to.

Paul was distraught, absolutely beside himself on the train, having received my text. I think there may also have been a sense of relief in me knowing about the drugs too. There was nothing left to hide. No more secrets.

Of course, this was now my dirty little secret too, and I hid it from everyone, feeling deeply ashamed. I didn't want anyone to judge him, or me, or tell me to leave him. After all, I was meant to be marrying the guy in two months! I loved this man, so damn much, despite all the chaos, but many people are sharp-tongued and quick to judge. This was another situation best left hidden.

When Paul eventually arrived at the rehabilitation centre, he was exhausted. The staff were waiting to greet him, and he was shown to his room. Once settled in, and the staff had explained the house rules, the doctor sat with Paul, and they discussed his addiction. He was given a course of vitamins by injection and set a strict timetable for therapy.

Paul spent a week detoxing with exercise, vitamin injections, a healthy balanced diet and twice-daily therapy sessions. For that short time, he was under someone else's watch, and I was relieved he was no longer my concern. I already had more than enough on my plate with Thomas and Jack.

When Paul returned a week later, he was like a new man: a sober one. He stood taller, and he was exuberant and full of life and enthusiasm. He'd lost weight and looked really well.

Paul joined a local gym and worked out three times a week. Everyone noticed the change in him, and his forty-four-year-old physique rivalled that of any twenty-year-old man. Not only was he physically at his peak, energetically he was on fire, and I could feel his new-found confidence.

A couple of months later, we married in a low-key intimate ceremony with a few family and friends and, of course, all four boys. It was a simple but magical day, and I was hopeful for a more balanced future, confident in Paul's ability to stay clean and sober.

REFUSING SCHOOL

JANUARY 2017

It was becoming increasingly difficult to get Jack up for school. He was still dead to the world at 7am and virtually impossible to wake. He'd begun complaining frequently of vague symptoms of illness or tiredness all the time.

It started gradually with the odd day off from school here and there; a headache one day, a stomach ache the next, but things deteriorated quickly. Within three months, the days off school were stretching into weeks.

There was always an excuse, but I was busy trying to juggle a job, two teenagers – one of whom was about to start GCSE exams – and a husband in recovery from alcoholism. It was easier to keep Jack away from school rather than deal with the inevitable showdowns before work.

Jack's school avoidance quickly escalated into refusing to leave the house at all, which would erupt into momentous rows I didn't have the time or energy to deal with before the school run. On several occasions, Jack bolted out of the flat and disappeared. Exasperated, I'd be left with no choice but to get Thomas in the car, and drive off, leaving Jack missing. It was the only way Thomas stood any chance of getting to his school exams on time – it was a twenty-minute drive away and we were up against peak traffic every time.

I'm not sure how, but I got Thomas to every exam just in time; however, both he and I had frayed nerves for the entire time. Poor Thomas – it was certainly not a calm prelude conducive to sitting exams, especially for a kid who was already feeling nervous and with no real confidence in his own academic ability.

By the time I'd get back home from dropping Thomas off, I would find Jack lurking sheepishly somewhere nearby. Filled with seething anger, I'd let him into the house, muttering under my breath, then make a mad dash to work for 9am. I had neither the time nor patience to listen to him or try to establish why he was getting in such a state before school.

Thomas had also been struggling at school in the lead up to his exams and had been showing signs of anxiety, but I'd been far too absorbed in Jack to notice. Jack was at the peak of his school refusal and at the time, John had moved into temporary accommodation after separating from Sarah and the subsequent sale of the family home. He was struggling with his own low mood, and it was affecting both the boys. Neither of them wanted to be in that environment and they both started making excuses to avoid going to John's.

Thomas' head of year called me one day at work – Thomas had not turned up to his afternoon lesson. A friend had directed the teacher to the toilets as he knew he was hiding in there. The teacher found Thomas sobbing in a cubicle. His teacher told me he never wanted to see a child in that state over being at school again.

That particular teacher took Thomas under his wing

and would meet regularly with him to offer him words of encouragement and liaise with his teachers to give him a little longer on assignments. He even arranged for a small, quiet room to sit his exams in, away from the large halls filled with hundreds of students.

Thomas was finding his schoolwork difficult to understand, but I didn't take the time to listen to him and put his discontent down to the complexity of our home life, teenage hormones, and the pressure of his exams.

Assumption is a dangerous thing.

During that time, I made countless calls to the school in tears, not knowing what to do. The school warned me I could face fines or even prosecution for Jack's absenteeism and I was terrified at the prospect. I'd often use this as a threat in an attempt to coerce Jack back to school, but it was in vain. Nothing seemed to alter or alleviate his disproportionate anxious outbursts before school.

I called the doctor, who listened sympathetically and offered to re-open a referral to CAMHS for me, once again warning me there would be a substantial wait. In the meantime, a private counsellor saw Jack weekly. It helped him a little to talk, but it was just a temporary fix until CAMHS were able to see him. At nearly £200 a month, it wasn't easy to sustain.

The Education Support Officer at Jack's school met with me on several occasions throughout his increasing absenteeism. They had put measures in place to help Jack. An exit card was issued so if he felt uncomfortable in class, he could show the card to the teacher and leave, but he felt too self-conscious to use it. They tried a reduced timetable, but nothing helped and by June, he was no longer attending school at all.

When school broke up that July, I breathed a sigh of relief. I no longer had to deal with the daily exhausting battles on school days. Looking back, I wish I had recognised this behaviour was as a symptom of Jack's anxiety, not just wilful, defiant behaviour as some people kept kindly suggesting.

The reality is that only a small percentage of children don't want to go to school because they can't be bothered. There is almost always an underlying reason, such as bullying or an undiagnosed mental-health issue such as anxiety or depression. School refusal can start at any age, without warning. It is always very distressing for both children and parents, and we were no exception.

I spent most of those six months in a state of high anxiety, shouting at Jack daily, bribing him, threatening him, removing his gadgets, and punishing him under a fearful cloud of prosecution by the education department, rather than realising my son was clearly not coping and in need of help.

LIFE AFTER SCHOOL

AUGUST-OCTOBER 2017

Results day approached, a day both Thomas and I dreaded. It's ridiculous that letters and numbers on a piece of paper should have such a profound effect on our children's futures, but apparently they do, and I take issue with this.

At what point did schools become so focused on academic results? My last year at school was the first to take GCSEs in 1987. Though we were encouraged to knuckle down and revise, we were never force-fed a study diet, whereby A levels and universities were glamorised as the most rewarding path into a glittering career. Not all kids are academically minded nor gifted, and further education is not suitable for everyone. Since leaving school at the age of sixteen, I've always worked and I've never been asked what exams I took at an interview, let alone the grades I achieved. I've never used a maths compass or protractor for that matter, nor found the need to set alight phosphorus in a controlled environment.

I wish I'd been taught how to cook, budget, bank and find the best insurance deal – all essential life skills children are not equipped with, and neither was I when I found myself out of home and fending for myself aged seventeen. The system is antiquated and outdated and we are not doing justice to our future generations by placing such high academic expectations on them whilst so young.

Thomas had passed just three of his nine exams, and the sense of failure he felt sent him spiralling into a deep depression. He had not achieved enough passes to be accepted to his school's sixth form, where most of his friends were going. Despite applying and asking for further consideration, his application was rejected – additional salt to rub into his already raw wounds. I arranged an interview with our local college to try to help him find a focus.

The advisor had a refreshing attitude to exam results and convinced Thomas that his life wasn't over because he didn't get different letters on a piece of paper. Somehow this revelation coming from a stranger had more impact than it had coming from me, and Thomas enrolled on a Computer Technology course, along with repeating English. He seemed brighter and more hopeful.

College started in mid-September, and Thomas appeared happy, apparently enjoying the course and making new friends. I was relieved he was settling in as Jack was deteriorating, so I switched my focus back to Jack. However, behind the scenes, things weren't going as well as I'd hoped.

A couple of weeks into the first term, I received a call from the college tutor advising me that Thomas had not arrived at his lesson. I called him, and he confessed he was sitting in the library and couldn't face class. Thomas was struggling to understand the assignment he had been given but was too shy to ask for help in front of his classmates. It was such a shame because Thomas was a real computer whizz and excelled in the subject at school until a change of teacher in Year 10 left the subject mostly taught by locums with no real consistency.

Thomas and I attended a meeting with his tutor, who wanted to reassure him that he could ask as many questions as he wanted. Again, I came away hopeful things would stay on track. With some extra support from the tutor and myself, Thomas received a distinction on his first assignment, which was promising.

However, it wasn't long before I began receiving regular calls about his absence from lessons, and after three weeks, I'd had enough. Instead of going to class, Thomas had been hiding in the library as he wasn't grasping the written work at all. The college was incredibly supportive and agreed after some discussion to test Thomas for dyslexia, as it appeared he was struggling with comprehension.

Thomas was subsequently diagnosed with dyslexia and offered extra support after classes. I was relieved, but equally upset. It was hard to comprehend how Thomas had managed to get through his entire school education without anyone noticing. Equally, I felt incredibly guilty for not realising myself and compounding his difficulties at school. I winced at the memory of the times I'd dismissed his attempts to convey how much he was struggling.

Hello, Guilt Monster ... it's been a while.

Thomas returned to class, but naturally his classmates wanted to know where he had been, and their curiosity made him feel uncomfortable and self-conscious. Thomas asked if he could study from home, which the college agreed to and set a timetable of assignments. For a while, Thomas seemed to be progressing with my support and tutoring at home.

Thomas returned from John's one morning not feeling

well and bolted straight for the bathroom. "*Mum...*" he wailed.

Running upstairs to the bathroom, I found him surrounded by vomit everywhere. I ushered him to his bed and began the mammoth clean-up; bathmat, towels, and everything else in the vomit's radius went in the bin. I gave up trying to salvage anything and did it in record time as Jack was asleep and blissfully unaware of what had happened.

This rather violent vomiting episode left Thomas feeling nauseous for many months after, which didn't help his mood. After about six months, he went to the doctor, and after tests, it was established he was lactose-intolerant. The bug had stripped his stomach of all its good bacteria, and he was unable to tolerate any dairy food whatsoever. That was a bit of a shock to the system for a teenager who loved pizza and chocolate. Thomas' diet had to change.

Thomas applied for a part-time job at a large department store. They didn't seem to care about his exam results, and he got the job, working weekend shifts. It boosted his self-esteem, and in the early months, he enjoyed earning his own money.

The following May, the college staff manager who had set the assignment goals resigned from her position, and one of the other tutors contacted me. Thomas had been given unrealistic goals by the outgoing teacher, she said, and the extension promised was not possible after all. The college felt he couldn't possibly complete the work in time and advised Thomas it was best to withdraw from the course and repeat it in the new academic year.

Eight months of work wasted. That was the straw that broke the educational camel's back for Thomas. He threw the towel in on study and vowed never to return.

During the summer of 2017, and without any conscious recognition by me, Jack continued to deteriorate. By this stage, he wasn't showering or sleeping in his bed, and I would often come home from work and find him asleep on his floor.

Calling CAMHS, I pushed for an update on his first appointment as he was already in their system. It was to be a further twelve weeks before CAMHS saw him, and during that waiting period, Jack deteriorated considerably.

Our days were filled with angry outbursts, slamming doors, swearing, and refusals to shower or leave the flat. Jack was a very angry, lost teenager who hibernated in his room day and night, becoming more and more withdrawn from everyone.

In mid-September, he had been unable to return to the new school year and we were caught in a draining loop of trying each day. The daily battles returned, my sheepish apologies to school became routine, as did my desperate attempts at bribery to get him there. Getting him back to school was my Holy Grail. It was the answer to all Jack's problems in my exhausted mind.

I returned from work one evening to find Jack curled up on his bedroom floor as he so often was, watching TV. "How are you feeling love?" I asked him soothingly.

Unexpectedly, he started to cry. Jack rarely cried. He would hold his tears inside. Jack believed boys shouldn't cry, and it was a sign of weakness to him. Thanks, society, for that one – he certainly didn't get that viewpoint from my parenting. '

'I wanted to kill myself, Mum. I put a knife to my heart, but couldn't do it... I called a helpline, and they made me feel calm. They told me to call you, but I waited for you to come home from work," Jack told me, in between sobs.

Frozen with shock and in disbelief at what I had just heard, an immense wave of guilt washed over me. *Where was I when my son needed me?* Working full-time, pretending everything was okay, and my son so low and desperate, he wanted to kill himself. What kind of mother was I, trying to carry on as usual? Things were far from ordinary, and my thirteen-year-old son, whom I fought *so* hard to bring into this world, was in so much distress, he wanted to die.

Instinctively, I leant over to embrace Jack, but he pushed me away. His self-loathing was palpable. This had all happened a few days earlier, but he had been too scared and embarrassed to tell me.

Leaving his room, I reassured him that chasing CAMHS was my priority in the morning, to get him the help he needed, and everything would be okay. There was nothing else to offer him.

Sleep eluded me that night. Leaving Jack alone in the house for four long days a week to go to work whilst he was in this fragile state was no longer an option. If he ever hurt himself, I would never forgive myself.

The following day, I contacted CAMHS and told them what had happened. They scheduled a home visit for late October. It was still six weeks away, but it was comforting just knowing they were coming.

After several days considering what to do about work, I decided to resign. It was a tough decision to make and sad, because I loved my job. It was a strange situation though: I worked for my brother but had never disclosed the full extent of what was unfolding at home with my own family, so my resignation came as a shock. But Jack's welfare had to come first.

Applying for a new part-time position nearer home became a priority but the employment market was brutal. After several interviews, I'd still heard nothing, so I took a chance and approached a company I'd worked for previously and thankfully, they were recruiting. Two team managers met me for an interview. Having previously worked with one of them, it was very informal. After explaining my situation, I was met with a great deal of understanding and empathy. They offered me a part-time position with the company starting that November, with flexible hours to work around Jack's appointments. That job and those particular managers were to prove lifesavers in the years to come.

The date of the first CAMHS appointment arrived. Jack was in a highly anxious state in anticipation of their arrival. In fact, he was in full fight mode that quickly turned to flight. I had to hold him down by the legs to stop him from climbing out of his second-floor window in an attempt to jump. "Get away from me. I'm not seeing them!" Fear flashed in his wide eyes.

Jack ran past me downstairs and grabbed a bottle of bleach from the kitchen cupboard, frantically poured a cup to drink, but the pungent smell snapped him out of it. He hurled the cup into the sink and grabbed a small, sharp knife from the drawer, pushing it into his neck. "I will kill myself. Leave me ... alone. I *hate* my life. I won't be a burden anymore to you!" Jack cried, fighting back tears.

I pleaded with him through hysterical tears to put the knife down, whilst Thomas stood behind me, holding my arm, visibly distressed and uncertain about what to do. This was the third time Jack had threatened in this way and it hadn't got any easier to witness.

Jack threw the knife down, crying, and ran past me upstairs, shrugging off my attempt to grab his arm and comfort him. His door slammed with enough force to shake the wall. Thomas and I exchanged helpless, bewildered glances. It was the most distressing incident yet, and it upset me knowing Thomas had witnessed it too.

Shortly after, two CAMHS staff arrived, and through my sobs, I explained what had just happened, along with giving them a rundown on the events of the previous few months.

"Okay, let us deal with this," one of the support workers gently offered.

Feeling entirely out of my depth for so long, an enormous sense of relief washed over me at that moment. Many emotions ran through my head, including fear of their judgment of my son's potential bad language and behaviour.

I led them upstairs to Jack's room, where he lay curled in a ball, with his bed covers pulled over his head. With my permission, they remained with Jack and sent me downstairs.

Standing at the bottom of the stairs, straining to listen, I heard them gently speak to my son for twenty minutes, attempting to coax him from under his covers, but he remained hidden. My cheeks flushed red with embarrassment, but they were calm and obviously used to this kind of behaviour. Jack eventually surfaced but kept a cap pulled firmly down over his face, hiding his shame.

It was clear his irrational response to their visit was from a place of pure fear. Jack was convinced that they had come to tell him off for his non-attendance at school, which, of course, wasn't the case. They were firm but compassionate, and once he realised that they were there to help him rather than punish him, he relaxed a little. Jack remained in his room with the support workers standing in his space, talking to him. It was agreed they would both be conducting home visits each week, two sessions a week. Relieved but terrified at the same time, I feared a repeat of the frightening episode.

As they left, one turned to me. "Here is a number for our emergency out-of-hours service. Please call if you have any concerns over Jack's behaviour or there are any more attempts to harm himself. Please also remove any knives and sharp objects from the house for the time being."

They left and I collapsed on the sofa in floods of tears, filled with relief that the appointment was over and that someone else was taking charge of this dire situation. The appointments continued, and Jack's anxiety thankfully lessened before each one.

CAMHS reduced the visits to one staff member weekly, and Jack formed a relationship with his support worker, Ben. He tried tirelessly to get Jack out of the house and back to school. It was a long and challenging journey lasting two years, but despite small milestones and goals being achieved, it ultimately failed to get Jack back into education.

Whilst Jack was now receiving therapy, Thomas' mood deteriorated, and I was dragging him from his bed most weekends, often distressed, to get him to his shifts. It was exceptionally stressful. I had gone through this with Jack's school refusal, but there was something much more formidable when dealing with absenteeism from a job. I was so preoccupied with the thought that he might lose his job, or this was somehow going to blight his entire future career path, that I failed to recognise the telltale symptoms of his depression. I think, to a certain extent, I was also in denial and didn't want to face the fact that I potentially had two sons with mental-health issues.

Thomas wasn't showering and started sleeping around the clock. He was having frequent angry outbursts and had become increasingly disconnected from his friends and family. After managing to persuade him to go to the bus stop for work, I would start receiving a string of desperate texts from him:

"I hate my life."

"I can't believe you are making me go."

"I feel so angry I want to hit someone on this bus!"

On a couple of occasions, I received more distressing messages:

"I want to throw myself in front of this bus."

How was I meant to respond to that? How could I possibly say anything that would help when he was standing on a busy roadside?

Thomas would always get to work and stay in contact with me via text the entire time, and I would spend his forty minutes travel time attempting to encourage him. When he would be due to start his shift, I'd breathe a sigh of relief. Sadly, the relief was often short-lived, and within half an hour or so, I'd often get a desperate text from Thomas, from his hiding-place in the work toilet: *"I can't do this, Mum, I don't know what to do."*

I'd try to encourage him via text, but it was fruitless, so I tried directing him to speak to his supervisor or manager to explain how he felt. Sometimes he would manage the entire shift, but more often than not, he would tell his manager he felt unwell and leave early. It was exasperating. To add fuel to the fire, when Thomas got paid, he'd often gamble his wages away within days.

This went on for some weeks until I took him to the doctor who signed him off work for a few weeks and referred him to CAMHS. Thomas was blessed with a very understanding boss, sympathetic to mental-health conditions, and it was a relief not to have to fight every weekend for a while.

I persuaded a local agency to see Thomas for gambling counselling, despite him being under eighteen. He attended several sessions but found talking about gambling made him think about it even more and subsequently want to gamble. The more isolated and low he became, the more he gambled. The agency suggested he went to Gamblers Anonymous meetings, but he was far too self-conscious at seventeen years old to attend a meeting for adults.

As CAMHS were already working with our family, Thomas' first appointment came through within six weeks. He sat in the clinic, his head hanging down, hood up and his long hair obscuring his face almost entirely. In the past, I would have barked at him to sit up straight and look at the person addressing him, but I was well used to this style of shutdown after witnessing Jack's behaviour during appointments.

Although shy, Thomas was well-mannered and would usually maintain eye contact with confidence and ease. Instead, here sat a slumped, miserable young man, finding it hard to articulate himself and struggling to find any joy in life. I sat next to him, large tears silently falling, but I had nothing left in me to care enough to wipe them away. Now I had two sons under the care of the mental-health team. What a failure of a mother I'd turned out to be. I felt utterly crushed.

After a lengthy assessment with the psychiatrist, Thomas was diagnosed with anxiety and depression. Thomas was assigned a caseworker who put in place a CBT care plan. The psychiatrist agreed that he would probably be better suited to working in a much smaller and quieter environment than the large department store where he was currently employed.

CAMHS referred Thomas to a local lottery-funded agency that specialised in working with young people who were considered at risk of unemployment through not studying. Thomas joined the agency and was about to begin a support program when he received a call to say that, sadly, they were unable to help him as he was still employed part-time. It was such a frustrating example of red tape for both the agency and Thomas.

Thomas began his CBT sessions and returned to work, but it wasn't long before he couldn't cope again. He was asked to attend a meeting with his manager. I joined him and they both agreed after some discussion that he would resign on health grounds. It was only a matter of time before he would have been sacked for his absenteeism through sickness, and we all agreed that it would be better to leave before that happened. Secretly, I felt a tremendous sense of relief as it meant I would no longer be fighting to get him to every shift. It also meant the specialised agency could help him.

A week or so later, Thomas rejoined the agency. They set about helping Thomas identify some goals to work towards and coach him to improve his confidence, attend social events, and fund some computer courses. Thomas remained working with them until their closure a year later due to lack of funding another casualty of inadequate funding for a very worthy project.

By this stage, I wasn't coping well at all. Our family's dysfunction felt relentless and overwhelming. I scraped through each day, crying, hiding my breakdowns in silence in the bathroom. It was a hopeless and dark place, and I felt very alone. It led me to avoid my family and friends, making endless excuses and hiding the shame I felt.

I couldn't bear to hear from friends who were going out and getting on with their lives and didn't want to see their holiday snaps or hear about their days out. That resentment festered inside me, and I'd send a short, veiled sarcastic response to their messages. I wanted them to know I didn't have a life anymore.

I didn't want to know about their children's success either: studying hard, passing exams, part-time jobs, girlfriends, boyfriends. Normality. It was salt in already painful, open wounds and I didn't want to be reminded of both my sons' dysfunction. Of course, underneath the resentment, I deeply cared for my friends and would be the first to congratulate them. That's the beautiful ambiguity of texts, no one can see the pain and tears behind those cheerful words.

I was still on social media at the time but found it excruciating to see what I perceived to be perfect families enjoying wonderful experiences whilst my youngest was curled in a ball on his bedroom floor, with his will to live disappearing daily. My eldest was depressed and gambling and my husband still drifting in and out of sobriety. After a while, I couldn't cope with seeing other people's regular lives, so I removed myself from social media and didn't return.

One day, Paul and I were sitting in a coffee shop, watching a family at a nearby table. They were laughing and enjoying their drinks, engaging in conversation. Every time they laughed, I envied them more. That envy turned to anger, then to tears, and eventually we had to get up and leave because I couldn't contain my sobs. I hated that family who were happily enjoying their afternoon together, oblivious to my stares. I hated that they had something we didn't: an ordinary family life.

Over time, I became more and more jaded by the perpetual depressive cycle we were all stuck in. It was a daily struggle just to find a purpose to do anything but get through the days. I isolated myself from everyone, including Paul. These were my children, not his, and this was my mess, my responsibility. It was easier to push him away than allow him to sail through the storm with me.

MOVING MEDITATION

MAY 2018

AFTER ALL THE daily battles with both Jack and Thomas, not to mention papering over Paul's fluctuating state of mind, I was utterly exhausted. One morning, following another difficult night with Jack, I finally got to bed at about 5.30am.

I woke up a couple of hours later and prepared for work in a numb state. Soon realising I couldn't gather myself together or stop crying, and that there was no way I would be able to manage my job, I called in sick.

Juggling work and home life felt overwhelming. Previously, I'd never have dreamt of risking my job or income, but at the time, I couldn't have cared less if my entire world fell apart around me. I simply didn't have the fight left in me to keep going.

A short while after, my boss called me back. In between sobs, I confessed to considering resigning, for, at that moment, the thought of work on top of everything else felt unmanageable. I was barely able to get my words out.

Concerned for my welfare, she calmly told me to call my doctor and explain my feelings. She gave me leave without question and told me to switch off from work and take some time out for myself.

My doctor offered to prescribe me antidepressants, but I declined and told her I would find an alternative way of coping, agreeing to contact CAMHS and access some help that way.

After a couple of weeks' wait, CAMHS assigned a family support worker who met with me weekly in a local coffee shop. It helped to sit and talk to someone objective and not emotionally involved in our situation. After a month of unreturned texts and emails, I called the office chasing my support worker, to be told she had resigned. It was a shame no one at CAMHS had bothered to tell me.

A week later, I joined a local hotel pool and began swimming a couple of times a week. I'd steal a few hours here and there, telling everyone I was at work, but instead sneak off to hide at the hotel. I bought myself a pair of waterproof headphones so I could listen to music whilst swimming.

The pool was blissfully empty during the day, and so I'd float around, often alone. I would swim laps, slowly, meditatively, back and forth, my mind wandering from time to time, but always falling back into the lyrics of song I was listening to. I would dive down and all that was audible was my music, with the faint hum of the filter boxes and gentle swirls of bubbles rising to the surface of the water.

Sometimes I'd cast my headphones to the side and submerge myself just enough so that all the noise would stop, both inside my head and out. I liked that silent space. It was as if the world and all my chaos stood still under the water. It was peaceful and comforting. It was without doubt, a form of moving meditation for me.

Sometimes I'd swim to the deep end and roll onto my

back and float, staring at the nothingness above. I'd let my long hair loose from its hairband and it would fall and float ethereally around me and I'd allow the gentle bob of the waves to take me to a different corner of the pool.

I'd pull my hands into a stretched point above my head, point my toes and lay on the surface of the water, motionless, my face almost immersed, until I felt myself slipping under and then move my body with effortless grace, diving down. Mother Mermaid. I felt weightless under the water, both in body and mind.

The water made me feel free. Just for that short time, and I know that time spent in the pool improved my well-being both physically and mentally. It was the little pocket of self-love that I gifted myself. No matter how bad the day had been, getting in that pool and swimming grounded me, and I would leave feeling more peaceful and ready to resume my role as a mother, wife, and caregiver with just a little more strength and grounding.

GOODBYE, SCHOOL

SEPTEMBER 2018

Throughout the previous twelve months, various agencies had become involved with Jack's care, as he had not attended school for over a year. The local authority offered him a place at a specialist school for children who had been out of mainstream schooling for some time. It provided a gradual return to study in a small and safe environment. The plan was to slowly build up Jack's confidence, enabling him to return to his school a few weeks later.

After multiple attempts to get Jack to attend at the start of term, the agencies involved scheduled a meeting to discuss the next steps. A week beforehand, a letter arrived from Jack's secondary school. Angry tears stung my face reading it. The local authority was considering an application for an education supervision order (ESO) if Jack was not attending school by October,

Unfamiliar with the term, I searched for its meaning on a government website, and what I found incensed me. An ESO is an order that the family court can apply to you if the local council feels your child needs extra help in education and you, as the parent, aren't cooperating. Jack wasn't going to school through a lack of trying or my laziness. My son was unwell, and it seemed no one was acknowledging that.

Arriving at the meeting, I stood outside with a tight chest, finding it difficult to breathe. My heart was racing. Knowing I would be confronting the staff responsible for sending me the letter filled me with apprehension. Not one to usually feel nervous before these appointments, this time I was representing my son, and there were seven people from various agencies also attending, along with John.

Signing in at the reception, everyone in the meeting room was waiting, all eyes fixed on me. It felt like a heavy weight was pushing on my chest and I struggled to breathe. Poor Jack, this is what he must have felt a lot of the time. It gave me a momentary understanding of his torturous days living with chronic anxiety.

Breathing deeply, I entered the room. After brief introductions, the meeting was underway, and the professionals, some of whom had never met Jack, expertly advised me how I was failing at parenting. At least that was my perception of their comments, though granted, I was exhausted, emotional and unable to be entirely objective. Still, I felt under attack and outnumbered.

One suggested that my son was defiant rather than struggling with a mental illness and that punishment was necessary. Wounded by their words and immediately defensive, my chest ached, and an angry lump threatened in my throat. "As you all sit here judging my son – some of you haven't even met him – I'd say to you, come and walk in my shoes for twenty-four hours and then tell me he's badly behaved. *He's sick for God's sake!*" I fumed at my captive audience, fighting back indignant tears.

I retrieved the letter from my bag. Now was the perfect

opportunity to ask for an explanation. "I'd like to address this letter." I proceeded to read the letter to the room, my voice quivering. "I've attended every appointment you have made. I've answered the door to every visitor. I've engaged with every agency that has contacted me. You give me an example of how I haven't cooperated with you!" I demanded. The fire of anger roared in my belly, replacing the tears.

The school and council representatives took turns to attempt to appease me. They reassured me it was policy, not personal, and that I could be prosecuted and face a fine of up to £3000 for Jack's lack of attendance – although it was unlikely if CAMHS presented medical evidence to the court.

"There is no way I'm going to court, I can't face it, and I don't have the energy or the funds to lose," I snapped.

John, who had been silent up until that point, spoke up: "I'll go to prison before either of us pay a fine over this."

At last, it felt like someone was on my side.

After some discussion, we agreed the specialist school staff would come to the house and take Jack to school. Doubtful, I agreed with them; the fear of court and fines weighing heavily on my mind. The meeting left me drained and anxious.

Monday came, and a support teacher arrived to collect Jack. She had visited twice before to familiarise him with her, as she would be helping him at school.

Jack came downstairs to meet her but avoided all eye contact, went straight to the wall facing it, pacing from side to side in a state of high anxiety. It was apparent to us both that it was not going to be possible to get Jack into her car, despite her gentle coaxing.

The school support worker made a couple more

attempts to get Jack into school with the same result. As she left for the third time without Jack, I stopped her outside the door and asked her what she thought I should do.

"Off the record, I can't tell you what to do, but if Jack were my son, I'd pull him out of school and let him get well."

She smiled warmly, and I thanked her. It was the third time I'd had 'off the record' chats with professionals working with Jack – all mothers – and all had suggested exactly the same thing. It was clear to me as his mum and full-time carer, he was a very unwell young man, and the persistent stress of trying to get him to return to school was exacerbating his illness.

After some discussion with Jack, we agreed to withdraw him from school. It would ultimately end the risk of prosecution. Sending that email formally withdrawing him from education gave me an immediate and overwhelming sense of relief. Now we could concentrate on getting Jack well.

"I'M SO LONELY, MUM"

OCTOBER–NOVEMBER 2018

Jack caught a stomach bug that lasted several days. Thankfully, he didn't throw up, but he lost a substantial amount of weight and barely slept. Despite not being sick, Jack was extremely anxious that he might vomit the entire time. In the early hours on the first night of his stomach bug, Jack came and woke me up and asked me if I would go and sit with him as he couldn't sleep.

After heading sleepily upstairs, too tired to try and reason with my son's anxious brain, I set up a makeshift bed on his floor with a dressing gown and cushion. It was hard and uncomfortable, but it was a sacrifice I was prepared to make if it allowed us both to get back to sleep.

Jack got into bed and kept apologising. "I'm so sorry, Mum, I didn't want to disturb you. I feel safer now you are here."

"It's okay, Jack, try to rest now. It's late, and we both need some sleep," I soothed.

It made me sad to see my son so anxious over something most people would shrug off as an annoyance.

"Please don't leave, Mum, okay? Just for tonight."

'I won't leave you, Jack," I whispered.

Jack drifted into sleep, and I slept fitfully and uncomfortably on his floor. The stomach bug continued and somehow, so did my presence on his floor for the next couple of nights. Jack didn't want me there. What fourteen-year-old teenager wants their mum in their room whilst they fall asleep? However, he needed my reassurance that he wouldn't throw up.

Many parents experience these episodes with their children when they are young, mopping up vomit in the wee hours and setting up makeshift beds on floors. Uncomfortable as it is, we do what we have to do at the time. Had it been more apparent to me then, what this seemingly innocent stint of comfort would have led to, I may have handled things differently. I'm not entirely sure how, though.

Jack recovered from his bug, but his sleep was severely disturbed once again. He was starting to fall asleep at 5pm, waking up in the early hours. Jack's entire body clock was out of rhythm. An unfortunate hangover from the bug was his need for me to sit in his room as he fell asleep as a safety measure. It started pretty innocently, but I didn't realise I was reenforcing his anxiety.

Luckily, my job afforded me the flexibility to work from home when needed, so I'd sit on Jack's floor working on my laptop until he was asleep. I'd sneak out of his room and finish my shift, before starting dinner for the rest of the family. Jack's would be plated up, so that when he woke, he could then eat his dinner as his breakfast.

This nightly regime slowly progressed to me being pulled into a very elaborate and exhausting nighttime routine lasting hours; it was to continue for many, many months. It also slowly laid the foundations for another anxiety disorder – obsessive-compulsive disorder.

During those months, I recall being sat on Jack's bed in darkness around 4am, waiting for him to fall asleep. This particular night, a blackbird started singing in the distance. We lived in a concrete jungle, the very heart of the town, filled with shops, clubs and bars and not a tree in sight, so it was very unusual to hear any birds other than squawking seagulls.

The sweet innocent song of the blackbird moved me to tears; a simple but beautiful gift nature had given to me amongst all the chaos. The little nature-loving girl that I used to be returned once more, just for those few moments, in awe of the blackbird's call. It kept me company for several more nights, and then just as suddenly as it had appeared, it disappeared, but it left a memory firmly in my heart.

During October and November, Jack had no contact with anyone other than me; he barely left his room. His mood slipped lower and lower. Due to Jack's unusual sleep habits, none of his friends were online, so he sat in an empty prison of his own mind, hour after hour.

One day I found him sitting on his floor, quietly crying. Jack was angry and hostile towards me because I'd discovered his tears. "*Get out! Leave me alone!*" he yelled. This was not unusual, especially if he was scared; however, his voice wavered, and he started to sob.

"What's wrong, what's the matter?" I pleaded, heart-broken at seeing my son suffering this way, day after day.

"I'm so lonely, Mum," Jack sobbed. "I have no one to talk to you but you. I can't talk to my friends. I hate my life, it's a prison, and I'm stuck in this room. I want to die, Mum. I can't go on like this..."

I was in pieces. How could I make this better or ease

Jack's pain? "I will speak to CAMHS and see what extra help we can get, okay?"

That was all I could offer Jack, but we both knew that gave neither of us much hope. Jack's weekly therapy sessions with CAMHS were consumed with getting him to leave the flat and attempt some form of education, not establishing his anxiety's underlying cause and treating it.

Leaning forward to stroke Jack's arm with tears dripping down my face, he pushed me away. Jack hated crying himself, but worse still, he hated seeing me cry. Jack bore full responsibility for my sadness – he felt he was ruining my life.

Masking my tears in front of Jack was easier, because if I didn't, he would turn that painful guilt inwards and self-harm when left alone. He would scratch at his hands until they were bloody and sore or hit his elbows on the wall next to where he sat.

Once downstairs, I slid down the wall, sobbing. It was the type of cry that is uncontrollable. It ached in my heart and stomach in a way that is difficult to describe; a physical, tangible pain – primal maternal protection, mixed with a sense of hopelessness.

A TOUCH OF MAGIC AND MADNESS

DECEMBER 2018

CHRISTMAS APPROACHED, but there was little seasonal joy in our flat. Two days before Christmas, Jack made a rare appearance in the lounge late at night. He had always loved Christmas as a child, but it had lost its shine with the arrival of mental illness.

Out of nowhere Jack spoke up: "I love Christmas, I love all the lights in town."

"Let's go and see them, Jack," Paul suggested, spontaneously.

Without thinking, Jack agreed. Before I knew it, all six of us were wrapped up warmly and leaving the flat, Billy the dog in tow. It was Jack's first time leaving the flat in almost six months.

It was a Saturday night, so the town was busy, but thankfully, the tipsy revellers were still at their office parties or in the pubs, so we were spared the usual drunken stumblers. We approached the central gardens, where spectacular lights adorned either side of the paths. A temporary outdoor ice rink had been set up there, bustling with exuberant skaters and a German bar playing seasonal tunes.

It felt warm and wonderful, despite the frosty December air.

We walked under a giant pyramid made from thousands of colourful lights. Jack looked up inside it, and just for a moment, the anxiety left his face and was replaced with childlike wonderment at the beautiful lights as they changed from colour to colour. "This is magical, Mum," he whispered to me.

"I know, Jack, isn't it just? It's so beautiful."

I smiled warmly at my son. Gulping down the lump in my throat, I put my arm through Paul's and walked on, whispering to him through tears: "I feel normal tonight."

Paul squeezed my arm soothingly. "I know darling, I know."

We arrived back home just before midnight, buoyant and chattering away like the old days. This was what our family *used* to be like: all together, united, the boys chatting and sharing stories. It had been over two years since we had been all together like that; I missed those days.

When we got back, Jack was drained from the walk but upbeat. I was elated and as ever, overly optimistic that this would be the start of some positive changes. Everyone went to bed except Jack, after all, he had just got up. As we all slept, he sat up all night watching TV in his room.

The following day Jack felt unwell; his stomach was hurting; he was tired and felt sick. Jack attributed this to the walk and vowed never to leave the flat again.

Christmas arrived, and tensions were running high between Paul's eldest son and himself. Paul was stressed and lacked the coping skills to deal with the rows and challenging behaviours. His son was also struggling with his own feelings, school and life at home with his mother – that's how he found himself temporarily living with us. We survived a tense and depressing Christmas Day, but on Boxing Day, things erupted.

I'd had a bottle of red wine earmarked as a gift for someone, but when I went to get it out of the hiding spot I'd stashed it in, it had been emptied and refilled with water. It was the classic trick of an alcoholic: drink now, worry later. Not only did I have to go and buy another bottle of wine, but, more importantly, Paul was drinking again and hadn't told me. What had happened to honesty and trust?

The trouble with any addiction is that it turns the addicted into a sneaky liar. They will do anything to get their hands on the fix, whether it's drink, drugs, gambling or, in my case, food. They'll trample over anything and everyone to satiate the desire and they'll try every trick in the book. They'll become adept at spinning stories, and telling lies becomes the norm. I'd seen it with Thomas' gambling, and I'd seen it with Paul's drinking. Paul's reaction to being rumbled was to go straight out to the off-licence and down a quarter bottle of vodka, some cheap ciders and return home drunk. We exploded into a furious row. A familiar feeling of dread and anger returned. This was all I needed. Thankfully both my kids were in their bedrooms chatting to friends online and blissfully unaware of the carnage unfolding beneath them.

We lived within ten metres of two local shops, both selling alcohol. Beyond them was a supermarket and another two off-licences, all within five minutes' walk. The central location was convenient because it offered round-the-clock access to food and drink, but it was also a massive disadvantage to an alcoholic. It meant Paul was constantly surrounded by available temptation, day and night, and there were constant reminders – discarded cans, bottles, and frequent street-drinkers. Moving wasn't an option – I'd bought a share in the flat from a housing association, so moving would entail selling my share and finding thousands of pounds in fees, not to mention finding somewhere new to live and all the upheaval.

I calmed down, mainly from exhaustion, and returned to what I thought I was good at: fixing things. I had to find a solution to this latest messed-up situation. Paul wanted to get sober again, but there was no possible way we could afford for him to go back to rehabilitation. However, we decided it might be a good idea to get him out of the flat and immediate area to sober up again. I found a cheap hotel in the town where he could stay, locked away with no money – just food being delivered by me.

The day after Boxing Day, as everyone else was watching Christmas movies with their loved ones and finishing off their festive treats, I was checking my alcoholic husband into a seedy hotel to sober up. *Happy fucking Christmas!*

Paul was bloated in the face, and his stomach had blown up like a barrel. He felt very unwell and confessed he had been drinking a lot more than he'd first told me. I left him at the hotel with a couple of days' worth of food and left him to it. Paul was in no fit state to see me for a while and the initial couple of days' withdrawals were the worst. In all honesty, I had no desire to see him either.

Paul's nights were restless; he couldn't sleep or even concentrate on the TV. I had no idea how it felt to be withdrawing from alcohol, but when I delivered his next batch of food I could see he was struggling. By day five, Paul was much better. He'd lost several pounds and had lost that watery, bloated look. He vowed to stay sober and return to AA meetings.

As things deteriorated with Jack at home, and my time became more consumed with both my sons, it began to impact on Paul and me. I didn't have, nor make the time to spend with him. Our weekends away were a distant memory, and naturally, our relationship suffered. Paul was secretly a little resentful, jealous perhaps, of the time I was spending with Jack. That resentment, along with the lack of quality time spent together, slowly started to affect our relationship.

SPIRALLING

JANUARY 2019

After fourteen long months waiting (and some tearful begging on my behalf) a psychiatrist from CAMHS finally visited Jack at home. The build-up to her visit had been tiresome. Jack was highly anxious about meeting someone new. His support worker, Ben, was on leave for four weeks, but between illness, Jack's sleep cycles and absent staff, it was four months in between visits – something I feel had a substantial impact on Jack's mental health.

After the apprehension of the psychiatrist's arrival, a sense of relief washed over me as Jack didn't mask his anxiety in front of her. Jack sat alone, avoiding eye contact, and scratching his hands uncomfortably as she probed him about his feelings. After a lengthy assessment, Jack finally had a diagnosis: severe specific phobia (emetophobia) and generalised anxiety disorder, both of which were considered life-altering in their severity.

It shouldn't have mattered to have found a label, however, Jack was relieved at being told what he was experiencing had a name. When the doctor confirmed that it was severe and affecting every aspect of his life, it comforted him somehow. Someone, aside from me, was listening and acknowledging what he was going through, and offering hope of recovery from this dreadful place.

The doctor discussed several medication options, and Jack explained his fears around it. At that time, he wouldn't even consider taking antidepressants due to the potential risk of throwing up as a side-effect. The doctor suggested an alternative treatment plan including more intense CBT, occupational therapy using some physical techniques for coping with anxiety, and the possibility of EMDR therapy (eye movement desensitisation and reprocessing).

The doctor left, and I felt momentarily elated – someone was finally validating my son was sick, not badly behaved. Then the inevitable tears overwhelmed me; I felt an odd mixture of relief and sadness at finally having a diagnosis.

Sadly, after fourteen months, Jack still hadn't been offered any of the suggested therapies, and the lack of adequate treatment for his anxiety disorder and phobia contributed to the rapid deterioration of his condition, along with the development of full-blown OCD.

Obsessive-compulsive disorder comprises two elements: obsessions and compulsions. People can experience obsessions, compulsions, or both, and they can cause a great deal of distress. Obsessions are intrusive and repetitive thoughts that don't go away; compulsions are behaviours or actions a person performs in order to feel safe. They become habitual when they give the sufferer temporary relief from their anxiety.

If left untreated, as in Jack's case, OCD can worsen to the point that the sufferer becomes unable to function normally in day-to-day life. It's not uncommon for someone with severe OCD to experience suicidal thoughts. Although I knew Jack had OCD, it took a further fifteen months for the CAMHS psychiatrist to diagnose Jack. During that time, it took complete control of his life ... and mine.

As the months passed without the right therapy, Jack's OCD worsened. His daily routines evolved into a series of safety-seeking compulsions that, if not followed, would lead to meltdowns of fear-filled, epic proportions. I was pulled unwittingly into the compulsions; it was easier to go along with Jack's OCD demands than disturb the entire household, especially at night.

Things deteriorated dramatically; slowly the compulsions grew. Sentences, or 'scripts' as Jack called them, became fixed and had to be repeated in the same tone repeatedly. The compulsions consumed hours of his day and night; he was so frustrated by them and his need to repeat them.

By this point, we were going through about a litre of hand soap a week during excessive hand-washing episodes, in a bid to alleviate his extreme feelings of contamination. Jack had weeping patches of eczema on his hands, wrists, upper arms, and elbows where he was washing his hands and arms so much each day. I had to bandage his hands and arms at night with emollients to ease them. But despite his noticeable deterioration, despite my pleas with CAMHS for therapy, Jack continued to sit on a waiting list and I was left to manage things as best I could.

Just before Christmas, Thomas' psychiatrist had reviewed his case and suggested he try some medication to improve his low mood. Although reluctant at first, Thomas agreed, and he started on a low dose of antidepressants. Initially, he didn't notice a great deal of change or experience any side effects. He was finding it hard to get up or motivated, and he was very low a lot of the time. Then Thomas' psychiatrist suggested upping his medication dose. Initially, he felt a little lifted, but within a few days, he started to swing from chronic insomnia – he was jittery and giggly and awake for twenty-four to thirty hours – to almost comatose episodes. During the latter, Thomas would sleep twenty to twenty-three hours a day and only stir to use the bathroom. Sometimes he didn't even eat or drink for the entire day.

After three months and without consulting his doctor, Thomas suddenly stopped taking the tablets, without tapering off them. I couldn't stop him – he was seventeen years old and it had been his choice to go on them, but he was not comfortable with the way they were making him feel.

Thomas' sleep pattern continued to be severely disturbed; he found it hard to either fall asleep or wake up. It wasn't unusual for Thomas to sleep seventeen hours in one stretch.

One Sunday night, at about 8pm, Thomas ran down the stairs with his coat and backpack and fled the flat without saying a word. It was very out of character for him.

Grabbing my shoes and coat in a frantic fumble, I ran after him, but he had already disappeared into the darkness. Thomas was a real homebody and loved being at home. He was not one for drinking or partying and rarely went out at night unless meeting a friend at the cinema.

I came back into the flat and attempted to call him but

there was no answer, so I immediately ran up to his room to search for clues for what might have sparked this uncharacteristic behaviour. There, lying on his bed, was his phone with messages pinging one after the other from several of his concerned friends. I contacted two of them and discovered he had told them he had hurt himself with a knife and was leaving.

Concerned for his welfare, I called the police and explained what had happened and what his friends had told me. I gave his description and what he was wearing, and they advised they would get a patrol car out looking for him. I called John and explained what had happened. He immediately went out to look for him, as did Paul.

Jack came out of his room to see what the commotion was. I outlined the story gently and without too much detail, but Jack knew Thomas better than anyone and recognised that this was entirely unexpected behaviour.

Just before midnight, the police arrived, along with Thomas. He had walked into the police station and asked them for help. As a precaution, they handcuffed him, in case he had the knife I had warned them about.

As I sat there with Thomas and the police, listening to them telling me how my son had surrendered himself at the police station in search of help, a myriad of emotions washed over me. How could I possibly cope with anymore? But I was relieved to see Thomas safely home and grateful to the police for their compassionate support. The police agreed to inform CAMHS of the incident.

When they left, Thomas didn't want to discuss the night's events and went straight to bed. He was embarrassed and clearly still upset over something. I gave him the space he needed and messaged his friends to let them know he was home safely.

The following day I checked on Thomas. He was sleeping deeply, and when I went to pull his covers up, I noticed his left arm – there were nine or so horizontal cuts across it. I had not seen them the night before. The cuts were superficial and already faintly scabbed, but they were very upsetting, nevertheless. What could have upset my son so much to hurt himself like that and run out of the house?

Later that morning when he awoke, he was much calmer. "It's over, Mum. I don't want to talk about it," he offered, flatly.

I gently brushed over the cuts on his arm, and he pulled away.

"It's nothing. I thought it would help me feel better, but it didn't. Don't worry, I won't do it again," he said, dismissively.

"Thomas, I'm always here for you. Please don't ever feel you can't talk to me again about anything troubling you, okay?" I said, reassuringly.

"Okay, Mum. Can we just stop talking about it now, please?"

Within weeks, Paul relapsed again. Difficulties with his son triggered the old demons within, and he started drinking again in an attempt to cope with the stress. Thankfully, he never touched the drugs after rehab. Just as well – the drinking was bad enough.

One day, Paul had a heated argument with his son (who'd been staying with us) and left the house. I went looking for him and found him barely coherent, urinating up against a wall in broad daylight in the busy town centre. Paul had consumed three-quarters of a litre of neat vodka in the fifteen minutes it had taken for me to find him. He'd wet himself and was shivering in just a T-shirt in the icy wind.

I wanted to slap his face, to snap him out of his stupor and wipe the irritating grin off his drunken face... Paul was meant to be my husband, the man standing by my side, supporting me, but instead, all I had was a dysfunctional drunk staggering in the street. I was angry and humiliated. *"What the fuck are you doing?"* I spat, venomously.

I didn't care if anyone around us saw or heard – I was utterly enraged. All I could think about was Paul's teenage son appearing around the corner at any minute. I was desperately trying to save him from seeing his father in that state.

I dragged Paul, literally, up the steep hill, got him into the flat and made him strip off his wet clothes and lie on the sofa, where he promptly passed out. His son had already left and never knew about the incident. My sons were upstairs and thankfully oblivious.

I was relieved – I'd averted yet another disaster, and nearly killed myself in the process once again. My nerves were frayed and my stomach in knots. I sat there silently watching Paul sleep, observing him snoring, reeking of stale drink and urine, with an odd mixture of love and revulsion.

As always, Paul was filled with remorse when he woke up. I felt sorry for him. When not drinking, he was a lovely, kind and caring man. He was a hard worker and always provided for us and would go out of his way to help anyone. But behind that lovely, compassionate man was a very lost, broken person.

Paul was becoming more mentally unstable and started regularly self-harming with sharp blades at work. Half the time, I didn't know he'd done it as he'd pick inconspicuous places on his body, hidden by clothes. He'd often wear socks to bed to cover the gashes on his ankle, and I was oblivious.

One night he forgot, and as he turned over in bed early the next morning, I caught sight of something dark on his skin. "What's that on your ankle, Paul?" I questioned.

"It's nothing," he muttered, pulling away from me.

It was too late. I flicked on the light and gasped at what I saw. Paul's ankle had about a dozen or so very dark, reasonably fresh and prominent scars across the inside of his ankle, crisscrossing in every direction. In the middle was a deep, fresh cut about 4cm long and about 2cm wide. It was oozing and dark red.

I started crying. These were not surface scratches. What the hell was this man feeling to mutilate himself in this way? "Oh, Paul, what did you do? Why. *Why?* "I cried.

"It's nothing, it's fine," he dismissed, clearly embarrassed and covering his ankle with his hand.

I pushed his hand away, wanting to see the macabre extent of his cuts. The large deep one was dark purple and crusty. Paul had used a blade cutter to slash himself but had cut a lot deeper than intended. The cut was substantially wide and probably should have had stitches. Paul must have nicked a small vein because he described how the blood had spurted out in a long, cotton-like string, pumping profusely. He'd panicked and grabbed a bonding agent, glueing his skin together, then wrapped it with some blue paper roll to stem the blood flow at his workbench, before cleaning his blood off the floor. Luckily, Paul worked alone in his workspace, so no one witnessed this shocking act of self-harm.

Running my finger over the crusty, angry-looking scab, I shuddered with shock and revulsion. It had happened three days earlier. I felt a strange mix of disgust and sadness for him, but misplaced guilt too. How could I not notice that

Paul was hurting this much? I'd seen the nicks on his arms and scratches before, but this was self-harm on a whole new level. Paul's ankle painted a morbid portrait – target practice for his internal pain – and I had no idea how to save him from himself.

"*You're such a bad wife, Emily,*" the Guilt Monster whispered.

A GENETIC GIFT?

I HAVE HAD my own experiences with mental illness, which began as a teenager, and it is something I have never truly acknowledged until recently. I can recall wandering into the kitchen at about the age of thirteen whilst my mother and stepfather were exchanging heated words about his gambling. She fell silent at my approach.

Still seething, and without warning, my stepfather grabbed a framed picture and angrily smashed it across the back of a dining chair, sending shards of glass flying in every direction across the kitchen floor. He pushed past me, muttering obscenities under his breath as he left.

The front door slammed, and my mother and I jumped with the ferocity of the bang.

Good riddance, you fucking bastard.

Without saying a word, my mother got on her hands and knees and started carefully collecting the shards of broken glass. She glanced up at me with apologetic, tear-filled eyes as I watched her picking up the pieces, both literally and metaphorically.

"Emily..." she started to say, but I cut her short. "Don't, Mum. Please don't..."

Rather than run to her for comfort, or instead, console her, I ran out of the house trembling with the aftershock of my stepfather's violent outburst. I walked for a couple of miles until I found a bench and sat down, crying. In my thirteen-year-old head, I had run away from home with no thought of where I was running to. The bench was my new refuge.

With no mobile phones back then for distraction, I had no choice but to sit within my own thoughts. I lacked the maturity to process what was happening in my mother's new marriage.

I'd gone from living with a man whose presence I'd never felt, to living with a man who made his presence very much known, in the loudest most terrifying ways. And so had my mother.

About two hours later, my mother pulled up in her car. She had been driving around looking for me. She sat down gently next to me, and we held each other tightly without saying a word. I could feel her apology and helplessness through the tightness of her grip. She was in over her head and making the best of what had fast become a bad situation.

She took me home; home, to a place where everything felt out control. I decided to take back control in my life the only way I knew how: I slowly stopped eating.

At the time, I was at an all-girls senior school and was always trying to be taller, slimmer, and more popular, to be liked by the other girls. I was moving through puberty and my body was changing shape, which led me to becoming very self-conscious about my weight. That, along with my volatile homelife and the rejection I felt over my father leaving, led to me to restrict my food intake.

It began subtly. I'd give away my packed lunch at school, or worse still, bin it. I'd take my dinner and our dog, Sam, to my room to do my homework and avoid the dinner table at all costs. I fed the dog my dinners most nights, having taken the smallest nibble of a vegetable or two. I was in control of what I was putting in my body and that felt powerful.

My obsession with food gradually led to anorexia and a couple of very worrying years for my mother as I dropped to just over six stones. Even so, I still hated the fat body I saw in the mirror.

It was 1986, and back then, my treatment consisted of an older doctor at the point of retirement telling me if I didn't start eating, he would admit me to the hospital and force me to eat through a feeding tube in my nose. He scolded me for upsetting my mother, who was sitting in the corner of the room, quietly crying.

I was absolutely petrified at the prospect of being hospitalised and force fed. I was also terrified of this doctor reprimanding me and remember feeling terribly guilty for hurting my mother – though I had never intended to upset her. The poor woman had enough to contend with. I vowed to try eating just a little bit more from then on, but it wasn't easy. You can't just tell an anorexic brain to eat. It's not that simple.

Not long after the doctor's appointment, I had a shower with a full face of makeup on, as you do as a fourteen-year-old. Stepping out of the shower, I caught sight of my reflection in the bathroom mirror. My mascara had run down my face in rivers, highlighting my sunken, shallow eye sockets. Long black streaks framed my facial features, and I looked skeletal. Glancing down, I saw my shoulders, the bones protruding across the top of my chest, then scanned down my body and saw my pelvis and hip bones jutting out. As if someone had lifted a veil from my eyes, I saw myself for the first time as others saw me: scrawny, thin, and pale. It was a turning point in my recovery.

Coming through the other side of anorexia, I returned to a more normalised eating pattern very slowly under the watchful eye of my mother and schoolteachers. However, the eating disorder left me with some very skewed thoughts about food, and I would inspect food labels for fat content and calories for many years to come, well into my early twenties.

After my father's death, I became obsessed with ensuring I'd turned the iron and cooker hob off. The stress of my father's death appeared to trigger a mild OCD. "Off off off off off..." I'd say aloud, tracing the knobs on the hob over and over, ensuring they were in the 'off' position. I could *see* they were off, but I couldn't accept they were off. My mind kept telling me to check, one more time, over and over. "Off, off, off, off, *off*! *Oh, for fuck's sake, Emily, they're off!*" I'd shout, losing patience with myself.

I'd do the same with the iron. Once I even made an excuse at work and drove home just to check it was off, which of course it was. It slowly progressed into checking the fridge was closed properly, and all the doors were locked, especially at night.

I became terrifyingly convinced someone would break in, and so created obstacles by the doors and left the dishwasher door down, which obstructed the back door. I placed long pieces of wood in the patio door frames so no one couldn't open them. I drove John mad with my barricades. It lasted several months and then suddenly disappeared after I returned to the UK.

It resurfaced three years later after my divorce, another period of great stress, whilst I was caught up in the emotional torture of my secret lover. I lived in a top-floor flat at the time, so I felt reasonably safe and didn't indulge in the door security compulsions again, but it didn't stop me from getting stuck in the hob and iron rituals once more. Once again, the OCD only stayed for a few months, and when I was more balanced, it disappeared and hasn't returned.

Jack had never witnessed any of this. The first occurrence was before he was born, and I hid the reemergence of these behaviours completely from my children.

I've never been a drinker, nor smoked or even enjoyed tea or coffee, so I didn't have the classic go-to when I struggled to cope. So instead, when life spun out of control with Paul, Thomas and Jack, I found myself turning to food. During the most difficult months I discovered food gave me imaginary comfort. It's not uncommon for people to turn to food to ease anxiety. A full tummy can give you a false sense of contentment, but it's just an illusion. Food, especially sugary food, can become just as addictive as drugs and alcohol.

As the challenging weeks rolled on, I found myself secretly eating vast quantities of food in short bursts: crisps, chocolate, cakes and fresh white bread with lashings of butter; all calorie-loaded, nutritionally useless stodge. As I was eating the food, I knew it was unnecessary and unhealthy for me, but I found it hard to stop. I was in denial that I had a problem, and it's incredible how powerful my brain was at convincing me otherwise.

My weight gradually increased, and that made me miserable. I joined an online slimming site and, for three months, stuck religiously to a strict calorie-counting regime. It gave me a sense of control over something again, and I lost a substantial amount of weight. But then my membership ended, and without the daily discipline, the desire to binge again slowly returned, predominantly at night. I was able to consciously witness my behaviour, though, so if I had an angry confrontation with Paul or felt stressed before an appointment for Jack, I knew I'd want to eat. Crunchy food was one of my favourites: sweet or savoury – it didn't matter. Biscuits and crisps were perfect for satisfying the urge; it was as if I was trying to bite through my anger.

Initially, I didn't gain weight after one or two binges which gave me an imaginary green light to do it again and again. Slowly but surely, though, I regained all the weight and then some. Things quickly got out of hand and before long, I was bingeing four to five nights a week. It was always in secret and always at night, and I'd hide the evidence at the bottom of the bin or stash food wrappers behind cushions if I heard one of the children approaching. I'd spend weeks yo-yo-ing up and down, starving myself and losing weight, then bingeing and regaining everything and more.

Food became my comforter, a self-destructive soothing blanket. I began to plan my binges. I'd feel tingles of excitement from the anticipation of eating beforehand and would go to a local shop after dinner and look at all the things I could eat.

One evening, even after the entire day's intake of three regular meals, I consumed an enormous amount of food during a two-hour bingeing session. It started with two family bags of crisps, five bars of chocolate, a large trifle, a box of chocolates, followed by a large bag of popcorn. It all had to be washed down with a drink, always sickly-sweet fruit juice, – it was not unusual for me to consume almost half a litre of fruit juice during a binge.

I went out again and bought a 1kg family bag of cheese savouries and ate all of them, cramming my mouth full, leaving just enough room to squeeze in some juice which would soften the food and make it easier to swallow. Then I ate a box of sickly caramel ice-creams, four in total. Eating until feeling nauseous and bloated, I then ate half a packet of biscuits and three large bowls of sugary cereal, all within a two hour-period. I'd easily consume around four to five thousand calories during one binge.

The crazy thing was I *knew* I shouldn't be doing it. My body would never want all that junk if given a choice. Once I started eating, the anticipatory excitement wore off almost instantly, and I munched through the food in a state of subconscious frenzy. It wasn't that satisfying to eat any of it, but I couldn't stop myself. It was as if something had taken over and stolen my willpower. I knew it was me, of course, but it was not me: Emily. I was observing this gluttonous feasting from outside of her.

The next day I felt ill, utterly poisoned inside with a toxic hangover from the vast amounts of sugar and fat. I felt downright miserable. I binged like that for three consecutive days. By the fourth night, despite feeling physically sick, I began another planned night of eating.

Mid-feeding frenzy, I decided to look up bingeing on the internet. I know it's never a healthy or accurate practice to play Dr Google and self-diagnose, however, I stumbled across a site dealing with binge-eating disorder and could identify with all of the associated behaviours. I burst into tears, then went to the kitchen and made two rounds of toast, sobbing as I ate them. I recognised I had a problem, but I felt out of control and unable to manage it alone.

I saw my doctor in late October 2019 and broke down. He was very sympathetic when I told him about my anorexia as a teen and my disordered thoughts about food. The doctor asked me to tell him what I was consuming during a binge. I felt ashamed to admit the truth, but he gave me little choice. It was as if I was reading out a sorry shopping list of processed food, though there was relief in being honest with someone at last. With my history and current food behaviours he agreed to refer me to an eating-disorder clinic for specialist counselling. He was aware of the family history with Jack, Paul, and Thomas and suggested I'd been hanging on for so long, the stress was now coming to the surface in its own way, through my eating. He told me it wasn't me consciously eating, it was a faulty part of my brain, and therapy could fix it.

Even knowing what I was consuming wasn't healthy or normal, when the doctor confirmed that I was eating an abnormal amount of food and it was like any other addiction, it hit home a lot harder. I left in tears. I was meant to be the strong one, meant to be keeping this ship afloat.

Now everything in my life felt out of my control, including me, so I rejoined the online slimming club that day and returned to a calorie-counting regime. It's against their advice if you have an eating disorder of any kind, but I knew it would be several weeks until the appointment came through from the clinic, and I didn't want to continue bingeing and ballooning in weight, so, I lied.

It gave me back a false sense of control, and the weight started to come off. More importantly, the bingeing stopped, temporarily. I later learned that the yo-yo dieting I was caught up in was one of the underlying causes of my bingeing. The constant deprivation of self-labelled 'naughty' foods would lead to inevitable binges of the same foods I'd spend all my time avoiding.

My referral for the eating-disorder clinic came through within a few weeks, and I met my psychologist in November. We began working through a self-guided recovery program together over the phone. It was a slow process and difficult to stick to, what with so much else going on at home. Deprivation and dieting often underpin bingeing. I stopped weighing myself daily, which, in turn, stopped me micromanaging the ounce fluctuations. When the need to binge arose, I tried to distract myself with writing, or texting a friend. I tried to keep myself occupied at night. Nighttime was always my danger zone.

In the past, when I'd finally got Jack settled at night, I used to reward myself with two or three chocolate bars. I stopped rewarding myself with sugary late-night snacks in 'my time', and as a result, my weight stabilised and very slowly started to drop. Food became less of a focus for a while and eating became easier without the constant underlying thoughts about how many calories were in the meal and how much weight I would put on.

I got halfway through my treatment for the eating disorder, and it was helping my eating patterns enormously. Still, like any therapy, it required me to be fully engaged and responsible for my recovery. I found the homework a challenge. Daily meal monitoring fell by the wayside several times. However, I continued to work with the program and have phone sessions with my psychologist until she contracted Covid, and sessions were suspended. I saw her absence as an excuse to quit and in April 2020, I foolishly withdrew myself from treatment. I'd convinced myself I had it under control, and it was an unnecessary annoyance to deal with on top of everything else.

One of the hardest parts of having developed another eating disorder was accepting that it is a mental-health disorder. I struggled to accept that I had a problem. *No, not I, I couldn't possibly...* I was the invincible one, tasked with saving everyone else. I couldn't do that job if I had succumbed to mental illness myself, and I judged it as my weakness, an inability to manage. And so began a phase of crucifying self-criticism.

Anorexia, OCD and binge-eating disorder all appeared in my life when it was at its most chaotic, and more importantly, out of my control. Although I was unable to witness it at the time, each disorder gave me a false sense of control over the situations I was in. I had also succumbed to depression more than once in my lifetime.

Another thought provoked that Guilt Monster of mine regularly: were all these disorders just different traits of a mental illness that I'd somehow bestowed on both my children through my genes?

BUFFERING THE MAYHEM

Over the course of twentysomething years, I have mastered the art of emotional labouring: the ability to smile outwardly through gritted teeth, disguising my own emotions whilst appeasing those around me. My mother inadvertently taught me that skill. However there have been times I couldn't force that fake smile no matter how hard I tried. I was angry my life had been tipped upside down by mental illness and addiction. I couldn't go out anywhere or make any plans and became a full-time, round-the-clock carer to three debilitated people. It wasn't a role I'd chosen or wanted.

I selfishly resented my youngest son at times for being sick. I punished him like it was a choice he was making, unable to see his illness for what it was, or to witness his pain and frustration because my own anger blinkered me to it.

Likewise, I wanted Thomas to pull himself out of his depression. He knew better than anyone what I was dealing with each day with Jack, so somehow, I expected him to sort himself out without my help. I needed him to stop gambling, to stop hiding away from life in his room and causing me additional stress.

I was angry with Paul too. His alcoholism threw a ticking time bomb into our lives that eventually exploded. The inevitable debris left only remnants of our old marriage for me to hold on to, to try and salvage. The strong man I needed beside me more than ever had gone. When things deteriorated with Jack, when he was needed the most, Paul became like another child, another responsibility to constantly worry about, leaving me flooded with resentment towards him.

At the time, I thought they all just needed to man up. What an awful, demeaning expression that is, and I'm embarrassed to admit I shouted it at them all at times, from a place of ignorance and desperation.

I became accustomed to buffering everyone's mayhem. I couldn't tell Paul about Thomas' gambling, nor of Jack's lack of progress, or tell my sons of Paul's drinking and self-harm, for that matter. And in the process, I juggled everyone's extreme imbalance with the well-meant intention of protecting them from each other. I was essentially lying to them all, most of the time. Most days, it was a job to remember whose truth I was dealing with at any given time.

Everyone's instability had to be absorbed somewhere and I was the perfect sponge, sucking it all up in silence, creating a personal whirlpool of seething chaos. From time to time, rather like a pressure cooker, the steam had to release to prevent an explosion. Sometimes though, letting off a little steam came too late and I blew.

My skin would crawl and itch from the inside at times with sheer frustration. Gritting my teeth, I'd quietly walk away from my sons to the sanctity of the tiny kitchen in my flat and grip the work surfaces tightly. I'd dig my fingernails into my palms, desperately wanting to scream and shout every known profanity you could imagine.

Most of the time, I didn't. I'd slam kitchen pans around with gusto and grab pencils from a pot on the windowsill and snap them. What I really wanted to do was snap their bloody necks at times, but what kind of mother would even think such thoughts?

Me. I am a mum – a loving, kind one, but I'm not unshakable. I'm still just a person with limits, and I'm honest enough to admit they all tested me regularly well beyond them. I began to question my moral compass at times, having such dark thoughts. I'm almost ashamed to voice them but recognise now it was just a symptom of desperation and frustration. Anger and frustration are part of our emotional makeup and should not be stifled. They are more likely to explode with devastating effects on the poor unsuspecting people around you when held in.

My family and I would have been much better served if I'd grabbed my keys, left the flat and gone to sit in my car. I could have shouted out that anger alone, without affecting anyone or directing it at them in personal attacks.

I'm not going to lie, I love my husband and children fiercely and would defend them to the end of time, but there were several times when I couldn't stand to be around any of them. There was no respite from their struggles, and I'd spend my time running from one person's crisis to the next. I was like a rag doll – with each one of them tugging at one of my limbs, pulling me in every direction. It was exhausting.

Each of them didn't fully know or understand the extent of the others' dysfunction. How could they? I'd hidden it so well, so how could they possibly know what I carried solely on my shoulders?

There were many occasions I'd walk out of the flat enraged, with nothing more than the coat on my back and the change in my pocket. I'd every intention of disappearing and never coming back. *Fuck them all! Let them be someone else's problem now, not mine.* But I couldn't bring myself to do it. Something stopped me, every time.

None of this is easy to admit – after all, I was the perfect earth-mother, 'butter wouldn't melt in her mouth' Emily. Some days I fucking *loathed* the sight of my own family because of their mental illness.

But I never stopped loving them. Ever.

INTERRUPTING OCD

JUNE 2019

Thomas continued attending his CBT sessions at the CAMHS clinic, and he seemed to find them helpful. His support worker was helping him to view life differently and turn overwhelming despondency into a little hope. Thomas appeared more optimistic, and I was relieved because his upturn in mood coincided with Jack's deterioration.

Thomas attended a review with the psychiatrist and confessed to having stopped his medication. The doctor was taken aback but agreed he was happy for Thomas to stop taking them if he felt uncomfortable with them.

Just after his eighteenth birthday in June, Thomas was discharged from CAMHS and advised to contact the adult services to get on their waiting list, which was approximately six months' long at that point. Somehow, some months later, Thomas missed his turn and had to reapply to go back on the waiting list, which he did.

We were back in the mental-health services waiting game, again.

Jack and I were both utterly exhausted by the beginning of summer 2019. Jack had become desperately low and suicidal again; his intrusive thoughts were consuming him day and night. By this stage, he had created several hundred compulsions he was forced to repeat each day by his brain in order to keep him safe, all taking hours to complete. OCD was fully in charge and overpowering his rational brain. Jack was completely debilitated by it at this point.

I called CAMHS and requested an urgent review by the child psychiatrist. It had been over six months since the doctor had seen Jack; he was no further up the waiting list for therapy and as a result, had deteriorated rapidly. OCD was a new and exhausting, yet still undiagnosed addition. Jack's doctor was away on extended leave, so CAMHS agreed a locum would visit him at home at the end of July for a review.

One day in late June, after a particularly challenging night, Jack came downstairs to talk to me. "Mum, I can't take any more of this. I don't want to keep living like this," he said flatly, with his head down. "Is there any way you can take me away, like, really far away from this country? I want to break these rituals, and I think it's the only way I can do it."

Stunned, my mind started whirring at the prospect of getting Jack out of the flat, let alone on a plane to another country. He'd not left the flat in six months, so it seemed an impossibility. I'd not seen this coming, nor ever contemplated such lunacy. A thousand thoughts were spinning around my head, least of all, how could we possibly afford this miracle trip?

"Okay, let me see what I can do, Jack. Are you sure this is what you want?" I offered, hesitantly.

"Yes, Mum. It's the only way," Jack said, somewhat pleadingly.

I was desperate for change too. The long nights and disturbed sleep were taking their toll on me; getting to bed about 5am most mornings and then up again by 9am for work left me exhausted and tearful most of the time. We were stuck in a punishing Ground Hog Day, and I struggled to see a way out of the situation. I'd agreed with Thomas to borrow the money he'd received from his recent eighteenth birthday on the proviso I would pay it back over the next few months, so I'd at least have a way to pay for this mad notion, should I be able to make it happen.

A few days later, I approached Jack about the holiday. We talked about flight times and hotels, and both agreed it would be best if I find a local flight as well as stay in a tranquil area with no other people to minimise his anxiety. It was all still conjecture, a pie-in-the-sky notion, and I wasn't sure it would happen. But after hours of searching, I found an afternoon flight to Lanzarote, staying in an old villa in the middle of nowhere, with a private pool and no other guests. As it was before the school holidays, it was still reasonably priced, and with Thomas' birthday money, I could just about afford it. Jack wanted Thomas to come too – he didn't want to make the trip without him – but Thomas was hesitant. He'd seen Jack in full anxiety mode many times over the previous two years and was naturally cautious.

Desperate for change for both Jack and myself left me willing to try anything. If Jack couldn't do it after all, well, at least I'd have tried. Paul was the only person I confided in. It was best if no one else knew; that way, no one could judge this absurd idea.

Showing Jack the holiday, he carefully checked the

flight times and villa photos. The flight left in sixteen days. I gave him a gentle ultimatum: we do this now or forget it. The school holidays were fast approaching when the prices would skyrocket, and I wouldn't stand a chance of affording it. Jack asked me to give him two days to decide, meaning two more days to avoid deciding.

The two days came and went. Finally, the moment had come – book the holiday or lose the villa and the only affordable option. Jack agreed to go. But as soon as it was booked, he began to panic. "I don't know if I can do this, Mum, but I know I have to because you can't waste your money."

"Okay, let's see what happens, Jack," I reassured him, though not feeling remotely comforted myself.

Still, nobody knew about the trip, only Paul. I certainly didn't want anyone to give Jack a hard time if he couldn't face his fears and get on the plane. I went about preparing for myself and the two boys to go away, not knowing whether it would happen or not. As the days ticked down, Jack became more anxious, and I was in turmoil inside, though doing my best to mask it. I was already dreading the Sunday afternoon we were scheduled to leave, and it was only Monday.

Thomas spoke to Jack often about the trip in the preceding days, having decided to make the trip himself and confidently assuming we were all going. He attempted to do everything possible to help his brother whilst constantly reassuring him that he could do it. I'm not sure I could have got through those days without Thomas' optimism and support.

Each day, Jack's anxiety grew. "I'm so scared, Mum. I don't think you realise how big this is for me."

"I do understand, Jack. Let's just see what happens, shall we?" I soothed.

Oh, I knew alright, only too well, having watched him suffer unbelievable torment during these last eighteen months at the mercy of anxiety and now OCD. Although Jack was terrified of every aspect of this trip, and I mean *every* aspect, he was acutely aware that it involved borrowing money in every direction to make it happen. Despite the crippling nature of his illness, underneath was my kind, caring kid, and it gave me hope when glimpses of his true nature surfaced at times.

Saturday night approached, and his anxiety was peaking, as expected. Jack had barely left his room in six months, let alone the flat, and had cocooned himself in one tiny space, fortified with hundreds of compulsions just to stay safe. He was undertaking a momentous challenge the next day.

We repeated the usual pre-bedtime routine, interjected several times with worried questions: "What if I don't fall asleep tonight? "What if I throw up?" "What if my ears pop?" "What if the plane crashes?"

What if, what if, what if?!

The endless '*what ifs*' left me a nervous wreck, exhausted both physically and mentally. As I sat quietly on his bed, my mind went into overdrive about the following day. Jack finally fell asleep; it was 4.23am.

Heading back to bed, painstakingly quietly, I tried to avoid waking Paul. Sleep eluded me. My mind was racing with a hundred thoughts that bled quickly from one to another and I could feel my heart racing. This was anxiety. It gave me an insight into the world my son lived in permanently.

I drifted off to sleep around 7am at a guess but was

awake again by 8am. Thomas got up and was ready to go. Scraping back my hair into a unbrushed ponytail, I quickly got dressed. Thomas and I were ready. Paul took the dog out for a walk. He felt it would be easier not to be in the house while we were getting ready. None of us knew if Jack would go, and the tension was gnawing at us all.

It was 11am and time to wake Jack up. My stomach was doing somersaults, and I could barely breathe. This entire trip hung on his mood and the realisation that today was the day we were going away. He woke up quickly, and it instantly dawned on him: it was *the* day. He sat up and complained almost immediately of a stomach ache. An inevitable rush of anxiety and adrenaline came over him, and as I'd feared, he began to panic.

We had to leave by noon for the airport at the very latest as the flight left at 2.30pm. I'd already checked in online, so I'd figured two hours was ample time to get through bag drop and security. Minimising the amount of time spent sitting at the airport would be our best option, knowing it would be extremely difficult for Jack.

Quictly and calmly, I offered Jack his travel clothes. He dressed and put on his shoes for the first time in months and came downstairs. Paul pulled the car up outside and waited to see if we would all appear. I'm not sure where Jack found the strength to push through his anxiety, but there was an iron will inside my son that drove him on. He gave himself no choice, and that was a potent tool for change.

We said our goodbyes to the dog and headed downstairs to the busy street. Thomas led the way with the suitcase, followed by Jack and me. Paul put the bag in the car, and we climbed in. It was the first time Jack had been out in natural daylight in almost a year.

"It feels funny to be in the car, Mum," he said, as we left

on the short journey to the airport. It was only the beginning but I felt ecstatic to have even got Jack that far.

Thomas and Jack chatted away together in the back of the car. Thomas was trying his best to distract his brother. Paul leant over and put his hand on mine as the traffic lights halted us. "You can do this, Emily, you're an amazing mum, and I admire you for even trying. I love you."

Squeezing Paul's hand back, tears began to sting my eyes. "I love you too," I whispered.

We reached the airport just after 12.30. Jack quickly got out of the car.

"Fuck!" he exclaimed. "Look at all these people, Mum, *look at all these people!*"

There was no point reprimanding Jack for his language; it was simply an outlet for his fear, and it was always worse when he was mid-anxiety attack. It wasn't directed at me, it was just a verbal expulsion of his anxious thoughts.

A strange stillness blanketed me and fuelled by adrenaline, my movements were almost robotic. Thomas led Jack across the road with the suitcase, and I said a hasty goodbye to Paul. Leaving his embrace was difficult. His arms around me felt safe and reassuring.

"You can do this," Paul reassured, witnessing the fear in my eyes. We hugged once more before I sprinted to catch up with the boys, turning briefly to wave a final farewell to Paul.

Once inside the airport terminal, the enormity of where he was hit Jack. He began swearing at himself as he pulled his cap down lower, convinced everyone was looking at him. As I steered him in the direction of the bag-drop section, my heart sank when I saw the length of the long queue. We had no choice but to join it.

It felt torturous to stand amongst people. Jack was

swaying from side to side, swearing and trying to avoid eye contact with anyone. He began to hit his head and pull his neck and shoulders up sharply. It was a way for him to discharge his overwhelming anxiety. Unfortunately, these behaviours only drew more attention to him, and he became more self-conscious and repeated the behaviours even more. Thomas attempted to reassure and distract him but Jack couldn't concentrate on anything; he was in full anxiety mode.

After what seemed like an eternity, we reached the front of the queue, and Jack managed to mask the movements and swearing long enough to get through the bag-drop procedure. We were travelling light: one suitcase between the three of us. This was no ordinary holiday; there had been no time for clothes shopping or planning outfits. I'd even forgotten to pack a jacket, so I had nothing warm to wear should the weather turn cold.

We headed to passport control. Whilst walking through the airport, Jack got away with swearing and hitting himself occasionally. It appeared no one noticed. However, once we reached passport control, we were back in a queue, in a confined space surrounded by people.

"Mum, everyone's looking at me! *Fuck, I hate this. I want to go home!*" Jack's anxiety was peaking once again.

"We can't go home now, Jack, you're doing so well" I offered calmly. Thankfully the queue was mercifully short and we headed to security.

"Take your hat off," barked a security guard.

I'm sure Jack's behaviour appeared suspicious. Here was a 5ft 8" lad, swearing and pacing, waiting to walk through the metal detector behind his brother. Thomas had sailed through with no beeps.

The security guard signalled Jack through the metal

detector with a wave of his hand, and it flashed red and beeped. He was directed to stand to one side. Jack turned to me, looking terrified. "Are they going to search me? I've got no fucking drugs on me. Why do they want to search me?" he muttered.

"Shh, just be quiet, Jack, stop swearing. You'll get us taken away!" I growled, desperately.

The security guard led me through, and again the detector beeped. Of course, there was nothing suspicious about my behaviour, nor any forbidden contraband shoved down my knickers. Still, there is something about these situations that makes me feel guilty by default. But at least it meant we would both be searched together. We removed our shoes, and a security guard patted each of us down separately before swabbing us, presumably for drugs.

Having passed all checks, we were waved through to collect our belongings. I was grateful Jack had contained his anxiety long enough to get through the search phase.

Thomas had already collected our hand luggage, and we were free to leave the security area. I walked ahead of the boys, leaving Jack in Thomas' care briefly to avoid seeing the state Jack was in. Cowardly of me, I know, but I was already exhausted and we had not even reached the departure lounge.

Thomas led us to the far end of the terminal and some empty seats, as far away as possible from anyone. We sat down to give Jack a chance to recover. Leaving Thomas in charge, I went and spent a small fortune on water and some boiled sweets for the plane.

Other families had filled the empty seats around Jack in my absence and when Thomas spotted me, he signalled for me to hurry up. "Jack's having a panic attack, Mum. Quick." Thomas looked worried.

I knelt at Jack's feet and held his knees.

"I can't breathe, Mum, I can't breathe, *I can't fucking do this...*" he gasped.

As I stroked his knees and soothed him by guiding his breath, Jack slowly calmed down. Thomas and I glanced at each other, almost certainly thinking the same thought. Neither of us thought we would be getting on that plane.

In front of us were a family of four: mum, dad and two young children. A little girl, maybe six, was clutching a teddy and excitedly hanging off her dad, asking questions about the plane. They were utterly oblivious to what was unfolding behind them.

I sat next to my two beautiful boys, one of whom was struggling in a way no one could see or possibly understand. This should have been a happy occasion. The airport was filled with families excitedly looking forward to their trip to the sunshine. I longed to be one of those normal families but had accepted it a long time ago; this was my normal. Even with this acceptance, sadness overwhelmed me at times – not for me, but for my son, who was being robbed of his teenage years.

"I'm such an idiot and a waste of space, swearing in front of little kids," Jack muttered, critically.

There was my sensitive, aware child, but there was nothing I could say or do to change his opinion of himself.

Our flight was announced shortly after. We were the first group to be called due to our seat numbers. We headed to the gate, and Thomas and I both ignored the swearing and anxious muttering. Facing forward, I wouldn't catch anyone's eye or judgment.

We were ushered out into a tunnel adjacent to the plane waiting on the tarmac. As the other passengers slowed in the tunnel, Jack's anxiety peaked at a level not seen before and certainly the worst since we'd left home. Thomas and I glanced at each other with the same hopeless expression. I'm so grateful to this day that no one in the queue made an issue of Jack's behaviour.

We walked out onto the tarmac. The engines were roaring, and I've never been so glad for the deafening noise, as Jack screamed, "*Fuck!*" at top volume and hit himself across his head. He was flooding with anxiety. Thankfully, the engines drowned the sound out.

Thomas steered us towards the back of the plane, where there was a shorter queue. We headed up the steps and onto the plane. The fact we had got Jack this far was a minor miracle. Thomas quickly found our seats and sat by the window, Jack in the middle and me in the aisle. From this position, I was able to shield Jack from other people and them from him. As he sat down and put his seatbelt on, he began to calm down.

I sent Paul a swift text to say we were on the plane. Paul had always been there, quietly encouraging me to try this trip.

"*He did it! That's amazing. Well done. I'm so proud of you both. I love you, Emily,*" Paul enthused.

"*I love you too, Paul. I'll text you when I get there.*" Then I switched off my phone.

The kids used to hold my hands for take-off when they were younger. Two young men who now towered above me didn't need to hold their mother's hand anymore, though their mother would have welcomed holding theirs. Flying was not my favourite pastime, but Jack's increasing distress over the preceding week had pushed my fear of flying aside.

As we settled into the flight, Jack turned to me smiling. "I'm glad we came on this trip now, Mum, I'm enjoying it."

"I'm so pleased, Jack," I said, rubbing his back and smiling.

As he returned to watching a show on his tablet, I turned my body towards the aisle and let the tears fall. Those few words had made the last few hours of hell melt away. It was the validation I so desperately needed to justify the crazy trip.

Jack settled and Thomas dozed by the window. The three-and-a-half-hour flight passed quickly and peacefully.

We landed at Lanzarote Airport and let everyone else disembark first. It was a short walk to passport control which was reasonably quiet. Jack was noticeably calmer there, and I was relieved the swearing had stopped. We sailed through to the baggage-reclaim area, and thankfully our suitcase was one of the first on the carousel. Thomas grabbed it, and we headed to the exit.

I'd arranged with the villa owner to pick us up from the airport. We found his wife, Suzanne, waiting as agreed by the lift. It was a short twenty-minute drive to the villa. Jack was very quiet. Suzanne pointed out a local supermarket about ten minutes' walk away from where we would be staying. We'd arrived on a Sunday evening, so all the shops were closed. The owners had very kindly brought in some essential food items for the first evening.

We reached the villa. It was in a very isolated place, a fifteen-minute drive to the nearest large supermarket or town. Once we arrived, Suzanne gave us a brief tour and then left us to our holiday. The villa was much bigger than our flat at home and traditionally Canarian. Wooden doors and tiled walls opened out through a large patio door to a beautiful private pool area, lined with mature palm trees.

Thomas took one look at the pool, opened the door and dived in, fully clothed. It was a childlike exuberance I'd not seen in a long time. My sons had grown up with a swimming pool in the back garden throughout their early years in Australia and Thomas was a confident swimmer.

Jack watched with amusement as Thomas winced at the cold water.

"That's a lot colder than I expected," he gasped, getting out as the cool wind blew around the garden. Lanzarote is known for its windy conditions, and that night was no exception.

There were two double bedrooms and a twin room. Jack asked if I'd share the twin with him, just for the first night. Reluctantly, I agreed, and Thomas jumped at the chance of his own double room with a pool view.

Jack had not been able to stomach food since the previous Saturday night, and he was still unable to eat anything substantial. Thomas and I tucked into some fresh local bread with ham, cheese, tomatoes, whilst Jack nibbled on fresh watermelon.

We were all pretty exhausted from the day's events, and as the boys fiddled with the TV trying to get it to work, I went and set up the single beds for the night. Something caught my eye in the corner of the room: an army of ants had found their way in and were marching behind the beds. Armed with a can of deodorant, I did my best to rid them from the room silently. The last thing I needed was for Jack to see ants crawling all over the floor and walls.

We settled into bed at 11pm, and as Jack watched another show on his tablet, I must have drifted off to sleep quickly. He woke me at 1am to say he was going to bed. "Goodnight, Mum," he whispered.

"Goodnight, Jack." I yawned sleepily. Jack fell asleep.

And just like that, ninetysomething nighttime compulsions were interrupted.

Woken about 7am by an itch on my face, I stretched lazily. It had been the longest uninterrupted sleep I'd enjoyed in over twelve months, and it felt momentarily wonderful. That was until I realised my bed was full of tiny ants, and they were crawling over my head and body. Within a few minutes, Jack woke up itching too and dived out of bed, freaked by the early morning invasion.

We headed to the spare room, but neither of us could fall back to sleep. It was impossible to ignore the itch, and it became clear our hair was full of ants. We both headed outside to the pool, intending to jump in and rid ourselves of them, but it was surprisingly chilly in the wind, and the pool was freezing.

"I have to shower, Mum. I can't stand this itching."

After Jack's shower, it was my turn. The shower tray was full of dead ants.

After dressing, Jack lay down on the sofa, watching me intently as if about to speak, yet unable to begin. I sensed his apprehension. "I feel like I'm drowning, Mum, like I can't breathe. I feel so unsafe here, but I feel selfish and ungrateful saying that to you," he confessed.

"Jack, you are neither selfish nor ungrateful. I'm not surprised you feel that way, but you are doing so well. It will get easier, you know. Shall we go and sit outside by the pool?" I enthused.

"I'm not, Mum, I don't like this feeling," Jack replied, not remotely comforted by my praise or reassurances.

Jack was flooding with anxiety, not uncommon given the sudden change of environment. He had been ripped out of his comfort zone, his little safe space at home and was overwhelmed by the change. I wasn't sure how to feel. Part of me wanted to relax, enjoy sunbathing, and slip into holiday mode, but this was no holiday; it was one long, tough therapy session.

It was our first day, and we needed food and fresh water. Thomas was keen to explore and help me. Jack reassured me he was okay to be left alone but pleaded for us to be quick.

When we got back to the villa, Jack was still lying on the sofa, and as Thomas and I tucked into lunch, Jack still couldn't stomach food.

Peter, the villa owner, turned up with an ant powder and treated the bedroom, assuring us we would be ant-free from then on. Thomas and I headed out to the pool. For the first time in two years, I began to actually relax. I had pressed pause on the disarray of my day-to-day life and it felt momentarily luxurious to sit in warm sunshine and simply do nothing but watch Thomas splashing about in the pool.

Jack watched us from inside and eventually ventured out, squinting in the bright sunshine. He sat at the edge of the pool and dangled his legs in the water. The sunlight warmed his back in between the chilly gusts of wind. It was the first time Jack had felt the sun on his body in almost three years. "It feels nice to feel the sun again." Jack smiled as he kicked the water with his feet.

I glanced at Thomas and we both smiled behind Jack. Everything, no matter how small it was, felt like a triumph and Thomas and I were Jack's constant cheerleaders.

Thomas tried to encourage his brother into the pool. "Come in, Jack, it's not so bad when you get used to the cold!"

"Maybe tomorrow," Jack replied, without any real conviction.

I prepared dinner, but still Jack couldn't face eating

anything. He joined us as we sat outside eating and candidly spoke to us both about how utterly lost and scared he felt.

"Jack, you've done so well. Look how much you've overcome just to be here," Thomas said encouragingly.

But Jack couldn't see it. "I want to go home, Mum. I don't think I can last another five days here, he said quietly, his head hanging low and shuffling his feet uncomfortably under the table.

"That's impossible, Jack. We *can't* go home!" I replied, exasperated. We had only been there for twenty-four hours. I ended the conversation.

It became apparent that I was going to be spending the week in the twin room with Jack. Thomas had already claimed the double en-suite, and Jack still didn't feel comfortable in his room alone.

After watching some TV, we all headed to bed at 11pm. When Thomas was safely out of earshot, Jack started again. "Mum ... can we please go home early?" he asked hesitantly.

Clearly he wasn't coping as everything was so unfamiliar, yet he didn't want to spoil the trip for his brother and me.

"We will discuss this tomorrow, Jack. It's not that simple. I can't just magic a flight back home."

I sighed as we settled into the beds – they were ant-free, thankfully.

Despite the high winds rattling the wooden front doors, I slept better than I had in many months, without interruption. I woke Jack at 9am and Thomas shortly after that. We needed food supplies for the week, but the local supermarket wouldn't provide enough, unless we planned on living on bread, crisps and fizzy drinks. My concern about

Jack was growing as he had not eaten anything for almost four days, other than some watermelon. Not even fresh bread or ice cream could tempt him. He felt too anxious to eat.

Jack couldn't face a car journey or a busy supermarket, so we agreed he would be okay if we locked the villa door and returned as soon as possible. Thomas and I managed to scrounge a lift to the nearest town from Peter who was working nearby. I'm glad we accepted the lift as the supermarket was a fifteen-minute drive away.

We had a tight budget of €80 for the week. Thomas eagerly planned the meals for each day for me and chose the ingredients too. This was one of the highlights of my holiday: shopping with my son. After many months of challenges, there was something simple and wonderful about our little shopping trip.

Once we'd finished, we headed to the bus stop, but soon realised it was a further hour until a bus arrived. The ice cream and meat wouldn't take too kindly to sitting in the Canarian sunshine for that long. I was also mindful that Jack would have been alone for almost two more hours by the time we got back. Thankfully, John had shown us where we could get a taxi , so we headed there instead.

In hindsight, the villa's isolation wasn't ideal given we had no transport and a minimal budget. The taxi was €12 so between that and the shopping we only had €40 left for the week. However, this was no ordinary trip. We wouldn't be going out for family meals at night nor venturing on excursions, so there wasn't any need for money. It was enough for me to have a change of scenery and some decent sleep.

When we returned to the villa, Jack was curled up on the sofa and relieved to see us. Thomas decided to go out for a swim, and Jack seized the opportunity again to ask about going home early.

I'd been avoiding the issue and hoped the new day would bring him more peace; that he would relax and start eating again. That wasn't the case. "Okay, I will call the airline now and see when the next flight is."

I remembered when booking the flights that the airline flew twice a week, so there was a good chance there was an earlier flight.

Jack watched me like a hawk from the lounge as I sat outside by the pool and called the airline. A flight was departing on Thursday, and mercifully, there were a handful of seats remaining, though there would be an additional fee to pay for changing flights. It would mean coming home three days early, but based on Jack's mental state, inability to eat and our very tight budget, I wasn't concerned about leaving early. We had achieved so much already, just getting there in the first place.

After calling Jack and Thomas together, I explained what the airline had said. Jack offered to pay the extra fee from his birthday money, and Thomas was just happy that his brother had overcome so much to get on the plane in the first place. It was agreed we'd travel back earlier, on the condition Jack ate, and we all tried to make the most of the remaining time on the island.

I called the airline back and changed our flights. That left us with two and a half days to salvage what we could of our holiday. A weight visibly lifted from Jack and he joined Thomas by the pool. Thomas was already in, splashing about. Jack sat on the side, dangling his legs in.

After a few minutes of observing Thomas, Jack turned to me. "Mum, I will go in if you will."

The freezing pool was not remotely enticing to me.

High winds had chilled the water dramatically overnight, so it was unpleasantly cold, however I wanted nothing more than for my son to feel the joy and freedom of being in water again. "Okay, you're on."

I went to the steps and, much to the boys' amusement, I clumsily launched myself into the cold water. After some hesitation at the temperature, Jack followed. Thomas threw Jack a giant inflatable doughnut, and with much laughter, he climbed in after us.

"I'd forgotten how good this feels, Mum," Jack exclaimed, laughing with childlike delight.

The two boys bobbed about, mock-fighting, racing in their doughnuts and splashing me.

Out of nowhere, an overwhelming surge of emotion came over me, and I made an excuse to use the bathroom.

"Don't be long, Mum! Come back soon!" Jack called after me.

Once in the privacy of the bedroom, I slid to the floor on my hands and knees and sobbed for several minutes; the kind of crying where your mouth opens, but no sound escapes; you can feel the overwhelming pressure of pure emotion through your chest.

It was primal. It was a release.

It had been so long since I had experienced any joy with my boys and I had watched Jack suffer immeasurably in a silent prison for two long years. But we'd done it. Jack had done it. We'd defied the odds of getting here and there he was, laughing like the kid he should be, enjoying the simple pleasure of swimming in the warm sunshine. It was why we made this crazy trip, this exact moment, and nobody could ever take it away from us. If nothing else ever happened, I would always have this memory of Jack and Thomas, my beautiful sons laughing together once again.

"Stay there, I want to get a picture of you!" I rushed out to the pool, upbeat and disguising my tears. I wanted to capture that moment forever – a little something to hold on to during the darkness. Neither boy was keen on having their photos taken, but they were too busy playing to notice me snap a picture.

Sometimes, even now, I'll look at the picture: Thomas and Jack floating in giant pink doughnuts, simply being kids, momentarily carefree. There's a look of utter joy on Jack's face and it had been over two years since I'd seen that cheeky, grin. The photo still makes me smile today … and cry.

We swam, dived and raced together for ninety minutes or so, surrounded by palm trees in the warm sunshine. The wind was still chilly when we got out of the pool, but I was too elated to care. I sent the photo to John and my mother. Now I could tell people what I had done. I was triumphant.

I cooked dinner for Thomas and myself, but Jack still couldn't face any food. We sat outside all together and chatted about the next day and what we could do. Jack agreed he would like to go for a walk and make the most of the holiday. The dip in the swimming pool had boosted his confidence in himself. Jack had witnessed that he could do things out of his usual routine, and nothing terrible would happen. It seems absurd saying that, but in Jack's world, everything posed a potential threat.

We enjoyed a peaceful evening, and Jack finally nibbled on some bread, the first thing he'd eaten in four days. Relief washed over me. I called Peter and explained we were leaving the villa early and the reasons why. He offered to drive us around the island the following day, free of charge as a gift, so that we could see some of Lanzarote on our last day.

The following day, Jack joined Thomas and me on our walk to the local supermarket for fresh bread. Jack had not been out for a walk for six months or been into a shop in twelve months. Inside, I was doing cartwheels of joy, though in those days, I rarely allowed my feelings to run away with me or make a fuss about Jack's progress. He hated attention being drawn to him. Behind his back, though, Thomas and I would pull wide eyes and give big thumbs-ups at his achievements.

Jack was excited, taking in all the unusual sights of this strange desert landscape, his senses clearly heightened through months of lack of exposure to the outside world. We reached the supermarket, and he approached the entrance without his usual hesitation. It was tiny, with one staff member. We stocked up on a few bits, primarily obscure-flavoured crisps and Spanish chocolate, and headed outside.

Sitting on the wall, sipping his drink, Jack observed his new surroundings. He'd always loved travelling and exploring new places. "It feels good to be here, Mum, to be outside again. I've missed so much, haven't I?"

"You're doing amazingly. This is just the beginning for you." Thomas interjected.

We sat for twenty minutes with our drinks, talking about places we'd all like to travel to. It felt normal, hopeful. For so long, there had been little hope. Jack had only spoken about dying, not living, let alone a future that might include travelling.

We headed back to the villa, and Jack had his first substantial food in five days: a cheese roll. We ate lunch outside and prepared for Peter's arrival. The inevitable anxiety started to rear its head. "How long are we going to be? I don't want to go now."

I calmly ignored all of it. "Jack, we can be as long as you feel comfortable."

Peter arrived, and we all climbed into his old jeep. He set off, giving us a running commentary on the island as he drove. He took us off-road across a windswept desert track. The dramatic cliffs were a sultry backdrop to the arid landscape. It was exceptionally bumpy, and I kept looking at Jack's face in the mirror. He looked decidedly uncomfortable.

Peter drove us to a local beach and told us to take as long as we wanted as he set off to eat tapas in a local bar. We had a short walk, but Jack was hesitant. The villa had become his new comfort zone. There were families everywhere and several children running around. The cold wind was whipping the sand up into a stinging spray, driving against our legs. It wasn't pleasant and Jack looked uncomfortable.

We headed back to Peter's jeep, as I texted him to say we were finished. The poor man barely had time for the chef to batter his calamari before we were back. Peter seemed puzzled to see us so soon. After all, it had only been ten minutes, and he was still wiping the food from his mouth after a hasty lunch.

Peter drove us back to the villa via a couple of detours to see the island from the best viewpoints. The boys were quiet as they listened to his stories of the island's history, volcanic eruptions, and earthquakes.

After shaking his hand warmly, we all thanked him for helping us see the island. It was above and beyond renting the villa to us, and we were all very grateful for his kindness.

We ate dinner together on Wednesday night. Jack's first full meal since Saturday. Afterwards, Jack asked if he could use my tablet. He hadn't told anyone he was going away as he was worried he might not go and end up looking foolish. Jack messaged his friends and was chatting for some time.

Out of the blue, he looked up. "I'm going out with my friends on Sunday, Mum." It had been thirteen months since he had ventured out with friends.

"Oh, that's great, Jack. Who's going out?" I said, trying to contain my excitement.

"Just my friends from school. We're just going to meet in town."

I smiled. "That's fantastic, Jack. They will be so happy to see you."

"Well, I've done this, so I want to keep pushing myself, Mum," he said.

Jack had made arrangements many times before to go out with friends but always found a way to back out on the day. The night before, he would start getting anxious and talk himself out of it. He would then sink into a low mood at his perceived failure and isolate himself entirely the following day.

We went to bed, and whilst drifting off to sleep, my mind wandered, thinking about the weekend, hoping Jack would be able to make it out on Sunday. At that moment, the return journey was a more concerning issue. If it were anything like the journey out there, we would all need nerves of steel to get through it.

We awoke early. Both Jack and I was anxious about the impending trip for different reasons. It was overcast and very windy.

I headed out to the supermarket alone for freshly baked bread. Walking alone always gave me space to think, over-think for the most part and I'd often have silent conversations with myself about my failings as a mother.

When I returned, Jack was sitting in the lounge, waiting. "Do you want to swim with me, Mum?" he asked, grinning.

I winced. "It's a bit cold, Jack."

Getting in a cold pool was not very appealing. The sky was heavy with thick clouds keeping the temperature down, and the wind chilled the air further. However, this was the first time Jack had asked me to do something fun and carefree in a long time and by the end of the day, we would be back home and certainly wouldn't have this opportunity again.

"Come on, Mum, it will be fun!" he pleaded.

I attempted to muster some enthusiasm. "Okay, okay, let's do it!"

Jack eased his way into the pool, step by step, giggling at the coldness. I followed, ducking my shoulders under quickly to lessen the torture. Once in and adjusted to the temperature, I began to relax. We spent forty minutes or so lapping, racing, laughing and splashing each other. For that brief time, we were just mother and son again. There was no shouting or meltdowns; no anxiety, no fear – just unadulterated pleasure. It was a joyous welcome break from the years of Jack's mental illness.

I packed the suitcase whilst the boys packed their bags, and before we knew it, Suzanne had arrived to collect us. When we arrived at Lanzarote airport, it was surprisingly large and bustling. We'd had such a speedy transition through passport control and baggage reclaim at the start of our trip, I hadn't noticed.

"Mum, look at all these people!" Jack cried.

Two coaches were disembarking, and all the passengers seemed to be heading towards the same queue as us. We swiftly joined the front of the line, and thankfully, it moved quickly.

"I'm sorry, ma'am, but this flight is full, and I cannot seat you together. The only thing you can do is ask on the flight if someone is prepared to swap with you," the desk clerk offered apologetically as we checked in.

My heart sank and Jack's eyes widened in fear. "Do something, Mum, please. I can't sit next to someone else."

Unprepared for this, I objected. "The lady who scheduled flights for me told me as long as we checked in two hours before, we would be seated together. My son has acute anxiety. We can't sit separately on the flight," I pleaded, but it was pointless.

"I'm sorry, ma'am, but there is nothing I can do: the flight is full. The best I can do is sit you near each other."

She turned the screen towards me. There were two seats separated by an aisle and one in front. We had no choice but to take the seats.

We headed through security without issue this time, and Jack was noticeably calmer than the day we departed. Thomas found some empty seats in the departure lounge, but the airport was exceptionally busy with multiple flights leaving and Jack's anxiety had started to climb. He was convinced that everyone was staring at him, when in fact, they were just going about their business buying duty-free and bustling towards the gates.

It was a very uncomfortable hour for us all. It was playing heavily on my mind how Jack might react on the plane next to someone else.

As soon as the flight was called, we jumped up and got to the front of the queue. Jack stood still beside Thomas and me, and despite the other passengers standing nearby, he masked his anxiety remarkably well and was noticeably calmer than when we'd left England. Those around us wouldn't have known he was a nervous wreck disguised by clothes and a baseball cap.

We eventually boarded our flight and were seated right at the back. Thomas settled in his seat a couple of rows ahead. Jack and I stood up, waiting for the other passengers to arrive, to see if we could ask them to swap. An exuberant young couple headed towards me, and Jack gestured to me not to ask them, shaking his head vehemently.

Finally, a middle-aged couple approached Jack's row, and he stood out of the way to let them into their seats. "Don't worry, Mum, I'll be alright, don't ask them," he whispered to me, and settled himself next to the couple.

It was a smooth flight, and we arrived home on time at 11pm. We disembarked quickly and zipped through an empty passport control. Paul was waiting outside for us, and within half an hour, we were all home.

That night, Jack headed to bed at 2am. I was still up chatting to Paul and filling him in on our few days away. Jack asked me to pop in and sit on his floor for a few minutes as he fell asleep. There were no rituals, no scripts, or compulsions; just my presence. Jack was asleep within minutes.

Sunday came around. Jack's achievements in Lanzarote still buoyed him but the usual anxious thoughts still arose. He wanted to cancel, but he knew he couldn't. Jack was excited about seeing his friends and had more confidence in himself than I'd seen in months. However, anxiety doesn't just go away upon request, and the same fears still sat with him.

Jack headed into the shower – a place that was like being on the set of a horror film for him. Everything posed a potential threat that could lead to disaster: the shampoo might sting his eyes; my razor might fall in and slice him; he might slip and land on the upturned plug which could spike him. The list was endless and exhausting. I couldn't begin to imagine what it was like to live inside his head with that level of anxiety.

Jack dressed and prepared to go out, pacing the floor, checking his clothes for final approval. He studied his hair, scrutinising it, before putting on a cap and pulling it down tightly. The build-up to excursions was always excruciating and nothing short of a military operation in their execution.

I stood in the background, attempting to minimise Jack's stress, allay his fears and put everything in place to help him get out of the door. Enabling, in other words. Despite all the usual stress-filled preparations, somehow it was different this time. There was no question of Jack cancelling. He had psyched himself up for going out to meet his friends for the first time in thirteen months, and this time, he was going. They called for him, and he left.

Jack had done it. He had pushed all his fears deep down to go and spend time with the friends who, thankfully, had remained in touch with him throughout the last two years.

Four blissful hours passed before he returned, exhausted, slightly sunburnt, but elated. It was to be the first of several more excursions to come.

FALLING APART

JULY 2019

The week after we returned from Lanzarote, Paul went to meet some friends at a music festival. He wanted me to join him, but at that point, it just wasn't possible to get away, even for a few hours; I'd resigned myself to full-time caring again. He set off, and as the day wore on, he sent me various pictures of the festival and the occasional one of him with his friends. "*Wish you could have come,*" he captioned one.

My heart sank. At that moment, I wanted nothing more than to be out on that warm, sunny, July afternoon, listening to live music, but Jack's illness had me trapped in a miserable cycle I couldn't permit myself to escape. It made me happy that Paul had gone and was enjoying himself.

The day passed slowly and Paul eventually ran out of phone charge. Unable to reach him by almost midnight, I messaged both friends he'd been with and asked if he was with them. Neither had seen him since 10pm. Already knowing the answer, I asked anyway: "*Was he drinking today?*"

"*Yes, he had a few beers,*" his friend replied.

They didn't know the extent of Paul's drinking problem,

so to them it was fun and games. Of course, they'd also had a skinful and were high on festival vibes.

By 5am Paul still hadn't returned. I'd been up late with Jack and when I did get to bed, I was unable to sleep. I was both exhausted and angry – and a little concerned – so I headed out to the local streets where he'd parked our van, knowing he had taken the bus to the festival. Sure enough, I found Paul in the van, sound asleep.

Enraged, I pounded the side of the van, which made Paul jolt out of his slumber. He pulled the door open and winced at me, rubbing his head. The van was strewn with empty cans of cider and a takeaway container with its half-eaten contents clumsily spilling out all over the floor. *Our* van floor.

Paul was still drunk and aggravated at being awoken so abruptly, but I couldn't have cared less and ripped into him, all guns blazing. "Where have you been all night?!" I demanded. "I sat up half the night worrying about you! You've got work in two hours."

"What? What time is it? I was sleeping. My phone ran out of charge," he muttered.

Paul was safe, but by then, I was in danger of spontaneously combusting in fury at his behaviour if I stayed anywhere near him. "*Fuck you, you selfish idiot!*" I spat and slammed the van door shut.

I walked off, smug in the knowledge that the loud thud would have most certainly hurt his already delicate head.

Heading home to bed, I managed just a couple of hours of sleep. Waking again at 8.30am and still seething, I headed back to the van for another showdown. *How dare he*, I thought to myself, having imaginary angry conversations with him the entire way back.

Paul was fast asleep. I thumped the side panel again,

this time not quite so aggressively. He sat up, rubbing his face. He pulled the van door open, and the smell hit me: the mix of stale alcohol, takeaway and faeces. In his drunken state, he'd attempted to use the van toilet and missed or spilled the contents, defecating down the side of the van and in his jeans. I wretched at the stench.

Paul was sitting in his underwear, fresh self-harming scars on his ankles, surrounded by the chaos of the night before, looking like death and clearly feeling it. He was a sorry, pathetic shadow of the person I loved. It felt like someone had punched me in the guts. Wiping away hot tears, I felt disgusted, exasperated, angry and sorry for Paul all at once. "Look at you... Look at this van. You were due into work an hour ago, Paul. Have you called in sick?" I cried.

The reality of the state he was in and his lateness for work hit Paul, and he went into full panic mode, scrambling around for his keys, phone and clothes.

"Calm down, calm down, Paul. Paul, *stop!*" I shouted as I grabbed his hands to stop his frantic behaviour.

I texted his boss from his phone, telling him Paul had had an upset stomach and wouldn't be in, apologising for the late notice. I then called the doctor and made an appointment for Paul that afternoon. I'd had enough: the drinking, the cutting, this carnage – it was all too much, and Paul needed help.

After making him clean up his mess, I dragged him home and made him shower, eat something, and tell me what had happened. There I was again, lying for him, covering up the chaos, and trying to fix him. I just couldn't help myself.

Paul was in quite a state. I'd not seen him that upset and scattered in a long time. He confessed he'd not been at work for most of the preceding week or the week before, when I was in Lanzarote with my sons. Paul had been leaving the house, going into work, and feeling so anxious and overwhelmed, he was leaving by mid-morning and staying out all day until home time. He was too scared to tell me. He felt like a failure: empty and emasculated.

Paul had been drinking again and admitted to keeping a bottle of vodka under his workbench and taking a swig whilst pretending to pick up a tool or a dropped pencil. My heart sank with a familiar feeling. So preoccupied with Jack and Thomas, I'd not noticed Paul slipping. I was usually so sharp at picking up the signs.

At the doctors', I sat crying as Paul recalled all the sordid details of his relapse: the cutting and the anxiety. He had drunk four more cans just to be able to face the doctor. My tears gave the doctor some indication of the chaos our lives were in. He signed him off work for three months, prescribed antidepressants, referred him to an adult mental-health program and an alcohol outpatient unit at the local hospital. I called his boss and explained about the medical certificate. They were very understanding and arranged a meeting the following week to discuss his sick pay.

Paul went to the hospital appointment the next day, and they talked through his drinking and anxiety. They advised him they would be in touch about alcoholism support, but they never did get in touch. The unit folded a few weeks later through lack of funding.

Paul was finding it increasingly difficult to cope at home with his state of mind, and I was struggling to cope with him and his chaotic behaviours.

We agreed that Paul would stay at a local campsite for him to get some space. He felt that being away from me, and all the drama at home, would somehow help. It would also mean that he would be away from the temptation of the off-licences on our doorstep. He gave me his bank card and had no money or access to it.

It was late July, the sun was shining, and the campsite was private and quiet. Paul set up a large awning and started to relax into camp life. I would visit most days, and for me, it was a welcome escape from the flat. Enjoying the outdoor escape, I would fuss about his camp, cook food on the stove, and we would go for walks with the dog.

I'd long since craved a more peaceful life, especially after town-centre living. I would be more than happy living out my years in a caravan in a field, self-sufficient and away from the madding crowds, much to the disgust of my family and children. I wanted to fulfil my bohemian dream of a simple life in the outdoors, and Paul was living it.

But it was no dream for Paul in reality. He was isolated and withdrawn from life, pretending to be happy but anxious and miserable inside. Paul couldn't feel anything; he was totally disconnected. He hid from other campers to avoid conversation and became awkward and distant. It seemed that my dream was becoming Paul's nightmare.

After about nine weeks, Paul received a call from the mental-health team and they went through his circumstances. He was placed on a waiting list for CBT and warned it would be quite a wait.

Paul stayed at the campsite for three months but eventually he decided he needed to be around people and life again. But he wasn't ready to return home; he didn't feel he could cope with the stressful circumstances and was still feeling fairly fragile. So he stayed locally, camping in the van on a road near the beach. It had everything he needed: a bed, gas, a toilet, and access to free fresh water from the beach taps. Part of him enjoyed the fact he could camp on one of the most affluent streets in the town, with the best view of the beach, for free. He fancied himself as a bit of a beatnik, a peaceful musician escaping the constraints of conventional society with just his van, guitar and a few minimal possessions.

However, the local residents in their vast mansions didn't care to share their vistas with a handful of van-lifers, so they complained to the council. A traffic warden was sent to move Paul and everyone else on and those that didn't were given parking tickets. Sweeping views of the sea were reserved exclusively for the people in the mansions, and four campervans along a two-mile stretch were somehow spoiling their view.

Paul relocated to a quiet, tree-lined street nearby and returned to work. He was at least sober, not self-harming, and seemed a little more settled.

YOU'LL JUST HAVE TO WAIT, AGAIN

AUGUST–OCTOBER 2019

THE CAMHS PSYCHIATRIST reviewed Jack shortly after we returned from Lanzarote. Sitting in my lounge with the psychiatrist and Ben as they listened to what Jack had achieved filled me with a sense of triumph.

Ben smiled. "I've got to be honest with you, Emily, I didn't think you would be able to pull it off, but I'm so glad for the family and you, Jack, that you did."

To think no one thought we could make that trip happen made it all the more rewarding that we did. The psychiatrist listened with interest to our account of the compulsions and schedules Jack was practicing pre-Lanzarote. Though he didn't diagnose OCD, he did acknowledge that Jack's anxiety was on the severe, life-altering scale, and we briefly discussed medications again. Jack was still resistant to trying any pharmaceuticals. After all, every single one listed nausea or vomiting and stomach upsets as potential side-effects and considering vomiting was his life-altering phobia, it was still out of the question for him.

The doctor agreed to place Jack on the waiting list for

intensive CBT, a higher level of therapy than he had been receiving. It angered me that despite being in the CAMHS system for twenty months, and his psychiatrist's therapy suggestion six months earlier, he was only now being placed on the waiting list at my insistence; a waiting list still at least six months long, and one I had been assured three months earlier by the CAMHS team leader he was already on.

In April, I had called CAMHS having heard nothing since Jack's visit from the psychiatrist three months earlier. It had taken an entire month of phone calls, left messages and emails to get a response back from the team leader, by which point I was incensed by their apparent wall of silence.

She couldn't find a plausible reason why Jack had not been placed on the waiting lists and promised to do so then without further delay. But that had been a lie – a promise to placate a distraught mother at the end of the phone and she failed to add Jack to the waiting lists too. It was an unforgiveable oversight by the staff involved. Someone had failed to do a simple task, twice, which would cause my son a substantial deterioration in his mental health. I questioned if they could expedite the waiting list given their error, but they both agreed that was not possible, without much explanation other than more severe cases were waiting.

Had I not requested the review, Jack would not have been reassessed and placed on a waiting list. It took a further ten months for my son to reach the top of that waiting list and fifteen months to access it. This was a dire consequence of the critical underfunding of the mental-health system in the UK.

In the month following our return, Jack continued to make progress with his recovery. He had ventured out three other times with friends but each excursion was preempted by several hours of anxious preparation. Despite overwhelming fears, he would make it out and enjoy time with his friends for several hours. When he returned, he was always happy – though exhausted as he would have to mask his anxieties in front of his friends. Jack's many fears hadn't gone away, he's just managed to suppress them.

In the weeks following our trip to Lanzarote, Jack had expressed a renewed interest in returning to school. I applied to the local authority and after a frustratingly long six-week wait, Jack was placed back on the roll of his original secondary school.

Everyone, including Jack, the school, and his support worker, felt he wasn't anywhere near able to cope with being back at a busy school with over 1,200 pupils. As a result, he was once again offered a place at the small school for children struggling with mainstream education. Jack and I were invited to a meeting at the school to discuss his attendance there.

A whole year had passed since he last attempted to go, and it was with amazement that I watched him get ready and into the car with far less anxiety than usual. Once there, Jack openly chatted with the teachers about how much he had been struggling. They were incredibly supportive, and it was agreed he would attend after half-term; just over a week away. A year earlier, he was pacing, facing a wall and unable to participate, and now he was sitting in a classroom, agreeing to come to school.

The end of half-term fast approached, and as it did, Jack's anxiety levels soared once more. After all, he'd been out of school for almost two and a half years. Ben visited Jack during half-term, and they chatted about how he could best approach going to school, despite the crippling schedule and new compulsions that had crept in since our return from Lanzarote.

Jack agreed he would wing it on the Sunday night before and attempt to eliminate them all in one go. I had my doubts, but Ben and I had witnessed Jack face his fears with incredible tenacity in going to Lanzarote. "I am excited. I can see a future now," Jack said, grinning.

Ben smiled. After working with Jack for just over two years, it must have been so rewarding to see this young man starting to emerge from the darkness. There had been so many sessions where Jack had sat for forty-five minutes, head down, uncommunicative; sessions where Ben had left because Jack had stormed out of the session, unable to face his fears and angry over the life he was missing out on.

"This is why I do this job, Jack, so I can help young men like you get their lives back," Ben said warmly.

I swallowed the lump in my throat. This was a good day; one I couldn't have foreseen just a few months earlier.

Thomas was such an incredible help and support during our impromptu trip to Lanzarote, and for some weeks after, he was visibly buoyed. During the summer months, he'd also seen a little more of his friends, and his connection to them helped improve his low mood. He was well aware though, that his friends would be leaving that September for various universities around the country, so he made the most of being in their company whilst he could. He seemed a little more settled and brighter, which was a welcome relief.

When September rolled around and Thomas' friends scattered to start their new lives, he spent more and more time isolated in his room. He would sometimes go for a week or ten days without speaking to anyone, and that isolation proved crippling. He started experiencing stomach cramps and bouts of diarrhoea which went on for days. After each episode, he would feel utterly wiped and go to bed and sleep for up to sixteen hours, which once again messed with his entire body clock. The doctor ran an exhaustive set of blood tests and concluded the gastric symptoms were irritable bowel syndrome (IBS), and the fatigue was down to the IBS and reoccurring depression.

During the autumn, Thomas had several appointments at the doctors', along with a podiatrist for a painful ingrowing toenail and the orthodontist. It was exasperating trying to get him to each appointment. Thomas was sleeping so erratically and for such long periods, he woke up anytime between 11am and 11pm. I had to reschedule the orthodontist three times as he just wouldn't wake up. On one occasion, I dragged him, groggy after only an hour of sleep, for his toe surgery. It made him impossibly grumpy – I never knew which version of Thomas I would get each day.

His main issue was isolation, and this inevitably led to gambling episodes. He eventually surrendered his bank card to me voluntarily and avoided having any money in his account at any time.

Thomas became more withdrawn again. His handful of friends were all away at university, he no longer played games online or spoke to anyone, and he slept for hours on end. It didn't matter how much I chastised him to get up, to shower, to move, I couldn't shout his depression out of him, though at times, I really tried.

SCHOOL TRIUMPH

NOVEMBER 2019

THE SUNDAY NIGHT before school went back was fraught. Jack was in a state of anxiety not seen since our holiday. However, there was a hint of steely determination, which was slightly different from the previous two years. Jack planned his night over and over and discussed all the possible scenarios.

Sadly, the interruption of his OCD compulsions in Lanzarote had been temporary. Jack had well over a hundred new OCD rituals he had to perform each night before bed, taking several hours – until around 2am – to complete. He believed that if he didn't do them, there would be terrible consequences. The rituals included lining up five empty antibacterial gel bottles in a row, four empty deodorant cans placed in specific positions, plus multiple episodes of counting, furniture-moving, and door-closing. A rational mind can see that lining up four empty deodorant cans in a row would neither cause nor prevent a disastrous fatal event, but Jack's mind wasn't logical. Can you imagine being trapped in such a restrictive and exhausting regime every single day?

I left Jack around 11pm and, for the most part, ignored his persistent concerns about dropping all his compulsions. There was nothing I could say, his rational mind wouldn't listen to me.

I felt on edge and prepared for a restless night. Sleep eluded me, and at 12.15am, Jack appeared looking for reassurance that he would be able to go to school. Soothing him as much as I could, I led him back upstairs. Thirty minutes later, he was back downstairs again and once more, I showed him back to his room and calmly instructed him to get into bed. Sleep eventually came to me, although it was fitful and disturbed throughout the night.

I woke early and headed out at 7am to collect my car. Living in the town centre meant we had no off-road parking, so leaving the car about a fifteen-minute walk away was the norm. It was raining and a miserably cold November morning. I was back in time to wake Jack at the agreed time of 7.30am.

Surprisingly, he woke up, but it was clear we would not be getting to school that morning. Jack had fallen asleep around 3am and had woken multiple times. The lack of sleep and anxious thoughts left him hot and nauseous. He was angry at himself and bitterly disappointed. *"I want to die..."* he wailed and pulled the covers back over his head. "I need more sleep, Mum. I can't do it..."

We agreed that I would call into the school and explain what had happened. The headteacher, Carole, was very supportive and told me just to keep trying each day. She acknowledged it was never going to be an easy transition and I felt reassured, not judged, by her patient and understanding attitude.

I left Jack to sleep until 9am and woke him once more. He was no less angry at himself.

"Jack..." I gently questioned... "how many compulsions did you have to do last night?"

"Two," he replied.

"How many do you usually have to do?"

Jack lay in bed, mentally counting until he lost the number at around seventy-eight. He paused for a moment. "About a hundred." His voice was a little lighter.

I sat next to him on his bed and stroked his arm, something he had rarely allowed in the last couple of years. "I've spoken to Carole. She said it is fine and understandable, and they hope to see you tomorrow. I'm so proud of you, Jack. You've eliminated almost a hundred compulsions, just like that. You still managed to sleep, and nothing happened to you," I enthused.

"Nothing's happened *yet*!" he quickly corrected.

"It will be just that little bit easier tonight, Jack, and tomorrow, you will hopefully be able to get there."

Jack's mood lifted. A visible sense of empowerment washed over him at the realisation he had broken all his compulsions the night before. Just because he had not made it into school that day, it was still a day of celebration.

As the day wore on into the evening, Jack's anxiety reared its head once more, and by 10.45pm, he was pacing downstairs, babbling about scenarios of falling asleep, timing and compulsions.

Grabbing him by the arms, I held him still in an attempt to ground and settle him.

"What if I can't sleep, Mum?" he repeated over and over again. His energy was frantic and unsettling.

Jack finally settled in his room by 11.15pm, and I agreed to wake him at 7.45am for another school attempt.

Later that night, around 2am, movement upstairs woke

me up. Immediately I knew he was unlikely to wake up on time in the morning, but I tried to remain optimistic.

Waking early, at around 5.50am, I tried to avoid predicting what might happen, but my brain was in overdrive. My stomach was unsettled, and I realised how much Jack's anxiety was affecting me too. It was soon 7.45am. Jack was fast asleep, and I was still hopeful.

My hope was short-lived. Jack was difficult to wake – and miserable. "I hate myself, "I'm useless," he cried. The self-criticism continued for a few minutes.

"How about you get dressed and try to go in for a little bit?" I said softly and gently. Raising my voice in this situation wouldn't achieve anything other than to trigger flight mode or cause him to withdraw entirely.

"No, I got to sleep at like 3am, Mum. I was up again at 5am. I feel ill – you think I am making excuses, but I'm not. I hate myself."

His self-loathing sat like a heavy cloud in the room. It was a losing battle and one I wasn't keen on fighting at that time of the morning. Jack fell back asleep, and I headed back to my bed, climbing in fully dressed.

Facing the inevitable call to explain Jack's absence made my heart sink. Once again, Carole empathised but advised me that she would have to review the situation in a week's time if he didn't make it in.

Hanging up the call, I pulled the covers over my head and sobbed. We were right back in the same place we'd been in a year earlier; and the year before that, with the initial school refusal. It was all so frustrating and exhausting. The only difference was we had journeyed through so much, and I had no choice but to carry on; despite this setback, Jack seemed a little stronger.

Jack woke at 9am, but he didn't surface from his room

until 1pm that afternoon. He showered and seemed a little less self-critical. "I'm going to pretend in my head that I'm not going tomorrow, Mum, so I don't feel ill," he suggested after showering.

Jack seemed a little more settled that night, with a sense of resignation that he had to do this or risk losing his place at the school. He appeared at about 8.30pm in the lounge and smiled at me. "I keep telling myself I'm excited about tomorrow, Mum. I'm trying to tell my brain that I feel well and that I'm going to be okay."

Pleased to witness this shift in him, I could feel the difference in his energy through his change in mindset. It gave me a little hope. "That's fantastic, Jack, that's what you need to do!" I enthused. He disappeared back upstairs.

Jack was far more relaxed that evening. He sat in Thomas' room, chatting with his brother until 11.30pm; something he had not been able to do for probably a year or more, as his strict schedules forbid him from deviating from a set routine, especially at night. As he settled into his room shortly after, I felt optimistic for the first time that week.

I awoke to him gently touching my head about 1am. "Mum, I don't feel well, my stomach hurts, and I'm worried that I won't be able to go to sleep."

"It's okay, love, it's just your anxiety. Try to get some sleep now, ok? Do you want me to come upstairs and help you settle down?" I offered.

"No, if you do that, it will become a schedule, and I don't want that," he said as he paced around the room.

"It won't become a schedule after one night, Jack. It's just for tonight to help you so you can get sleep ready for tomorrow," I suggested.

"It will be in my brain. I'm going back up now, Mum. Sorry to wake you up again." His tone was apologetic, and I knew he recognised how much he depended on me and how grateful he was, even if at times his anxious state prevented him from showing it.

The alarm went off at 7am, and immediately I felt unwell. The previous few days had taken a toll on me, making me feel anxious and teary. I'd never followed a particular faith, but at times, I'd found myself praying to a god to help my son, often in floods of tears and sometimes on my knees, hands clasped, literally begging for help.

On the walk to the car, I chanted: "Please, help me get Jack to school today. Please help him wake up..." I repeated it over and over, like a desperate mantra.

Walking back into the flat, my heart was racing with nervousness, wondering if Jack would get up and go. Upon waking, he groaned at the realisation it was 7.45am, and that meant school. "Please leave me, Mum. I can't do it..."

I left him alone. I retreated back down to the kitchen, my hands in prayer, begging, pleading with something unseen to help, through tears of desperation.

Jack appeared a few minutes later, shivering, teeth chattering and anxious, but he was up, and that was progress. He dressed and cleaned his teeth and fiddled with his hair, smoothing the bits that were sticking up. He checked and double-checked his clothes and appearance. "What if I change my mind in the car, Mum?" he questioned.

"Then we turn around and come home, Jack," I reassured him.

He was unable to stomach breakfast or even a drink. We headed out the door to the car, and I knew at that moment, it was actually going to happen.

One of Jack's friends went to the same school. We pulled up nearby and waited for him. They had prearranged to meet in the car park of the local shop nearby.

Although he was understandably nervous, there was a different air about Jack. I had spent so long caring for him, and his needs were so great it was as if I was caring for a child of five years old most of the time.

His friend arrived, and Jack said goodbye.

"I'm so proud of you, Jack. Have a great day, and I'll pick you up at 1.30."

After watching him walk towards school, I drove away. I'd waited two and a half years for that moment. I cried the entire journey home; happy tears mixed with relief, pride, and a little hope.

Just like any mother of a child starting school for the first time, I called up at 10.30am to see how he was doing and was transferred to Carole. She delighted in telling me he was in class and engaging. Her genuine enthusiasm was heartwarming. Jack's attendance, smart appearance and engagement had made her day. Mine too.

I collected Jack at 1.30pm as arranged. He was excited to tell me about the school, the teachers, the other pupils and what they had been studying that morning. He was witty, enthused, and upbeat. It was hard to remember the last time I'd seen him like that, but it must have been at least three years.

We got home, and Jack played happily with Billy. Out of the blue, he asked if we could take the dog to the beach. I was taken aback. It had been about eighteen months since we'd walked to the beach together, despite it being only five minutes away. In a flash, I was up and had the dog's lead on, ready to go, not wanting to miss this rare opportunity.

It was a cold, damp and grey November day but the heavy rain clouds only enhanced the coast's rugged beauty. Jack and Billy ran along the beach together, darting over mounds of sand and avoiding the waves. Their unadulterated joy was infectious. I took a picture of myself with Jack, wanting to keep a memory of this wonderful day. Jack didn't object for once; he even smiled.

Later that afternoon, Jack complained of a headache and wasn't keen on eating. This went on into the night, and I suspected it was the aftermath of several days of constant anxiety, along with all the running on the beach. Jack hadn't had an active physical life for over two years, so this day had proved a little overwhelming.

His headache continued into the night until he eventually fell asleep at about 2am. Jack was tired and miserable the following day, still complaining of a headache, and didn't get to school. This pattern continued for the remainder of the week, and Jack was unable to attend. It seemed he had a virus, which, combined with all the emotional build-up to school, wiped him out for days.

Despite this, there was a different feeling about him. A couple of times, he voluntarily embraced me in a warm hug or allowed me to hug him. This was something that he'd rejected for at least two years. I felt it had been due to his self-loathing and I often winced at some of the derogatory comments he made about himself. Jack didn't love himself, let alone like himself, so he shunned any form of physical contact with me. Jack would reject compliments or dismiss me when I told him I loved him. This simple ordinary gesture to most people was uncharacteristic for him but heartwarming and further evidence that there was hope of him emerging from this illness.

As the days wore on, Jack's sleep cycle worsened, and he was now falling asleep around 4am so it was impossible to wake him at 8am for school. I was sucked back into the inevitable and familiar loop of calling into the school every morning to apologise for his non-attendance. I struggled to sleep and found myself waking from around 4am every morning, listening for movement upstairs. Every few days, Jack's sleep would shift slightly later, delayed by one compulsion or another.

Christmas was approaching once more, and his school would soon break up for the holidays. I met with Carole and the Education Support Officer – we discussed his absenteeism and how we were both working round the clock tirelessly to help him fix his sleep pattern. At this point, Jack desperately wanted to get back to school, and they agreed to allow me to continue to try and improve his sleep over the Christmas holidays and start back at the beginning of January.

As the days rolled into weeks, Jack's mood was noticeably dipping once more, and he lost all confidence in his ability to return to school. It was so incredibly frustrating for him – and me. It was so disheartening having to witness this step backwards, having felt such excitement and relief on that day he went to school.

When school broke up in December, relief filled me for I no longer had to do the dreaded daily calls and remained optimistic that we could fix this sleep situation over the holidays.

THE GOD OF BATHROOM DOOR

DECEMBER 2019

Christmas Day arrived. Jack had fallen asleep at about 5am so it was pointless attempting to wake him up before lunchtime. I remember wanting Christmas Day to be different, just as they portray in TV adverts – happy families gathered together in their matching pyjamas, opening presents. But it wasn't going to be like that in our house. You see, mental illness doesn't pause for special occasions; it doesn't give you a day off. There is rarely any respite from it, and Christmas Day is no exception.

Jack felt just as anxious as usual, in fact, more so because he knew Paul's sons were coming over. Jack wasn't interested in opening his presents; there was no excitement and very little joy.

I loved Jack, but I hated his illness, because it robbed him and us of precious family moments. I grieved for the happy-go-lucky kid who would jump out of bed at the crack of dawn to find his stocking and bound excitedly into the lounge to open presents. My son, who would eat far too much chocolate instead of breakfast at some ungodly hour on Christmas morning. My son, who would laugh and giggle and play excitedly with his new toys. I missed that version of Jack so much.

Paul had returned home briefly for Christmas and could sense my tension. I wanted everything to be normal. He hugged me and gently reassured me. "It is what it is. Let's just get through the day."

Jack decided he wanted to shower, but taking a shower was not that simple for him. Everything had to be organised: toilet seat placed down, followed by handwashing; fresh clothes placed in the bathroom, but not touching anything that could 'contaminate' them; a new bottle of shower gel. It was an exhausting routine.

As Jack was about to step into the bathroom to shower, he started to panic. "I can't do this today, Mum. I'm not coming down to open presents. I don't feel well.'

His anxiety was palpable. But after so many months of these episodes, I learned to just let go, but it was easier said than done. I put so much pressure on myself for this Christmas day to be perfect, to be different from every other.

"Okay, Jack, I'm sorry you feel that way. You can stay in your room, and if you feel hungry later, you can have some dinner," I said, unemotionally, resigning myself to the fact this day would be like any other.

Jack closed the door and got in the shower. I went to head downstairs but stopped and slumped on the landing instead, defeated. I was grateful to be in a dark hallway; it disguised the deluge of tears pouring down my face. "Please, please, *please*... help my son," I mouthed to the door in front of me, my hands clasped tightly in silent prayer, the tears dripping down my cheeks.

I could hear Jack rambling to himself in the shower about how ill he felt. And then he stopped. "Mum, I think I feel a bit better now. The feeling is going. I don't know if I can eat, but I will try and come down to open presents just for a little bit, okay?" he shouted cheerfully through the door as he stepped out of the shower.

"That's great, Jack. Just come downstairs and see how you feel," I replied, silently thanking the God of Bathroom Door for answering my desperate plea.

Jack opened the bathroom door and realised I'd been crying. Quite unexpectedly, he beckoned me to him as he stood dripping, wrapped in a towel. "Come here, Mum." He smiled warmly and pulled me in, placing my head on his shoulder. "Let it out, Mum. You know I hate to see you crying but let it out. It's okay, Mum."

Leaning on his shoulder, I let the sobs come. "I love you," I whispered, in between sobs. "Thank you, Jack," I muttered after a minute or so. It was an unusually touching moment between mother and son, and for the first time, the roles were reversed. My fifteen-year-old son who towered above me, was comforting me.

Paul's boys arrived at 4pm with all the usual Christmas excitement and buoyancy of teenagers, bringing with them a fresh injection of energy. Jack and Thomas joined us, and we all opened presents together. Jack's discomfort was evident to me, but we got through the obligatory gift-giving; shortly after, he thanked everyone for his presents and returned to the safety of his room.

I went to the kitchen and silently cried, holding onto the stove to steady myself and tilting my head back to stop the tears from falling, but they fell anyway. Wiping my face and nose, I composed myself, grabbing the platter of nibbles and heading back to the lounge smiling. "Right, who wants some food?" I asked, as if nothing out of the ordinary had happened. No one noticed I'd been crying. We ate dinner without Jack, and Paul took his boys back home. We had survived Christmas Day.

Later that evening, Paul and I sat and watched TV, and I sought solace in every type of snack, leftovers, chocolate and crisps available. I ate until I felt like I'd explode and continued to eat non-stop day and night for the next three days until I felt physically ill. Food was, without doubt, my coping mechanism.

The Christmas holidays came and went, and things didn't improve; in fact, they deteriorated. Jack was not able to fall asleep until 5am every morning, his mind now consumed with fears around returning to school. The more he tried to correct his sleep, the more elusive sleep became.

One morning he appeared at 8am and woke me up. "Mum, I can't fall asleep," he wailed in desperation.

I got up and followed him to his room.

"Can you stay with me, Mum, until I fall asleep?"

It had been some time since I'd seen him so worked up. "Yes, Jack, I will stay until you fall asleep," I reassured him.

"It's so bright in here, Mum, I'll never fall asleep now.'"

The winter sunshine was already flooding in around his blinds.

"Right, wait there."

My frustration was evident in my tone. Muttering under my breath, I grabbed two bedsheets from the airing cupboard and clumsily hung them from his blinds in an attempt to darken the room. Jack settled in bed, and after a string of protests, he finally fell asleep just before 9am. The rest of the house was getting up, and he was just going to bed. He didn't wake up until 3pm.

The rest of the day was horrendous. Jack was miserable and low and didn't leave his bed nor stomach food until 10pm that night. Thankfully the next day, he fell asleep around 5am without the need for me to be there. Just as well, as I had no intention of being pulled back into his bedtime compulsions, having spent nine months of the previous year sitting with him every night.

My relief was short-lived, unfortunately. Two days later, Jack appeared at 5.30am and gently woke me by touching my head. "I can't sleep, Mum. Can you come up? I'm so sorry to wake you," he whispered, trying not to wake Paul.

And so, the routine began again, pulling me right back into sitting with Jack between 5am and 6am every morning, watching as he completed ritual after ritual. I believed I was being helpful and safeguarding him from harm, but instead, I inadvertently reenforced his OCD's cruel threats and made things far worse.

Jack's behaviours bled into my world, particularly around my trips to the bathroom or food preparation in the kitchen. I should have challenged his disordered thoughts but I didn't, and therefore I unwittingly encouraged his dysfunctional behaviour. I lacked the skill and understanding of OCD; without the correct therapy to support him to break down the compulsions bit by bit, I was just muddling along and making things much worse.

Sometimes I'd sit there quietly watching Jack perform some irrational, irritating ritual before bed, such as straightening a book a millimetre from left to right for six or seven minutes until he got it exactly right. Inside my head, I'd scream, "*For fuck's sake, stop!*" but of course, I didn't say it out loud.

Screaming at OCD does nothing but exacerbate the anxiety associated with the compulsion and double the time taken. Often this would increase the repetitions exponentially. I learnt that one the hard way.

On the occasions I did lose my patience and raise my voice in frustration, Jack would get even more anxious and repeat the process again and again. So, I learnt the art of silently screaming and sat watching the concentration and frustration on my son's tired face as he repeated a behaviour over and over, realising it was considerably more difficult and annoying to my poor son. It was simply heartbreaking.

SUICIDAL

FEBRUARY 2020

As JANUARY ROLLED into February and the next review meeting approached, it was becoming apparent that my chances of getting Jack back into school were slowly slipping away. Jack had not made it there once during January.

Jack's nighttime routines were destroying his life, bit by bit. I watched him slip away yet again. After about six weeks of attempting to fix his sleep patterns every single night by getting into bed earlier, he snapped.

One night, Jack began pacing around the lounge in manic circles. "I can't take this, Mum. I can't take this anymore. My skin is crawling. I need to get out of here, *I need to get out of here!*" he reeled over and over.

He ran into the kitchen and turned on the hob in an attempt to burn himself. Luckily, I'd turned it off at the wall so it wouldn't heat up.

He ran back to the lounge, marching in a crazed state.

I started to cry. "Please, Jack, stop. Calm down, come here, let me help you."

He pulled away and started searching for sharp objects.

I considered calling an ambulance, genuinely concerned Jack was going to harm himself.

As if with divine timing, Thomas, oblivious to the commotion, came bounding downstairs. He happened to catch Jack mid-pace in the hallway. "Alright?" he asked unknowingly.

"Not really," Jack muttered under his breath.

"Come with me, Jack. I want to show you something." He ushered Jack upstairs to his room.

Listening on the stairs, I could hear Thomas talking, and after some time, Jack answered. Within ten minutes or so, Jack had calmed down and Thomas had unknowingly diffused a potential implosion.

Quite by chance, Paul had returned that night as the weather was dreadful and he needed a break from van life. He was in the bath and blissfully unaware of the drama unfolding downstairs at the time. (Thank goodness – I hated it when he witnessed the meltdowns.) However, when he came down, I could barely speak and couldn't contain my tears.

"What's wrong, Emily? Talk to me..." Paul said encouragingly.

It was the first time in a very long time Jack had been that distressed, and it had shaken me. I blurted out what had happened in between sobs, and Paul held me tightly, unsure of what to say. Neither of us slept well that night.

About two years earlier I had been feeling utterly overwhelmed. I remember driving home from work one day, in a dangerous auto pilot state, somewhat aware, yet not fully conscious of the traffic around me as my head was swirling, preoccupied with a thousand thoughts about Jack, Paul and Thomas. As I neared an industrial estate, I saw a large grey building and I remember thinking that if I put my foot down and drove into that wall at speed, it would all just stop, and that nothingness would be easier than facing this life every day.

It felt as if every atom of my being was in freefall, and I had no grounding, no anchor point in that moment. I didn't feel like me. I felt separated from my body – just a consciousness in a frantic state. It was a surreal experience, and utterly terrifying.

I was approaching a roundabout and the cars in front braked, forcing me to react and brake hard – that was enough to interrupt the dark thoughts.

So shaken by the experience, I pulled into the industrial estate and parked up. I was shaking and crying hysterically. How could I have even entertained the thought of ending my own life?

As upsetting and unsettling as it was at the time, I'm now grateful for that experience for it gave me an insight into what all three of my men must have felt at times.

By January 2020, Jack was struggling to find a purpose in his life, and I could understand his desperation. It appeared the only function his OCD didn't seem to control was his breathing. After a couple of years of suicidal periods, I had nothing left to offer as reassurance; I was too exhausted.

I can remember sitting him down calmly one night after one such conversation about the purpose of his life. "Jack, I love you with all my heart and I don't want you to kill yourself, but I cannot stop you. I am your mum, and I will always be here for you if you need me and you are not alone," I offered calmly, rubbing his back, before getting up and walking away.

Just before completing this book, I met with Paul for a walk, and we sat on a bench together in the warm autumn sunshine. It was a brief moment of peace and clarity for Paul in between episodes of deep depression. Paul glanced at me with an anticipatory stare. "What's wrong Paul? Talk to me..." I gently enquired, knowing he wanted to say something.

" Emily..." Paul's face crumpled, trying hard to contain small sobs. "Emily – I looked around my room for somewhere to hang myself last week..."

"Oh Paul... Please don't ever sit alone in those feelings again. Promise me?"

I gripped Paul's shoulder in a silent-but-strong gesture of solidarity and support. This was not the first time I had heard Paul confess thoughts about killing himself. But this time my reaction was very different: I was calm, not hysterical. The sustained chaos of the last three years had given me strength to witness those situations, without trying to rescue anyone. It had given me clarity too – I could love this man, I could love my sons, but I couldn't protect them from their own mental shadows anymore. They had to seek their own healing.

There is the belief held by some that people who talk about suicide, rather than attempting it, are just crying out for help and unlikely to carry it through. It had been said to me on more than one occasion by different people, that they didn't believe Jack would hurt himself; almost dismissing his desperation. Their words were little comfort.

When your child is so miserable, so desperate with life and imprisoned in their mind – and on endless waiting lists for therapy – their feelings of hopelessness are genuine. In Jack's case, he was not saying these things for attention. When he was physically exhausted and he couldn't take any more of the struggle, he genuinely meant it. I knew my son inside out. I knew that at times, he genuinely felt that dying would be easier than continuing to live.

When you battle through infertility to bring a child into this world, it is all the more painful knowing that they want to take the life that you fought so hard to bring about away.

About two years after Thomas was born, I discovered complications from his birth had left me infertile and unable to have more children naturally. I desperately wanted a second child; I didn't want Thomas to be an only child, but I needed a distraction from the heartbreak that my father's cancer had brought into my life.

The same consultant who repaired the physical damage from Thomas' birth through two subsequent surgeries, happened to be the head of the hospital fertility clinic I had been referred to. After twelve months of exhaustive rounds of hormonal injections and negative pregnancy tests, he realised an important screening test has been overlooked and referred me immediately.

Within days, I underwent a rather unpleasant test where dye was injected through my cervix into my uterus with the intention of watching the dye spill out through the fallopian tubes. This would indicate any problems that could be preventing pregnancy. I lay back and watched the dye light up my uterus on the screen, though it trickled in rather than flooded. I am no gynaecological expert, but even I could see something wasn't quite right. Although it emptied through my left fallopian tube, there was no sign of any dye leaving my right one. After the test was complete, the doctor told me to go and wait upstairs in the fertility clinic while he prepared the report.

My consultant called me into his office an hour later and gave me the news I feared. A month after Thomas' birth, I'd retained some placenta that had become infected, requiring surgery to remove it. My womb, already fragile from pregnancy and birth, had not taken too well to further trauma. Instead of healing normally, scar tissue formed and fused my uterus together. My right fallopian tube had been completely blocked by it. I was diagnosed with Asherman Syndrome and therefore my chances of getting pregnant and sustaining a pregnancy were very slim.

I burst into tears. My consultant was kind and spoke softly, attempting to soothe me, but he offered little comfort. He told me to take some time to absorb the information and adjust to the idea of not being able to have any more children. In his opinion, it was unlikely my body would cope with carrying another child, even if I could get pregnant.

I felt winded; drained of all breath. The consultant's words had punched the energy right out of me. I'd been on a pointless fertility rollercoaster for a year – injections, medications, scans, regimented sex – all for nothing and all under a cloud of my father's cancer and subsequent death. But worse still, I felt robbed of the choices I wanted to make as a woman. I was thirty-one years old. A choice that should have been a reproductive right as a young woman had been snuffed out.

Sensing my reluctance to leave his office and face reality, the consultant shuffled my notes and read the latest entries on my file. I'd been into the clinic the morning before my test for my usual bloods to be taken and follicles to be checked and measured. "You have one egg that is almost ready in your left ovary and your progesterone levels are looking good. How about we give it one last shot with this egg? We can try artificial insemination in the clinic this time."

I looked up from my lap, interrupting the tears from hitting my knees.

"Emily, you have nothing to lose by trying, but I can't offer you any guarantees. If this attempt is unsuccessful, I will have no choice but to recommend you stop fertility treatment. I'm deeply sorry," he offered gently, but I had not heard the last part of the conversation; only the first. There was still a chance and that was all I cared about in that moment.

Two days later I went back to the clinic for an injection to trigger the follicle to release. The next day I drove back to the hospital with a small pot of hope, wrapped in foil and tucked between my breasts to keep John's sperm warm and alive on the journey. It wasn't your typical conception and there was definitely no romance involved. Nine excruciatingly long days later, I got the results of a blood test from the clinic.

After three surgeries, countless injections, umpteen scans and being told it was almost impossible, my body had managed it and Thomas would have a baby brother or sister after all. All the heartache, all the pain of surgeries and tests and trauma of fertility treatment evaporated in three words: "You are pregnant."

I tried so hard to convince Jack how much I loved him, how I had wanted him so desperately before he was even born and I told him, more than once, the story of how John and I had battled to conceive him. I told him how he had fought to come into this world, but nothing I said changed how he felt.

I didn't tell CAMHS about the suicidal episodes in 2020. I should have, as it may have helped Jack progress on the waiting list. When Jack had first told CAMHS he wanted to kill himself in 2017, they had questioned him about how he planned to do it. But Jack didn't have a clear intention at that time, and it had been many months since he had called the suicide helpline whilst waiting for his first visit from CAMHS.

His support worker told Jack not to threaten me with his suicide as it was unfair to me. His tone reminded me of a parent scolding a disobedient child, as if Jack's suicidal talk was a deliberate act of emotional bullying. Being fraught at the time and grateful to have the professional help on hand, I didn't give his comments much thought, but have since felt that they were a little harsh on Jack. Perhaps some young people do wield suicidal talk as a tactic to shock, or elicit a response from their parents, but many don't and I knew my son wasn't bluffing.

Whilst writing this book, two of my dearest friend's children have both attempted suicide whilst struggling with their mental health. Thankfully both survived their attempts, yet their parents overwhelming heartbreak and distress was a stark reminder that the risk of suicide amongst young people is very real and it made me keep a much closer eye on my own sons.

The response from CAMHS two years earlier had stopped me from telling them when Jack started talking about it again. I was scared they would not take him seriously, that they would dismiss his feelings again, and that would be enough to tip him over the edge. I now regret not telling CAMHS and realised sometime after that it was simply me trying to control a situation that was way beyond my control.

Throughout this time, Jack sat on a waiting list for high-intensity CBT. He went from first on the list to second place as a staff member left the unit. Until they recruited new staff, only one therapist in the area was qualified to deliver the level of therapy my son needed. There was just one therapist covering a vast geographical area with a very long waiting list.

CAMHS advised me that although Jack would return to the top of the list in due course, should another young person present at higher risk of harm to themselves or others, they would take priority over Jack. And they did. Month after month rolled by, and five months later, he was still waiting to get back to the top of the list.

The Child and Adolescent Mental Health Services are simply another critically underfunded limb of our health service. As a result, children's lives are fractured by undiagnosed and untreated mental-health disorders because there isn't enough funding allocated to recruit adequate staff numbers. I believe this may worsen as the full effects of the pandemic on young people's mental health start to emerge. Without staff to provide the necessary therapy and support to meet the growing demand for their services, families are being let down. A child should not be on a waiting list for over twelve months for therapy when diagnosed with a life-altering mental-health condition. A young person should not have to wait months to see a doctor for a medical review if their condition deteriorates.

The staff I dealt with were always courteous and very apologetic over delays. Can you imagine how hard their job must be telling desperate parents, probably daily, that there are no appointments for the foreseeable future? And believe me, in that place, you *are* a desperate parent, and you turn to the experts in the hope of a way out of the darkness. If they are unable to help you, it can be a terrifying place to find yourself.

The delay in therapy due to the extraordinarily long waiting lists, without doubt, contributed to Jack's deterioration. The staff acknowledged this and apologised for their part in that deterioration. Whilst it felt satisfying to have that acknowledgement, it didn't alter the situation nor make it any easier to cope with.

I called the psychiatrist's secretary in early February 2020, having already asked for a review appointment in October 2019 and heard nothing. She explained that they only had two doctors and that they were now sharing the additional responsibility of covering a nearby in-patient unit due to staff shortages. She advised me that there were no appointments, nothing at all. She couldn't even say that the doctor could see him by April or May 2020.

I apologised to her for her position and felt sorry for this lady, desperately trying to juggle patients and angry parents. You could hear the hopelessness and apprehension in her voice, having to deliver such news to me. And these delays were *before* the pandemic hit.

At the beginning of this journey, I would have roared

down the phone at the unacceptability of this outrageous situation but it was too far down the line for that now. Shouting at the secretary would not create an earlier appointment to become available. She thanked me for not losing my head and suggested that if it was too difficult to cope, to get back in touch with her. I let out an unintentional laugh and told her I'd passed the point of not coping about a year earlier. We both knew it wouldn't change a thing.

I AM AN ENABLER

JANUARY 2020

THE RUMBLINGS of Covid had just begun around the world but at that stage, the first lockdown hadn't yet begun in the UK. Later in the month, I called Ben to see if we could shuffle that afternoon's appointment to later as Jack had not fallen asleep until nearly 8am. He agreed, but the conversation then steered towards how things had been going in the previous two weeks. After explaining what had been going on, we both agreed that my efforts to manage the OCD compulsions were not working. Ben told me I was enabling Jack.

What the hell was I meant to do at 6am when my son was going into a meltdown, unable to sleep, pacing, about to undertake hours of pointless OCD rituals? As far as I was concerned, I was safeguarding him, *not* enabling.

But actually, Ben was right. At the time, I just couldn't see it.

There is a negative connotation to the word enabler, perhaps a little stigma, as if it's a deliberate act of a loved one to knowingly support problematic behaviour. Although it always starts from a place of love and a desire to help, it rarely ends well and encourages the issues to be covered up rather than allow the person to succeed at making the changes needed. An enabler encourages – usually unintentionally – self-destructive behaviour in others.

Hello, my name is Emily, and I *am* an enabler. I didn't mean for it to happen – it just did, and I became the classic enabler to all three of my men. Rather than empowering them by giving them the means to cope with their own situations and allowing them to face their problems, I unwittingly enabled them. It's not that I supported Paul's drinking, Thomas' gambling, or wanted Jack to have OCD, but to some extent I felt that if I didn't help them all in their various situations, the outcome for all of us would have been far worse. I was also cushioning each one from knowing the extent of each other's dysfunction, but in doing so, I prevented them (especially Paul and Thomas) from seeing the consequences of their addictive behaviour, and therefore seeking help.

With Jack, my enabling reinforced the strength of his OCD thoughts. I supported his compulsions by sitting with him, a reassuring presence hour after hour, whilst he completed one ritual after another. In doing so, I was reinforcing the lies his OCD was telling him; I was confirming the threats were real – Jack really was in danger, and he *must* carry out those compulsions to make him safe. I unknowingly fattened up that parasite in his brain. When Thomas gambled and lost money, I'd help him find ways to replace his money, therefore diminishing the consequences of his actions.

I feel foolish now, in retrospect, but at the time, I was just mopping up the aftermath of one crisis before moving onto the next one, unaware my actions were throwing petrol on a dysfunctional pyre that was already burning out of control.

From time to time, Paul would run out of money because he was drinking most of it away and prioritising alcohol over food; the only food he was eating was what I gave him. I'd meet him most days, and if he was out of money, I'd buy some drink to stop his shakes or buy him a sandwich if he hadn't eaten. Paul once told me if he had no food, he would have gone through the bins to find some, and I was mortified at the thought of that. I simply couldn't risk the embarrassment and shame I'd feel if someone I knew saw him doing that. Had I left Paul without food or drink, he may well have sunk to rock bottom a lot faster without me constantly trying to cushion him from hitting it. But the reality was, he was only ever going to heal from hitting that dark and miserable place himself.

Paul had requested, both through his GP and a local alcohol support group, to go on a waiting list for detox and rehabilitation. The rehab centres were closed due to the pandemic, and there simply wasn't much funded help for alcohol detox. Paul was placed on a waiting list but it was weeks, if not months, long. He had no choice but to reduce his intake alone and join online support meetings.

Paul was barely recognisable to me. He looked ill, bloated in the face and stomach by the alcohol's effects and a shaky, anxious mess. This was not my handsome happy-go-lucky husband. He was long gone, and with the best of intentions, I was doing my bit to aid his addiction and keep him stuck in that chaotic state.

In his unbalanced mind, Paul decided we had separated, and to all intents and purposes, we had. We didn't live together anymore; we didn't spend much time together and we'd separated our finances. But we never had 'that' conversation, and I continued trying to be a wife whilst missing what was staring me in the face. My husband had disconnected from me, emotionally checked out from our marriage, and was in the full-blown grip of depression and alcoholism. There was nothing I could do but sit back and observe the inevitable car crash that lay ahead.

"You're colluding with him," Ben advised me.

Colluding... Now there's a word probably best *not* said to an exhausted mother trying her best. I was perhaps overly sensitive and saw most suggestions as criticism, but this particular comment hit a nerve and sent me into defence mode. It was a poor choice of word, given the meaning.

Bursting into angry tears, I blustered: "You're not listening to me. I've been waiting for over twelve months for the therapy Jack needs. How am I meant to just stop helping him, stop enabling him without the correct therapy to back me up? "I didn't give poor Ben a chance to respond. "I'm sorry, I can't do this..." I said, and hung up on him.

Standing in an empty shop doorway, I sobbed until I was exhausted. Why did everything have to feel like a constant battle?

I texted Ben and apologised for hanging up so abruptly. He replied sometime later, acknowledging my upset and cancelled the later appointment we'd arranged. It meant I didn't have to face CAMHS that afternoon, which was just as well – I didn't have any fight left in me that day.

NO LONGER THE WOMAN I WAS

FEBRUARY 2020

THE NEXT DAY was the final review meeting at the school, joined by the Education Support Officer from Jack's secondary school and Ben. I had been dreading this meeting as I knew the inevitable was coming. After all, I had only managed to get Jack to one session in four months, and they couldn't hold the place indefinitely when other children were waiting. I also felt embarrassed knowing I'd be facing Ben again after hanging up on him.

I was grateful to be the first to arrive at the meeting as it always felt a little uncomfortable walking into these meetings after everyone else. Jack was relying on me to be his voice, but that day I felt edgy and defensive. I was right to be. It turned out that the ESO had been advised by the local authority that Jack's place was being terminated after the meeting.

"Wait... they can't do that?" I protested at the news even though I'd expected no less. After all, they couldn't just remove the place without providing an alternative provision for Jack's education. The ESO apologised and said that the decision had been received via email.

Everything I'd been holding onto for the last four months, all that energy and upset day after day, trying to make it happen; the sleep disruption and my brief elation at Jack attending school, disintegrated right there. Standing up, I burst into tears. "Sorry ... I just ... can't take anymore..."

I hurried out, heading for the school entrance where I found a seat and began sobbing uncontrollably. It really hurt. The pain in my chest was pure emotion rising up and it couldn't be contained.

A moment later, Carole appeared with a box of tissues and attempted to soothe me.

"What am I meant to do?" I wailed loudly. "Nobody is listening to me. Jack's still waiting for his therapy. I've got no *fucking* help!" I was wild. Carole looked on uncomfortably, unsure how to appease me. But in that moment, I didn't care about my tears or foul language.

It took a few minutes to ground myself enough to return to the meeting and apologise for the outburst. The staff welcomed me back soothingly. These same staff had been on this journey with me for over two years and could see my desperation. They agreed that they would go back to the local authority and arrange a meeting at my request.

I wanted to meet the decision-maker face-to-face. I wanted them to know we were a real family with real feelings who were struggling. I felt I was at least owed some information on an alternative educational provision in person, rather than via a faceless email. I asked them to keep Jack's place open in the meantime, clinging on for dear life to any last threads of hope.

I left the meeting and didn't look back, knowing it would probably be the last time I'd set foot in that school. It was a shame, but it was about time I accepted that this option had been well and truly exhausted.

The next afternoon, unprepared to wait, I contacted the local authority myself. I'd built myself up for a verbal showdown, but it wasn't required. A very kind and softly spoken lady explained that the local authority had already removed my son from the school roll. In fact, his place had already been given to another student a couple of months earlier in December, but no one had bothered to inform me. I'd spent all of January in a state of high stress, as had Jack, attempting nightly to fix his sleep, and calling in every day to report his absenteeism for a school place that no longer belonged to him.

The lady explained that there had been a communication breakdown and after a brief pause, she suggested that perhaps no one had wanted to tell me the bad news earlier. I'm not entirely sure how I kept my composure at that revelation. Knowing the staff involved, I don't believe that was the case at all, but it had caused an unforgivable delay in exploring alternative options and an extraordinary amount of unnecessary stress. Thankfully, this person supported Jack's desire to study and achieve some grades if possible. She rushed through an application for funded online study which was arranged within two weeks.

It was agreed that Jack would start Functional Skills in English and Maths online. GCSEs were out of the question as it was approaching the beginning of March. It took some time for Jack to accept he could not study for his GCSEs. He'd been in denial, and when faced with the reality of three years' lost education, it hit him hard. Jack's mood sank, and it took some persuasion to get him to accept that Functional Skills would be an acceptable step into further education at college.

As his sleep was still so disrupted, the online education provider agreed to try some late-afternoon lessons, and a daily timetable was established. The first attempt at an online maths lesson was painful. Jack sat next to me with headphones on, but as soon as the teacher greeted him, he fled the room in absolute terror. He started hyperventilating, and a full panic attack ensued in the hallway. I was frantic and tried to calm him, whilst typing an explanation to the teacher, who was left wondering what was going on.

The lesson was cut short, and it was undeniable that this was going to take some time. My heart sank. If this was Jack's reaction to the teacher just saying hello via anonymous audio, how on earth would we get through five days a week of lessons?

After several more attempts, the online school abandoned Jack's lessons, and set work for him to do when he could manage it around his sleep and compulsions. Jack managed a few English assignments and seemed to enjoy them, but the free time to study was dwindling fast. By this point, Jack spent all his waking hours in one OCD compulsion after another. He remained on the CAMHS waiting list for high-intensity therapy and every week brought further deterioration.

Paul had struggled for many months with the situation at home. He was exceptionally patient and compassionate and never judged Jack but he could see that Jack was really struggling. Because of his own battles with anxiety for years, he had great empathy. Paul's frustration lay with the lack of support I was getting; he wanted to help me but didn't know how.

I pushed Paul to the sidelines, unconsciously initially, but it became a conscious movement to hold him at arm's length as time progressed. If he wasn't around me, I wouldn't have to worry about his opinion on the exhausting nighttime routines or lack of progress and change.

Somewhere during this chaos we had been living in, he'd lost his happy-go-lucky wife; the one who always used to smile, the strong one. I'd become a tearful mess most of the time. Jack's compulsions were consuming his young life and I slowly found myself woven into many of them. When he eventually slept, I'd try to meet Paul, support Thomas, and run errands with no thought of giving myself any time out or self-care.

I remember those days well: at times feeling utterly exhausted, drained by everyone else's shattered states and my endeavouring to prop them all up. I was still holding on so tightly to unrealistic outcomes. Supposing I could just get Jack to college, Paul sober and Thomas settled, everything would be okay ... wouldn't it? None of this was my responsibility to fix, though, and the more I tried to control my environment, the more frantic and unstable I became. And as a result, I destabilised my family, who were heavily reliant on my strength and balance.

I arranged my entire existence around Jack's OCD. It owned me completely, and I was its reluctant slave. Sometimes my involvement in his compulsions would take twelve to sixteen hours, day and night, so I catnapped whenever possible. Days would pass where I'd get three or four hours of sleep at most. I wore the same old clothes for a week at a time and would fall asleep in those same clothes. I didn't shower for days, sometimes for almost two weeks at a time. My long hair stayed pulled into a messy knot on top of my head, and when I did eventually wash it, it was painfully matted; just trying to detangle it would leave me in tears.

But it didn't matter to me because I didn't care about myself, and I never saw anyone anyway, so my appearance seemed insignificant. Unable to work or go out, I distanced myself from friends and never really disclosed my feelings to anyone, not even my own family, who remained oblivious to the desperation I felt. I rarely looked in a mirror, and when I did, I didn't notice the dark circles under my eyes or the grey hairs that had snuck in. I only saw an ageing, overweight woman that I'd learned to loathe.

I had fallen a long way from the woman who arrived back from India eight years earlier, confident and self-assured all those years before. Of course, Paul still loved me deeply, even though I had little love left for myself anymore. We didn't nurture our relationship; we had so little time left for romance, we drifted.

Paul had spent months on end sleeping in our campervan parked a couple of miles away. The disconnection between us had a profound effect on his mental health. Paul spent a long time out of work, struggling daily with his direction and place in life, feeling displaced and isolated. In his mind, he had now lost his second family unit and I was giving almost all my attention to my sons, leaving little time left for him. Paul relapsed, turning back to drink to numb the pain, which marked the beginning of yet another very difficult and destructive period.

One evening, Paul was back at home for a night or two when Thomas lost a large sum in an online gambling scam and, as a result, thumped his desk loudly. The noise startled us all, and as usual, I ran upstairs to try and contain the latest drama. Thomas was angry and desperately trying to control his feelings, but the more I tried to smooth things over and shut him up, the more he kicked off.

Unable to contain his anger, Thomas jumped up and punched his chair several times, swearing. Paul bolted upstairs as I left Thomas' room and demanded to know what was going on. Fleeing downstairs, my stomach was in knots and my head in a spin. I'd been keeping Thomas' gambling a secret from Paul.

Paul and I exploded in angry words at each other. I struggled to breathe, a heavy weight crushing my chest. "*Leave...me...alone... I can't take this anymore*!" I shouted, on the verge of screaming at Paul.

I was pacing the kitchen floor, crashing pots, wide-eyed and in an animalistic, almost primal state. It's the closest I've ever got to a total loss of emotional control, and it was very frightening for me. Paul told me some days later that he was terrified I would hurt myself or smash the flat to pieces that night. I came very close to doing both.

I grabbed my coat, determined to drive as far away as possible in my car and never come back. Everything I'd been feeling, everything I'd been holding onto, came tumbling out in between sobs.

Paul knelt beside me, holding me firmly by the hands in an attempt to calm me. I'd been a human pressure-cooker, my emotions simmering for months while I tried to contain everyone's mental illness and protect them all from each other. "I can't breathe, Paul. Look at what I have created. This is *all* my fault!"

I sat reeling off all the issues my sons were facing, like some sad catalogue. "I'm constantly walking on eggshells around you, around everyone, biting my tongue, terrified you're going to blow up at me, worried you will judge my kids. I feel paranoid when you're here and can't cope with this stress anymore." I collapsed into uncontrollable, loud sobs.

The truths had been blurted out without any rational filter in that moment, and those words were to have quite an effect on Paul in the following day or so. But right then, he was calm, soothing, and he held me tightly.

When I was calmer, he gently wiped my soggy face and stroked my hair out of my eyes. "I love you, Emily, but tonight I have seen how much you are struggling, and I'm not helping you by being here. I can see you need time to breathe, and I'm going to give you that space." Paul smiled warmly, gathered some belongings, and quietly left.

Numb and drained, I sat alone in my chair, staring into emptiness. There was relief too. I *wanted* Paul to go; it was easier without him.

My boys had heard every word spoken in our compact flat. Thomas appeared first, then Jack a little later. I spent the next two hours convincing Jack that he was not destroying my marriage and giving him reasons to keep living. Jack was talking about the pointlessness of his life almost daily, and it was exhausting at the best of times, but after that explosive episode, I was drained and had nothing left to offer him.

By the following afternoon, my words had sunk in with Paul and his resentments bubbled to the surface. We exchanged angry texts well into the evening, and by 9.30pm, I could no longer handle the knots in my stomach.

One of my character traits has always been to not let go in a fight, or walk away and allow the dust to settle. I hate disharmony and have always attempted to resolve a situation there and then, which is not always helpful or productive. Sometimes people need time to cool down.

Jumping in my car, I drove around the streets until I

found Paul sitting in the van, drinking. He was startled at my arrival so late at night and not in the mood to chat calmly as I'd hoped. Our heated words spilt out of the van, onto the street, and we both were left wondering how to salvage our marriage. It's very easy for angry, tired and desperate egos to get a hold of these situations and take over; for things to be said that a rational mind later regrets deeply.

We parted, Paul slamming the van door and me driving off; foot to the floor to show him the depth of my anger in one final petulant display.

I got into bed and pulled the duvet over my head. It felt safe and warm and whilst under there, I didn't have to face anything. I didn't sleep well that night at all; I was tossing and turning, wondering how we could go on in a marriage as fractured as it was and still manage to care for my children's health without once considering my own.

Most mornings, the realisation of how bad things were would hit me within a moment or two of waking, and my stomach would turn over. I'd feel physically nauseous. That day was no exception. I checked my phone. Paul had texted with an apology. We agreed to meet for lunch, just the two of us, to talk.

Looking at my reflection in the mirror, I barely recognised myself. That day I wanted to look and feel like the old me again and show my husband this marriage was worth hanging on for, but I had not been taking care of myself.

I washed my limp hair; it was long overdue and I blow-dried it for the first time in months. After applying some makeup, I put on some jeans, a jumper and a colourful scarf – something I'd not done in a long, long time. I'd been stuck in dishevelled black clothes for months on end.

Walking into the café we'd arranged to meet at, I found Paul sitting there waiting for me. His face softened when he saw me, and he gently smiled. He held me close and I began to cry. "You look beautiful, Emily. I'm so sorry, I love you so much," he soothed.

We sat close together, hanging onto each other for comfort. After lunch we made a vow to spend time together every week, no matter what. We owed it to each other to rediscover our love and nurture our connection; we had journeyed through so much in the previous years – it would be such a shame to give up at this latest hurdle. Paul agreed to stop drinking, and he did, for a short while.

Living in the van overwhelmed Paul at times, and rightly so. Not many people could withstand living in a 4ft van with no adequate heating at the best of times, let alone through a British winter. It was a particularly wet winter too, with persistent rain for days on end. The van sprung a leak above the back door, and Paul was woken most nights by cold rain dripping on him. The bedding would become progressively soaked by the early hours. That, along with the cold and cramped conditions, proved too much.

Paul had been woken several times by people either peering in or tapping on the windows. One attempted break-in in the early hours resulted in the passenger window being smashed by a rock. Paul no longer felt safe and booked himself into a cheap hotel just around the corner for a week; the short break proved to be a welcome respite from the cold, damp van.

It was clear after a few days at the hotel that he couldn't return to van living. Paul had to find somewhere else to live but didn't feel ready to return home to the flat. Things were simply too strained and a little claustrophobic for him. He said it no longer felt like his home anymore, and he thought it was best for us all if he stayed away.

Paul found a single room to rent nearby, and he moved

in immediately. He made it his own and enjoyed the peace. Paul's sleep would not be disturbed by my nightly routines with Jack, and he settled in comfortably to his new place. I felt relieved, both for him and me.

Although not conventional, it worked well for us to begin with. Of course I missed Paul, but at the time, I thought it would rescue our marriage and save my sanity. We still saw each other each day. I filled his fridge with home-cooked meals and washed his clothes, but he always had his safe, quiet space to retreat to. Paul gave me the freedom to care for Jack, and he had the peace to nurture his own mental health.

COVID – LIFE GRINDS TO A HALT

MARCH 2020

MARCH ROLLED ON, and the country went into its first national lockdown on March 23 2020. From that day onwards, everything changed.

How strange that it took a global pandemic to force everyone to experience Jack's world – a world in which he had lived for over twelve months; a new world that now insisted on extra handwashing, masks, antibacterial gel and being locked away inside. Jack wouldn't feel like the odd-one-out in gloves and a mask anymore. It became the new norm for the outside world, and now everyone was the same as Jack: all forced to stay inside and protect themselves from the invisible threat of a deadly germ.

But Jack didn't care that the world had joined him – he loved the first lockdown because it helped him overcome his crippling social anxiety and venture outside for the first time in many months to walk the deserted streets. Jack also loved being able to chat to his friends online when they would usually have been at school. Whilst lockdowns brought isolation to so many, they gave Jack both freedom and re-connection, albeit digitally.

The lockdowns were double-edged swords for me, though. I welcomed the break from facing other people's normality, and they lifted the pressure from me of Paul's sons asking to come and stay. Whilst they isolated at their mothers, I didn't have to explain our strange situation to them. I wouldn't have known where to begin and I was too weary to try.

But the lockdowns slowed down access to the mental-health services my son so desperately needed. They also prevented me from spending any quality time with Paul aside from a daily walk, albeit socially distanced. They restricted the rehabilitation services too and caused a backlog in the medical support Paul needed.

Like many other young people, Thomas struggled with his mental health even more during the national lockdowns. Every time a new restriction was announced or an extension to the last, he became angrier and more disillusioned with life. By the middle of the third one, he was edging back into his depression.

Nothing was open. The government restrictions permitted us to leave the house once a day for exercise, but during the depths of that British winter, the weather was abysmal. Dark, cold wintry days fluctuated from bitter cold and overcast to storms and icy rain. It wasn't exactly enticing.

Thomas saw his friends three times during that year of lockdowns. The sense of disconnection from his family and friends, along with relentless boredom, left him depressed and doubtful about his future and his place in this new uncertain world. He wasn't alone in those thoughts – many young people felt the same and still do.

In 2019, Jack had introduced his brother to the world of Japanese anime – hand-drawn, computer animation originating from Japan. The stories varied widely, from futuristic fantasy to historical tales, romance, and pretty much any subject you could imagine, with a distinct art style that had quite a cult following. Thomas watched a show and was quickly hooked on this new medium he'd stumbled upon. It offered escapism from the mundane. He learnt a few words in Japanese and began to experiment with Asian food. More importantly, Thomas decided to plan a trip to Japan in 2020 and began saving for it. It gave him a goal, and that goal meant there was a future and something to aim for; something to look forward to.

But when the first lockdown was announced, Thomas' trip was cancelled. The one thing that was offering him a glimmer of light, had to be postponed. He resented the pandemic for interrupting his one point of focus. Thomas is just one of many millions whose mental health suffered due to the pandemic's effect on day-to-day life. The full extent of the impact on global mental health has yet to be established and documented. Still, I'm sure we will feel the ripples from Covid financially, socially and from a mental-health perspective for a long, long time to come.

I remember feeling anxious the first day the restrictions were lifted in April 2021, and it seemed like every man, woman, child, dog, cyclist and skateboard rider decided to come into the town for their first sweet taste of freedom in months. People were staggering out of pubs, drunk and singing. Crowds were rushing to buy clothes, queuing in long lines that snaked around the shops. It was a post-lockdown frenzy, and I was overwhelmed by the crowds, having barely seen anyone for the entire winter. I preferred the streets when they were empty.

I'd faced crowds at Delhi train station alone, and that was the definition of crowded, yet I couldn't cope with my own town centre post-lockdown. I fled for the safety of my flat shortly after venturing out. In some ways, I enjoyed the solitude of lockdowns. I didn't have to see people and they gave me a valid excuse to hide.

At the beginning of April, Jack's Functional Skills exams were cancelled, along with every other students' exams, when the country was plunged into educational chaos. I secretly breathed a sigh of relief. In all honesty, there would have been very little realistic chance for Jack to be exam-ready. Jack was barely able to engage in lessons, let alone spend the necessary hours revising.

The online education provider agreed that he could submit work, hoping that it could be graded, and a predicted exam grade granted. However, it was early days, and no one knew what would happen come July. I agreed to encourage him to do the set work when he felt able.

Despite my best efforts it was impossible to get Jack to focus on English assignments when he was declining in front of my eyes. It was clear he was too unwell to study, and he was withdrawn from education once again by the online provider. They asked if I had applied for an Education, Health & Care Plan (EHCP) – I'd never heard of the term.

An EHCP identifies educational, health and social needs and sets out the additional support to meet those needs of a young person who may require extra support with education. Not once in three years, despite being under the care of various educational departments, had anyone ever offered me this option. Had I applied, Jack could have received additional funding towards his education up to the age of twenty-five. There was a backlog in applications and with the pandemic, I was warned it may take up to nine months to process an application, probably longer. Once again, Jack had been let down, but I had no fight left to contest it.

By mid-April, Jack's compulsions were at their peak, and he was spending a torturous eighteen hours a day performing OCD compulsions. The only relief was the six or so hours when he slept.

I was growing increasingly concerned by his deterioration. CAMHS had stopped all home visits due to the pandemic, and my only link to them was a weekly catch-up call with me as, more often than not, Jack was asleep when they called.

I can't even begin to describe my frustration and the sheer exasperation I would feel watching him repeat these seemingly pointless compulsions. There was simply no logic to them whatsoever, but to Jack, they were essential to keep him safe from some invisible threat.

Jack's frustration and sense of powerlessness were so overwhelming at times. He would explode into uncontrollable rages, mostly directed inwards towards himself, and occasionally towards me. These explosions would often involve objects around him. He would kick the sofa, punch cushions, send unbreakable things flying whilst releasing short, swift growls and swearing outbursts.

During those episodes, there was a look in his eyes that scared me. He often spoke of a voice in his head that demanded of him constantly and it terrified me. Was this more than OCD?

Very occasionally, when he allowed himself to, he would slump and sob after such releases. Jack usually withheld his emotions and rarely permitted himself to cry.

These violent outbursts were increasing in frequency and with a deepening level of aggressive behaviour. They were usually triggered by sheer frustration at not being able to complete a compulsion. I learned to dodge the bullets because sometimes just an eye roll or exasperated huff of disapproval from me was enough to spark an outburst.

It was hard to keep my cool during these episodes, and I came exceptionally close to calling the police on a couple of occasions. Perhaps if I had, Jack might have accessed therapy faster, but it's a tough call for a parent to call the police on their child. Exhausted by his relentless compulsions and unpredictable behaviour left me scared of the ramifications of involving the police.

I remember pleading with John for help around that time, but I'm not sure what he could have done. John had never fully understood Jack's illness and as Jack had not stayed at Johns place for over two years, their time spent together had been minimal. I'd basically become a single parent. John blamed me to some degree for my part in Jack's deterioration and he saw my role as Jack's enabler as a huge part of the problem. It was, and now I can witness that too, but one thing is certain – no one can ever say I didn't try my best to help my sons in the only way I knew how. I loved them, just too hard.

Whilst Jack had reached crisis point, Paul wasn't far behind. I'd steal moments away to see Paul and bring him food and wash his clothes, and we'd manage half an hour together most days. Paul had finally started CBT after a nine month wait just before the first lockdown, but it put a swift end to face-to-face visits. Paul missed a couple of calls and left messages, then never followed it up, so the CBT stopped altogether. This was his pattern: start something and give up after a while.

Paul was prescribed a different antidepressant and after a few weeks on the new medication, he slowly began withdrawing from me. He felt increasingly numb, to the extent he couldn't feel love for me or even his children. The new medication was numbing everything.

During the further isolation of the lockdowns, in an attempt to stop the noise in his head, to feel more normal, or to just feel anything at all instead numb, Paul relapsed and slipped back into drinking. It was easy to hide it from me because we weren't spending any significant time together. Sometimes he was shaky and anxious around me when we met, and he never seemed to have any money, but I dismissed the signs, just grateful to see him and escape the flat for a few moments.

We met one afternoon and sat on a wall near his bedsit.

"I can't offer you anything Paul, it's not fair to you. You deserve better than this, you deserve someone else," I said apologetically through tears, unable to see an end in sight.

I'd set aside his dysfunctional behaviour for the most part and was listening to my Guilt Monster once again. After all, this was my fault we were all in this awful situation.

"Shh..." Paul whispered reassuringly as he kissed me gently on my forehead.

Paul never really said much more, and physical touch decreased between us. He stopped holding my hand when we were together; he was distant and didn't seem comfortable around me.

I have always maintained that intimacy is the glue that binds a relationship together and sets it apart from friendship. Without it, you are simply housemates. The trouble was, we weren't even housemates anymore.

A couple of weeks later, I went to meet Paul and we sat on the wall in awkward silence for a few minutes.

"I had to tell my children we are separated to stop them asking to come and stay at the flat. Do you know how hard that was for me?" Paul questioned with irritation in his voice.

"I know, and I'm sorry, okay?" I hung my head.

"I can't feel anything for you. I don't know what's wrong with me, Emily. I don't even want to get out of bed half the time. I appreciate everything you do for me, but I see you as a good friend these days," he offered apologetically.

Taken aback and deeply hurt, his comments stung. Sure, our lives were upside down, and the arrangements were unconventional, but I'd not checked out of our marriage once, continuing to do everything I could for my husband. I loved him deeply, but in reality, couldn't offer him anything more. Telling his children made it seem real to him, but not to me – I was denying the separation and was still hanging on in there for dear life. I couldn't fail at a second marriage. I couldn't let another man leave me.

By this time, Paul was binge-drinking heavily and mixing alcohol with his antidepressants, negating any possible benefit from taking them. During one binge, Paul drank about eighty cans of very cheap cider over a four-day period. I say cider, but it was the budget variety made purely from chemicals and without a hint of apple. When he was on one of these benders, his personality would alter entirely, and he became either defensive and resentful about our circumstances, or sad and overly emotional in his texts.

My Paul was still in there somewhere, under the layers of debilitation, alcoholism and depression – I saw glimpses of him. Paul was broken, but despite his fragile state and the self-hatred he harboured for himself, he was a kind man who never intentionally hurt me.

But Paul slowly withdrew from me entirely. We were barely friends by the end of the first lockdown, and he just about tolerated seeing me because he felt no connection to anything or anyone, including me. When he felt that way, which was most of the time, he became very angry with himself and isolated himself even more in an attempt to avoid hurting me. Sometimes his withdrawal was a relief; it was one less person to worry about.

NOT ENOUGH OF A CRISIS

APRIL 2020

EASTER WEEKEND WAS A PARTICULARLY low point for us all. Jack had exploded into a rage on the landing over a particular compulsion not feeling right, having spent seven hours caught in a ritual. He grabbed the exercise bike and dragged it to the top of the stairs, ready to launch it down. It was heavy and cumbersome and would have caused considerable damage to the walls and stairs.

Thankfully, it was awkward to move across the carpet, and he didn't quite get to throw it before I threw myself in front of him and the bike, blocking both, screaming, "*No!*"

He leant over me, and I cowered on the floor underneath him. This person was unrecognisable as my son. Jack's eyes were wide and angry and filled with frustration and fear. It was terrifying. I was scared of my own child.

Jack pushed past me and ran downstairs, straight to the kitchen. I heard a kitchen drawer fling open, and by the time I got down the stairs, he was at the bottom of the steps with a butcher's knife held to his neck. Jack's eyes were wild, his nostrils flaring like some crazed animal, breathing rapidly through gritted teeth. *"I'll do it, fuck off away from me, or I will do it!"* he growled.

"Put the knife down, Jack," I said as calmly as possible, stepping gingerly down the steps towards him.

"Fuck off! Leave me alone. I want to die! I can't take this anymore!" he wailed.

As I approached Jack, he pulled the knife from his neck and plunged it into the wall next to him. "Arghhh!" he roared.

He'd gouged a huge chunk of plaster out of the wall. The blade couldn't grip into the plaster and the knife clattered to the floor. Jack ran back upstairs and locked himself in the bathroom.

Grabbing the knife and all the others in the kitchen, I hid them before heading back upstairs. Using a screwdriver to unlock the door, I ignored Jack's protests to leave him alone. He sat on the floor in the bathroom, his head in his hands. "I don't even know who I am any more, Mum. I can't stop this noise in my head." He looked at me, absolutely terrified. "I feel like I'm standing on the streets of New York. People are laughing and talking, and cars are beeping – there's so much noise. Am I going mad, Mum?"

Thomas sat on the landing outside the bathroom, casting fearful glances across at me. Neither of us knew what to do.

After Jack calmed down, I called the CAMHS out-of-hours crisis team but got an answering machine as it was Easter Friday. I left a message for someone to call me back urgently but heard nothing that night.

The following day another explosion erupted. One of Jack's compulsions had taken two hours because it just didn't 'feel' right. It seems unbelievable to some people, but it was our reality. I was losing the will to live after two hours and snapped angrily at him. Jack kicked over the clothes airer sending all the wet washing flying in a violent outburst. Reacting with equal anger, I threatened to call John and the police. Jack grabbed my phone, and we fell on the bed, wrestling over it, pushing and pulling each other. Neither of us would give up.

Thomas heard the commotion and came downstairs. Without saying a word, he grabbed Jack's neck to restrain him, blocking his ability to breathe. It was the first time I'd witnessed Thomas intervening in such a forceful way. "I'm not having this anymore," he said defiantly.

Jack was like a caged animal fighting his brother's restraint but I got my phone back. Jack pushed Thomas away with one almighty surge of angry energy, and Thomas released his neck. Jack grabbed his shoes and fled the flat. Thomas was Jack's last ally, so to see his brother turn on him and restrain him was too much for Jack to cope with.

"We better go after him, Mum," Thomas pleaded. "What if he hurts himself?"

I sat motionless. I knew Jack was capable of hurting himself but was exhausted and just for a moment or so, I wanted to let him go. I didn't want to fight this anymore.

A few moments later, I snapped back into responsible reality, and we left the flat to search for Jack. Thomas called John, telling him what had happened. John drove over, and we went three separate ways to start searching, staying in touch with each other by phone.

I headed to the beach area as Jack had spoken previously about choosing the beach to drown himself. After about twenty minutes I spotted him and called Thomas. We were close enough to wave to each other near the beach road. Jack spotted us approaching and bolted. We gave chase, but we both lost him. Jack simply disappeared.

Sometime later, John called me. He had found Jack and persuaded him to get into the car. Jack stayed with John for four hours, calming down.

Thomas walked me home, and I curled up on my bed and sobbed for nearly an hour until there was nothing left inside me to cry. Desperate for a break, I asked John to keep Jack overnight, but it was too much for Jack. He couldn't cope being out of his environment, his safe space, and everything at John's was 'contaminated'.

Jack came home around 10pm, and there was an uneasy calm between us. He apologised and then saw Thomas, and they apologised to each other.

After John left, all the subsequent OCD rituals still had to be completed for Jack to be able to move on and settle. I got to bed at 4am the following morning.

On Easter Monday, Jack spent sixteen hours repeating compulsions and by then, I had gone beyond the point of coping alone and called the out-of-hours crisis team again. I got the same answering machine. During the lockdown, CAMHS patients were given a 24-hour mental-health support line. Calling them, I explained what was happening and how I couldn't reach the crisis team. They promised to contact them for me, and within a couple of hours, the CAMHS crisis team returned my call.

I explained what had happened over the weekend and that Jack was still on a waiting list for CBT and a review with the psychiatrist. They advised that unless my son was experiencing psychosis or was a danger to himself or others, it wasn't appropriate for them to visit. Our situation was not deemed to be enough of a crisis. I was floored by their response and burst into tears. "How much more of a crisis do we need to be in to get help? He had a knife to his throat!" I sobbed.

Up until that moment, I had been able to contain these episodes myself but I felt out of my depth as they escalated. The crisis team promised to get me a call back from CAMHS.

At the beginning of my children's journey into anxiety and depression, I was bewildered and had no idea how to cope with their mood swings and suicidal feelings. Nothing prepares you for loving someone with a mental illness. It is exhausting to both the person and the loved ones coping with their fluctuating mental state. You feel your way through the days, reacting to each experience, and your life adapts around them, often with great resistance and difficulty.

During that dreadful spring of 2020, I experienced a whole spectrum of emotions: anger, frustration, sadness, love, revulsion, guilt, fury. I felt all of them, swirling about inside me, weighing me down. I was robotically performing life, living some sort of sub-existence under the oppressive rule of a mental illness beast who had taken over all our lives.

When I say I felt anger, I mean *rage*; blood-boiling rage that I couldn't allow myself to vent. It simmered dangerously, temporarily contained under the surface until someone or something triggered me. When I snapped and blew, oh boy, did I explode.

I released that rage verbally on the three people closest to me: screaming, shouting, and swearing at the people I loved the most. It was carnage and very unsettling for everyone. Nothing was ever achieved by projecting all my pent-up anger on them in a slew of foul language and hurtful digs; it was always incredibly damaging. I'm ashamed of that behaviour now.

A couple of days after Easter, and after seven months of waiting, Jack's psychiatrist called and listened to my account of Jack's deterioration. She diagnosed OCD on a severe scale, and we discussed medication again. She said that sectioning him was an option but only as a last resort: the in-patient unit probably wasn't the best environment for Jack with his contamination OCD. In any case, the unit was full and not accepting any admissions during lockdown.

The CBT therapist contacted me a day later and advised that Jack was being made a priority and offered me online appointments. But of course, Jack's sleep was so disrupted, we just couldn't make a time work. I felt stuck in a torturous loop: Jack was mentally unwell and after fifteen months on a waiting list, he had finally been offered therapy but couldn't engage with it because of his erratic sleep.

Jack was spending every waking minute caught in compulsions, often all night too, leaving him falling asleep, exhausted, at some point during the day. Everything he did would involve an OCD compulsion. It would start upon waking: Jack would have to get out of bed a certain way, and if it didn't feel right, he would get back in and repeat the action over and over again until it did.

Jack would have to dress in a specific order, and again, if it didn't feel right, he'd pull his T-shirt back off and on, repeatedly, until it did. A lot of Jack's compulsions were based on feelings. Things had to feel a certain way and I think only someone with OCD could possibly understand this frustrating requirement. Sometimes the feeling had to be paired with a specific number of repetitions. One or two repetitions were never enough. The number three was banned, deemed unlucky and guaranteed to cause a consequence. Sometimes it was four, but if that didn't feel right, compulsions were doubled to eight, sixteen, up to 128 or even 256.

OCD can be like the arcade game where you use a hammer to hit frogs down. As soon as you hit one down, another pops up elsewhere. Jack's OCD was like that. He'd conquer one element and feel triumphant, only for it to pop up elsewhere in another form a day or so later. OCD loves to control you, so when you take back the control in some form or another, it fights back, with a vengeance.

When given his dinner or a snack, Jack would naturally thank me. Somehow that customary thank you morphed into a compulsion. It started as one thank you, which became four, then sixteen. Jack would say thank you over and over. I tried walking away, often muttering in frustration, but Jack would become anxious and worked up, and it was just easier, though not at all helpful, to go along with it.

At its worst, I remember standing on the stairs with him on the landing outside his room. Jack had just collected his dinner. My phone was in my pocket, and I glanced at the time. The thank you compulsion continued for seventeen minutes.

"For fuck's sake!" Jack shouted when it finally felt right, and he stormed into his room, with his cold dinner. That incident caused Jack to avoid eating, and he started to skip meals just to dodge the thank-you compulsion.

This went on for about three months until one day, he tried running up the stairs after saying thank you four times and bolted into his room and closed the door. It worked, and he was able to do the same for the next two weeks until it finally relaxed to saying it just once from then on.

Something so simple and basic to you or me, crippled Jack for three months. Most of the time, I didn't pay attention, but when I did, it would make me so sad to witness Jack's overwhelming compulsions over the most mundane tasks.

I had become so used to Jack being restrictive with his food it had become the norm in our household. He would go through phases of repetitively eating the same food day after day. Jack referred to foods being 'banned' in his mind. For example, if Jack ate a particular meal and felt unwell that day, felt overly tired, or was unable to fall asleep, he would attribute the disruption to his routine to that meal and ban that food type again, often for months at a time.

As his OCD intensified, untreated, it would tell him there would be a dire consequence to eating a certain food. Of course, there was no consequence and his inability to sleep or ill feeling was always caused by his underlying anxiety. It had nothing to do with a bowl of cereal or a piece of toast, but in Jack's head, it did.

Every single day for seven months, he was forced to eat the same thing: a ham sandwich with a packet of crisps. Jack called it lunch, but it could be eaten at 4am if his OCD told him to. It didn't matter what time of day or night he ate it, he'd still call it lunch.

Even Billy the dog knew this routine and would jump up eagerly, although a little sleepily if in the early hours, and sit patiently waiting next to Jack for his little ham treat. Billy would place his paw on Jack's arm patiently and it would make Jack giggle. It was one of the small joys for Jack that cut through the frustrations of these punishing routines. Billy was more than a just a dog, he was Jack's best friend, a therapeutic companion and often the only one that could make Jack smile.

GLIMMERS OF HOPE

MAY 2020

DURING THE FIRST lockdown in spring 2020, Jack decided – amongst all his OCD chaos – that he wanted to apply for college. All of his friends had applied, and he wanted to give it a go. It seemed unthinkable given his current state of mind, but I jumped at any thread of hope.

Jack applied for a science course and a few weeks later, the college scheduled an interview. Then I received a call one day out of the blue. The science lecturer had picked up his application and was calling students a little earlier than scheduled to get the ball rolling. He asked if Jack was available for a phone interview but Jack was just about to start his shower schedule. He'd come out of the bathroom as he heard his name mentioned. Jack shook his head at me in sheer terror. I told the lecturer he was in the shower and arranged a call back in thirty minutes.

Jack jumped in the shower and proceeded to have the fastest shower he'd had in months. Just over twenty minutes later, he was dressed and downstairs in time for the call. When the lecturer called back, Jack went mute. He'd never had an interview before, but I was grateful it wasn't face-to-face. The lecturer tried to gather from him why he was interested in that course, and he started to warm up and chat a little about his interest in science.

I never doubted Jack's academic ability – he was a bright, articulate boy – but this illness had robbed him of almost his entire secondary education thus far. The prospect of college seemed out of reach.

Jack was determined, though. In between the dreadful days – and there were so many of those – there were glimmers of hope for a future and I nurtured his dreams when he spoke of them as much as possible. He *had* to have hope.

The lecturer was warm and engaging. He'd had a little history about Jack from me beforehand so he put Jack at ease quickly. He reassured him that despite not having gained his GCSEs in English or Maths, they would love to welcome him on the course. The plan was for him to study Functional Skills alongside his science course.

Jack had successfully passed his interview and was offered a place at college. He was delighted; somebody wanted him despite his lack of grades. It gave him a sense of normality and he could level with his peers. It gave him such a boost, and it was great to see him smile again. We vowed to work together over the summer to get him well and ready for college.

A TORTUROUS SEASON

JUNE 2020

Jack desperately wanted a normalised sleep pattern. He didn't want to be sleeping in the day and up all night, but sometimes the OCD rituals could take up to six hours just so he could get into bed, by which time dawn would be breaking.

Jack spent two long and arduous years fighting his sleep patterns, constantly trying to adjust his sleep back into a reasonable routine by getting into bed a little earlier each day. The more he tried, the more his OCD multiplied and taunted him. He was terrified of staying up for extended periods to improve his sleep: OCD told him it would make him sick.

Jack's complexion was sallow and grey; substantial dark-brown circles encased his eyes. The lack of daylight, fresh air and exercise led to a very pale and unwell-looking young man.

Avoidance became Jack's best friend but also his worst enemy. He would hide in his room for hours at a time, distracting his intrusive thoughts and avoiding his compulsions. I don't blame him; Jack's OCD was in full control, and who would want to sit for hours at a time completing mundane but compulsory and often painful rituals?

One day, around 10am, he was still avoiding the compulsions and hadn't been to sleep. Exasperated by his hours of avoidance, I angrily burst into his room and gave him an ultimatum: "Get in that bed now, Jack, or I'm walking out. I'm leaving you and won't be helping you again."

I knew this would hit a nerve because I was Jack's safety blanket. Without me, he felt incapable of functioning.

"Go then, I don't care..." he muttered.

Jack didn't believe me, for I'd blustered like this many times but never followed through. This time was different though. I'd had enough. I was walking off the job.

Grabbing my phone, a coat and the dog, I left the flat. It was raining, but Billy and I walked along the beach, happily passing almost two hours away, just wandering. It felt so good to be free. My phone vibrated in my pocket. It was Jack calling.

Waves of guilt came over me, but I didn't let on and calmly told him I'd be back in ten minutes. I was only a minute or so away but needed that time to calm and prepare myself for the fall-out from my absence and the impending four- or five-hour compulsion shift that lay ahead.

When I returned, Jack was sitting on the stairs waiting for me. It was apparent from his red eyes that he'd been crying. He went into his room to start his compulsions, two hours later than planned. By the time he went to sleep, it was nearly 5pm.

Looking at my laptop later that evening, I found over a dozen open tabs where Jack had been searching for different articles and videos on OCD:

Will I ever be normal?

Teens with OCD
Can I overcome OCD?
How to beat OCD
Do teens with OCD commit suicide?
Suicide rates for people with OCD
Washing hands with OCD

The list went on and on and it broke my heart.

There were also two tabs for suicide helplines.

For weeks during the Covid lockdowns, Jack's sleep was gradually rolling forward due to the time spent performing rituals. He was falling asleep later and later each day until eventually, he was not getting to bed until late afternoon. Thomas tried to convince him that if he could just stay up a few more hours, he would correct his sleep pattern, but Jack was having none of it. Or rather, his OCD wasn't.

A couple of days after my walk-out protest, Jack was still up at 9pm and quite out of the blue, decided to stay up that night. He lasted until 1am.

It was new and terrifying territory for him and he pleaded with me to sleep on his floor in case of some dire consequence from this bold move. I didn't mind too much – I was relieved knowing my sleep would be uninterrupted for once and proceeded to make a bed up on the floor. I slept soundly until 9am – my first full night's sleep in over a year.

Jack got up and was upbeat, like a new kid altogether. He asked to go for a walk with the dog to the beach. He'd not been out for over six months, so I seized the moment and dragged Thomas with us.

Despite the lockdown, we were still permitted to take our daily exercise, and there were very few people around, which suited Jack. For the first time in many, many months, we walked all together to the beach. The sun was shining. It was a crisp, fresh day, and the boys played happily with the dog on the beach. Jack was beaming.

We enjoyed the most wonderful ninety minutes wandering and strolling back home through the town gardens. Halfway home, Jack's sense of achievement was at an all-time high, and he asked if he could use my phone to call John. He was always so excited when he felt he'd achieved something, and to Jack, fixing his sleep was monumental.

After a quick chat on the phone, we headed to collect the car and visit John. Jack was like that: all, or nothing, and when he got a burst of confidence, he wanted to do everything he'd been missing out on for months. We spent about four hours outside the house that day, which was just remarkable after months locked away.

Jack's exuberance lasted several days whilst his sleep remained semi-normalised, but within a week, it had reverted to nocturnal, and his mood sunk along with the change. It was such a frustrating rollercoaster.

By the summer of 2020, Jack, Paul, Thomas and I had all reached our own personal breaking points. The only person privy to everyone's deterioration was me, for I was still shielding everyone from the others' demise. I wrapped them all in cotton wool, cushioning them from their own torment. I didn't afford myself the same care: I just wrapped myself in more food.

By this point, Jack had restricted himself to three home-cooked dinners eaten in rotation. They were all beef dishes because they reduced the chance of food poisoning, and other meats and fish were strictly forbidden. Jack was bored stiff and hated the repetitiveness, but these meals made him feel safe and in control. I obliged as it saved me worrying about what to feed him.

Jack would permit himself a few snacks a day: always the same food. He'd go through phases of these rigid food patterns, and although the food might change every few months, the underlying controlled style of eating remained. He even measured the amount of water he drank daily. He would have to take eight sips after dinner and so many sips before bed. Glasses were banned for their contamination risk.

Even when talking to his friends online, he would count the sentences and words they spoke. Of course, they had no idea. There was no downtime from this crippling illness; OCD bled into every aspect of Jack's waking life. It would take him four to six hours just to complete the pre-sleep compulsions before bed, most of which were utterly ridiculous and illogical to the outsider.

Paul's mental health continued to deteriorate during the summer. He became agoraphobic, crippled with social anxiety, and struggled to leave his room for fear of bumping into people and having to hold a conversation in the communal kitchen. (He admitted sometime later that when we met up for our walks, he couldn't wait to leave and get back to the safety of his room.) Of course, I often sensed his discomfort around me and other people, but at the time, I just accepted it. Between his behaviour, the boys' downward spiral and the pandemic, nothing felt familiar anymore.

Thomas was miserable and disillusioned with life under lockdown, and it was impossible for him not be affected by the isolation. Just like many others, he did not see his friends or his extended family for many months. The disconnection and boredom was heightened by his already present depression, and this led him to start gambling again; just small dripfeed spends at first, but they soon escalated into larger sums. Thomas rarely won – the losses running into hundreds of pounds – yet he constantly chased the elusive wins; he craved the dopamine high.

As things deteriorated with Jack, and I remained disconnected from Paul, I slowly and unconsciously slipped back into bingeing. Before long, I was bingeing several nights a week, fully aware of my behaviour but too exhausted to do anything about it. Food became my one escape, a damaging drug to get through the agonising days. I ballooned by three stones in weight. It was the heaviest I'd ever been and was thoroughly miserable. I thought about food constantly.

Just like any addiction, it was a very destructive pattern to fall into. It made me a sneaky eater and I'd hide my bingeing from my kids. It was much easier to satisfy my addiction without Paul living there. There was no one to call me out for this behaviour.

I'd plan my bingeing episodes and I'd only ever allow myself to eat until midnight because in my twisted thoughts, I always intended to stop then and return to healthy eating the following day. I rarely did though. The euphoric escape food offered me was momentary; the anticipation was the most pleasurable part. The split second the food was consumed, I'd be overwhelmed by self-loathing and frustration.

I'd catch myself speaking out loud to myself whilst

preparing the large haul of food, trying to prevent myself from doing it: "You're going to regret this tomorrow. You don't need this..." But it never stopped me. The urge was far too strong and powerful. It overrode my rational mind and beat me every time. I knew it was unhealthy and unnecessary, that I wouldn't consciously choose to put all that rubbish in my body, but I couldn't seem to stop it. I would pick up a packet of biscuits and stare at the contents for a moment or two, willing myself to overpower the urge to eat them. What was it all for anyway? A few moments of pleasure followed by hours of guilt and regret. But the binger within me always won. I had a sensible dialogue running in my mind like a commentary – a conscientious monologue of what I *should* be doing – but that voice barely got a look in.

Insults were not confined to within my head. If I walked past the full-length mirror (which I mostly avoided) I'd berate myself out loud with a sickening venom that I wouldn't dare dream of saying to anyone else: "You're so fat. Look at you, you *fat bitch*!" I'd pat my stomach which resembled a heavily pregnant woman after yet another enormous binge.

I'd go from that mirror straight to the kitchen to find something else to eat because, well, who cared? I was already so overweight, it wouldn't matter. I loathed myself. Sometimes I would cry as the binge was nearing its end; tears of powerlessness and self-disgust.

The inevitable regret I'd feel after each binge would merge in with waves of self-hatred, mixed in with guilt at my self-declared failure as a mother and wife. I'd just add all those feelings to the pot of family chaos; just another ingredient to the madness mix that was bubbling away and threatening to boil over every day.

I was in denial that the eating disorder was back, this

time with a vengeance, and avoided re-referring myself to the eating-disorder clinic. As a result, my bingeing continued to spiral out of control.

I continued to meet Paul a couple of times a week, albeit briefly. I was fighting to keep my head above water with Jack's deterioration and juggling Paul's drinking and mood swings, Thomas' gambling, and my bingeing, along with the obvious breakdown of our marriage. I was spinning a dozen plates all at once, but now they were crashing down all around me.

After one particularly challenging day with Jack, I finally snapped. "I'm packing my bags and leaving you all!" I shrieked. "Look after yourself. I don't care anymore. *I can't fucking take it anymore!*" I screamed and burst into angry, exhausted tears, wild with indescribable contempt.

"Go then, see if I care!" Jack yelled in reply.

"I will then. I'll do it," I spat back at him and ran up to Thomas' room where I threw myself on his bed, face down, sobbing.

Every exhausted inch of my mind and body wanted to grab a few things and disappear; I didn't care where. I just wanted to run away, to shut down. I craved sleep and was sick to death of the responsibility of supporting them. Who was taking care of *me*? No one. I certainly wasn't.

Thomas sat next to me and held me. "What's wrong, Mum? What happened?" he asked, visibly disturbed by the state I was in.

"I can't do it anymore, Thomas. I can't take this anymore. I need a break," I sobbed.

"Mum, go. Please book a hotel. We will be okay. I will look after him. Jack will just have to get on with it without you," he pleaded.

Thomas had been watching my inability to cope deteriorate over the preceding weeks. I often turned to him for support, but my instability was undermining his own fragile balance. It unnerved him to see me fall apart. At the time, I was oblivious to the impact it was having on all of them.

Even with Thomas' encouragement, I couldn't let go enough to permit myself a break. I just couldn't bring myself to do it and felt such an overwhelming responsibility to stay. Perhaps on some subconscious level, I needed them to need me. I had to put up with all their shit, their mood swings, their imbalance. I had to love them unconditionally so that they would love me back.

I had been tied up in emotional bondage most of my adult life, tethered to the roles of a loving wife and mother with invisible chains from my own sense of unworthiness. It was probably underpinned by a deep subconscious sense of rejection I'd felt from my father's absence and him subsequently leaving me as a teenager. It was painful being left and feeling abandoned. I remembered that pain and could never inflict that same pain on my children. It was a pattern I'd carried through my entire life since my father emigrated, followed by my mother moving away when I was seventeen. I'd told myself everyone I'd ever loved deeply had left me. It must have been my fault somehow; I must be unlovable.

So, I compensated by giving everything I had to everyone in my life ever after, regardless of the personal cost. This whole situation was the *piece de resistance* of my self-inflicted emotional bondage and I had been building to this climax for years. Nobody was pinning me down, nobody was physically stopping me from going anywhere, just me, and I simply wouldn't allow myself to cut through those chains, or give myself permission to step away, albeit it briefly.

I continued to threaten to leave Jack weekly but

couldn't bring myself to do it. Instead, I muddled along, surviving the daily chaos, oblivious to the impact my threats were having on Jack. The more I threatened to leave, the more unstable he became.

I'd thought about reaching out to Steve once more, the man whose foundation course I had completed many years before. It had a profound healing effect on me, and I'd never felt more empowered or equipped to face life's challenges than after I'd completed it and applied the disciplines daily. Over time though, I'd fallen so far off the wagon from that practice that I couldn't bring myself to approach him. As a result, the wheels well and truly came off.

OWNING THE NIGHT

JULY 2020

As much as the pandemic interrupted our lives and slowed access to the mental-health services we so desperately needed, it gifted Jack a sense of safety which allowed him to walk unnoticed whilst the rest of the world remained locked away. Walking became a daily occurrence partly because Jack enjoyed it, but mostly because his OCD dictated that he *had* to do it.

Often, Jack and I would walk at night once his other compulsions were complete. Unfortunately, if Jack's catalogue of compulsions were delayed through his inability to satiate his OCD's demands, we'd end up walking at 2, 3, and even 4am. In fact, during the series of Covid lockdowns, we walked our way around the entire clock.

During the early weeks, Jack was very uncomfortable passing other people in the street, but as the days passed and his confidence grew, he became more comfortable with our nighttime ventures. We always followed the same route, dictated by his OCD. The only time we deviated was when he felt spooked by an exuberant drunk person, noisily heading in our direction. Suddenly Jack would dart in a different direction, and I'd run to catch up. We certainly met some characters during our night walks.

One evening, we walked past a man sitting on the kerb near us. It was 3am and we had no choice but to pass him. He was obliterated on drink, a bottle of spirits still clasped in his hands. He was rocking and muttered incoherently as we passed and by the time we'd walked four- or five-metres beyond him, he was lying on his back on the side of the road. He was singing loudly whilst cycling his legs in the air.

On another night, we passed an older lady at a bus stop. "Come here, you bastard. I am going to strangle you!" she slurred loudly, apparently at no one – though we feared it might be us.

We swiftly crossed the road and soon realised she was shouting at an equally inebriated man jaywalking along the middle of the road. Luckily, there was no traffic as it was nearly 3.30am. The drunken man shouted some muffled profanities back at her and we could still hear them swearing at each other as we returned home.

Then there was a one-legged, wheelchair-bound homeless man who appeared from nowhere around a corner, wheeling up to us just after 4am asking for change. He caught me offguard, and I hurriedly muttered that I had nothing before scurrying up the hill as fast as I could. Jack was wary of the drug addicts and homeless people, but I was rarely so, though their appearance from the shadows like that spooked even me.

The town centre was colourful at the best of times, but there was something about that window between 12am and 4am that was exciting and a little terrifying. It never really seemed to sleep; there were always sounds or movements in the shadows. We would laugh once we were home in the safety of the flat, but there were a few occasions when people's behaviour frightened us.

We heard countless drug deals taking place as we passed shady characters on street corners. We laughed at the number of men we caught sneaking into the local brothel, embarrassed to be seen sharing the same path as us – one in, one out sometimes. There was a whole new world out there, an often dark and seedy one, but it was always interesting and exciting to Jack. His only experience for several years had been watching life online, from inside his room.

There was also something quite magical and exhilarating walking the streets in the middle of the night. Jack always said he felt like he owned the night, especially if we passed no one. It was eerily apocalyptic during lockdown, but in a terrifyingly beautiful way. Our experience changed depending on the time we ventured out. It almost became a game of sorts, and we'd guess who lived behind the windows we saw lit up at night. We knew every inch of the roads we walked; every house, every flat, shop and rubbish bin. We'd peek voyeuristically into the lives of people who were still up at 4am: the ones who sat on their computers by windows; the invisible tenant we never saw but who must have kept their poor neighbours up night after night with the TV blaring until the small hours; the man who slept on his sofa in the basement flat, night after night, curtains open; the street sweepers in their little carts, and the night cleaners who cleaned the betting shop and local pubs.

We watched the supermarket night staff restock the shelves long after the town had emptied. We observed the local kebab shop mopping up and closing at 3am – and giggled at the seagulls swooping into shred their rubbish bags, searching for scattered chips. They would annihilate a black bag in minutes, and by the time we looped back around, the road would be littered with rubbish.

One night we disturbed some rats by commercial bins in an alleyway. They scattered everywhere with such speed, I squealed. We laughed afterwards, and 'spot the rats' soon became part of our nightly game.

For all that darkness, for all the dirt and the squalid things we saw, there was beauty too. Sometimes we would stop and look up at the stars together. Jack would marvel at them; the simplest things would enthrall him. Because Jack had been locked inside his own mind – and room – for three years, he would look at all things with childlike wonder, and it was infectious. He would often stop mid-conversation to look up at the wispy clouds moving across the black sky or the moon when it was full.

One night, we headed out at about 3.30am. It was stormy outside, but that didn't stop us: OCD doesn't pause for inclement weather.

Jack was giggling like a little child at the wind and rain hitting his face, and he suddenly sprinted up the road. When I caught up, he was laughing, infectiously. "I feel *free*, Mum," he cried, life dancing in his eyes.

Jack and I continued to walk every day. The walks became a highlight during a truly dreadful time and broke the monotony of the OCD rituals.

Paul never knew about these walks – I didn't dare tell him. It was difficult enough dealing with Thomas' protective reaction: he was terrified that something would happen to me whilst walking these streets at such strange times.

I half expected to bump into Paul at one of the late-night off-licences during our walks – but thankfully we never did. It meant I didn't have to justify the ludicrous dictatorship of Jack's OCD to Paul, nor explain to Jack the extent of Paul's drinking.

Jack and I often reminisce about those middle-of-the-night walks. They belonged just to us, our secret adventures, and as disruptive and exhausting as they were to me, there was a tiny part of me that mourned them when the lockdowns ended. Jack taught me to pause and witness the beauty around me. I'd become too disconnected from life outside our mental mayhem to notice it.

ROCK BOTTOM

AUGUST 2020

SECRETLY CRAVING a change of scene and some much-needed sleep, I suggested we stay in a local hotel to help disrupt the punishing routine Jack and I were caught in. The hotels had recently reopened after the summer lockdown, and despite it being early August, it was still quiet. Our trip to Lanzarote had been so successful in interrupting rituals and helping fix Jack's sleep, it was worth a shot.

"I don't know, Mum. I'm not sure I can do it," he said doubtfully.

I left it at that but mentioned it a few times over the following two weeks. By mid-August, Jack was thoroughly fed up, and he finally agreed. I excitedly booked a local budget hotel for two nights for the following day and went and checked in alone the next afternoon.

Lying on the twin bed, I smoothed out the linen and admired the texture of the crisp, white cotton, and the novelty of sleeping in a real bed. Mine was a sofa bed in the lounge that doubled as my bedroom in our small flat. It felt momentarily luxurious with its big fluffy pillows, air-conditioning and a large TV on the wall. The bathroom was beautiful, and I was hopeful of a long soak in the big bathtub. I headed home and showed Jack the pictures I'd taken of the room to try and entice him further and allowed myself to get excited.

It was late afternoon and Jack had only just woken up, so he had a long night ahead. I didn't envisage us arriving at the hotel until around dawn once he'd finished all his many rituals, but I'd accepted that. After spending the entire night completing compulsions, he finally finished around 9am and was ready to go to the hotel. I was shattered from sitting with him all night but the lure of sleeping in a real bed energised me.

"Mum. I'm too scared. What if it's busy at the hotel entrance. I can't deal with all the people."

I was bubbling with a mixture of frustration and disappointment. I'd already paid for the room and there was no hope of getting a refund. "Come on, Jack, let's just try. It won't be busy at 9am," I muttered, trying so hard to remain calm and not allow the anger to surface in my tone.

Jack relented, and we headed out of the door. We walked for about three minutes along the street when a couple appeared from a local guest house with their suitcases. Jack strode on ahead until a family of five appeared around the corner, approaching us. "I can't do this." I'm going home, *I'm not going*!" he shouted. Jack spun around and disappeared in the direction of our flat.

Momentarily frozen, I stood there, watching him disappear as the family walked past, giggling, laughing and chatting away as ordinary people do. I stood motionless and let my disappointment sink away for a moment or two, then reality settled in: we weren't going, and I'd wasted money on a room I'd never sleep in.

I headed home and found Jack pacing by the flat door.

He went straight to his room and slammed the door, his frustration with himself and his guilt over wasted money weighing heavily on him.

What I should have done was go to the hotel alone to sleep anyway and leave him to it, even for just a few hours, but I had allowed myself to become prisoner of his OCD.

Two days later, I returned to the hotel and handed back the key. I told them we hadn't used the room, not bothering to elaborate why; the receptionist wouldn't understand anyway. Never mind, I'd tried at least.

Sleep continued to dominate Jack's days and nights. His entire days' rituals and moods were dependent upon sleep, or the lack of it. No matter how hard both Thomas and I tried to reason with him that it would be easier to just let things naturally roll forward by staying up a little bit later each day, Jack's brain could not accept it.

One particular morning, he was still awake at 11am. He'd been up for about sixteen hours and was tired but fed up with this monotonous routine. Checking in on him, he looked anxious and exhausted. "I don't know what to do about my sleep, Mum." Then he searched something on his computer. "Right, that's it, I'm staying up!' he exclaimed, as if he'd had an injection of energy.

"What?" I questioned.

He'd searched, "*Can I fix my sleep pattern by rolling it back*" and there wasn't a single search or comment relating to it, which had swung it for him.

So he did as he said, rather excitedly despite his tiredness, and ended up staying up almost thirty hours. He went to bed at 1am and slept soundly until 9am. He didn't die from it, as he though he might, in fact, he felt okay. It was a pivotal point for Jack and marked a turning point in a two-year internal battle he had encountered with his sleep.

By the end of August, Paul decided he couldn't stomach drinking anymore – literally. He'd been feeling increasingly unwell and his stomach was tender and bloated like a barrel. He'd been kept up a couple of nights in the week before with excruciating stomach pains, to the point where he'd almost called an ambulance – Paul was not one to complain, so he must have been in agony. The pain subsided after a couple of hours, and he attributed it to something he'd eaten.

Paul closed himself into his room and went cold turkey for three long days, despite being warned not to stop drinking suddenly. It was a foolish thing to do as his body could have gone into shock from the sudden alcohol withdrawal, but he was determined to give up. The local addiction clinic had warned him not to stop drinking altogether but to wean himself off gradually, but he didn't listen and later that night he started shaking. It passed and foolishly, he didn't call an ambulance.

Paul couldn't face anyone, not even me, and started experiencing flu-like symptoms, sweating profusely. His stomach pain returned in the early hours of his third night of detoxing. Rather than call for help, he took painkillers and lay on the floor until it passed.

The next day was our wedding anniversary. Paul felt he was through the worst of the detox, and we arranged to meet for a walk. It seemed futile to acknowledge our anniversary given the current circumstances, but I somehow felt obliged. I still loved this man deeply and was concerned for him.

It was a cloudy day but dry. His appearance stunned me. "Paul, your eyes are yellow... Your skin is yellow!" He was a luminous lemon colour, and it was very apparent in the natural light.

He dismissed my observation instantly: "I'm fine. It's nothing."

Grabbing my phone, I quickly took a picture of his eyes and face to show him. There was no disputing it. Paul was jaundiced. "Right, let's go back to your place and call 111 and ask for their advice," I suggested.

"No, no, I'm fine. I'll just see how I am tomorrow. I can't be bothered with the hassle of the hospital. I'm tired and don't feel well."

'I gave him no opportunity to protest. 'Paul, you're jaundiced. Your body doesn't turn yellow for no reason. I'm calling them!"

As soon as we were back at his place, we called the NHS helpline and they took all his information. Within half an hour, a doctor called back and instructed Paul to attend an appointment at the local hospital within the hour and pack a bag – there was a good chance he would be staying.

Paul was admitted to the hospital and kept in for five days. His liver readings were significantly elevated, and he had an infection in his gallbladder, which explained the pain he had been experiencing. These factors had caused his body to produce excessive amounts of bilirubin which had turned his skin and eyes yellow.

As the days progressed, the yellow tinge spread throughout his body. Paul was very unwell at the time of admission, and the doctor warned him if he had waited another day to come in, he would have been in trouble. Paul's liver was fatty and struggling. Although the drinking had not necessarily caused the liver issues, it certainly hadn't helped.

The doctor decided to give Paul a medical detox whilst in hospital as he felt he was still experiencing withdrawals. It was something he'd hoped for, for some time. They pumped him with antibiotics for the gall-bladder infection and vitamins by an IV drip, and he started to feel better than he had in a long, long time.

The liver consultant came to see him before his discharge and warned him that given the state of his liver, he should refrain from heavy drinking again as any irritants would see his liver deteriorate – and much quicker next time.

It was a huge wake-up call for Paul and when he left the hospital, he enrolled with an online alcohol support group and attended daily meet-ups online.

CLIMBING MOUNTAINS

SEPTEMBER-OCTOBER 2020

As THE COLLEGE induction day loomed closer, it was apparent Jack wasn't any better. Sure, a compulsion here and there had been squashed but only for a new and equally irritating one to appear. Jack's sleep was still all over the place, but he seemed determined to try college and push himself. He'd been out walking every day and had slowly built his confidence.

A couple of weeks before college was due to commence, his contamination fears started to increase. Jack started washing his hands excessively again, spending anywhere between twenty to forty minutes, often going through an entire bottle of hand soap in one go. At the time, I didn't think much of it. It was annoying, but I was well used to all his illogical rituals and to me, it was just another irritating and expensive one.

It was early September, and the induction day was two days away. As if from nowhere and after months of sleep issues, Jack corrected his sleep. It was incredible and perfectly timed.

The night before, he was naturally very anxious and

struggled to sleep until 4.30am. It was very doubtful he was going to be able to wake up after just three and a half hours, but I tried anyway.

To my utter astonishment, Jack woke up at 8.15am. Adrenaline pulled him out of his sleep and he started to shake; his teeth were chattering and he couldn't stomach water, let alone food. We had about twenty minutes to get out of the door and reach college.

After a quick trip to the bathroom, he ran down to the kitchen and started to wash his hands. It took twenty-three minutes. My heart was pounding, and I desperately tried to stay calm externally, but inside I was imploding with panic. You couldn't hurry this process along at the best of times, but introduce an important deadline like college, and it became a stressful tension-fuelled nightmare.

"I'm not going. Look at the time!" Jack wailed.

I said nothing. Soap was splattered all over him, the floor and cupboards. Even Billy had a few foamy mounds on his back. It was a hazard he risked every time he joined us in the kitchen.

College started at 9am. It was already 8.50am, and we lived twenty minutes' drive away. Jack grabbed his bag, a mask and ran out of the door; no food, no drink, just some pens. There was a hidden reserve of determination that Jack could tap into at times.

As we approached the college road, my heart sank. Roadworks had commenced, and we were detoured for about ten minutes.

"You might as well turn around and go home. I'm not walking in this late," Jack protested.

"I can't turn around, Jack," I sighed as we sat in bumper-to-bumper, rush-hour traffic.

When we finally reached college, it was 9.20am. I'd

convinced myself he wouldn't go in, but from somewhere, Jack found a remarkable sense of courage and grabbed his bag.

"Right, I'm doing it. Bye, Mum. I'll be walking home..."

And with that, he jumped out of the car and headed towards the college without a single backward glance. I sat there for ten minutes in disbelief, sure he wouldn't stay, but Jack didn't reappear.

Driving home, I cried and shouted and screamed and sobbed the entire journey back, releasing months of pent-up feelings in a very primal way. Like a cat on a hot tin roof, I paced all day, half expecting to be called by the college and told he was mid-panic attack and to come and collect him, but the call never came.

At 1.30pm, I gave in and called to see if Jack was doing okay and still there. The college confirmed he was there, and although he hadn't said a word all day, he seemed okay.

I felt triumphant and filled with a strange mix of shock, relief and sheer pride. This was monumental: Jack may as well have climbed Mount Everest. Coping with little sleep and hours upon hours of OCD compulsions, contamination fears and chronic anxiety, the idea of going to a new college, especially so late, seemed impossible, but he'd done it.

It was 4.30pm when Jack arrived home: exhausted, starving, hungry and gasping for a drink. He had managed to find his way back and had walked the 4.5 miles home. Despite his tiredness, he was exuberant and proud of his own achievement. The walk alone was a massive milestone in itself. About two miles of it stretched along one of the busiest high streets in our town. It would have exposed him to many people, busy shops, and bustling traffic, which would be overwhelming for Jack under normal circumstances.

Jack was elated and, despite his mammoth trip home, still wanted to go walking with Thomas and me. Jack and Thomas chatted as I trudged behind. I had learnt to really savour these ordinary moments; they were few and far between. However, my imagination ran riot with thoughts of a brighter future, and in my foolish naïvety, I somehow believed that Jack was cured and that college would be the answer to all my prayers.

Jack was understandably exhausted that night and fell asleep sitting up against his bed. I found him around midnight and gently ushered him into his bed fully clothed.

I attempted to wake him at 8am ready for the second induction day at college but without luck. He was dead to the world until nearly 11am, clearly exhausted from the previous day's adrenaline-fuelled day. When he woke, he was frustrated at himself for sleeping through and missing college, but they weren't too concerned by his absence as they were fully aware of the circumstances.

About a week before college began, Jack's contamination fears had started to ramp up, and he became very obsessive over handwashing. Not giving it much attention, I'd assumed it was due to a fear of Covid. But this wasn't the case. Jack was terrified of the hidden germs inside the flat, not outside it. The family bathroom had been the epicentre of his contamination OCD for some time, but with the added anxiety of attending college, Jack's OCD was multiplying at a rapid rate and now everything was feeling contaminated, including the floor, wall, surfaces, clothes – the list was growing.

In the days following his first day at college, things escalated. He was struggling to get dressed. Every clothing item was painstakingly picked up and put down multiple times before he could put it on. It was discarded as contaminated if it happened to touch his leg or the wall, or me. Washing his clothes daily became the norm as it wasn't uncommon for him to go through three changes of clothes a day. Every single detail of his life was a series of numbered, repetitive actions carried out with meticulous perfection. It was utterly engulfing him and driving me insane.

Jack felt an overwhelming need to put gloves on in the house to prevent his hands becoming contaminated. I bought boxes of 100 catering gloves, and Jack would painstakingly remove one at a time from the tightly packed box. Often the gloves would come out stuck together, and his OCD simply wouldn't accept that; at times I'd stand there for twenty minutes as he selected the right glove. The ones that didn't feel right were tossed to the floor: discarded and deemed unusable. Jack's frustration was so upsetting to witness, and inside I was always either fighting a lump in my throat or wanting to scream, "*Hurry the fuck up!!*" But of course, I didn't.

At his peak, Jack went through two hundred gloves in four days, most of which were recycled by me when he wasn't looking.

"I'm so fucking useless, Mum. I can't even pick a glove or dress properly," he'd exclaimed when the frustration finally overwhelmed him. "I don't deserve to go to college, I'm not mature enough. I'm like a baby."

It was hard to know how to respond. But honestly, twenty long minutes, sometimes longer, just to pick two gloves out of a box was so irritating. Making shopping lists or mentally calculating money or something equally benign allowed me to pass the time. I just wanted some normality for Jack, but for me too.

Jack would not return to his room after going to the bathroom because his whole body and clothes felt contaminated. The only place he felt safe was sitting on my bed in the bedroom-cum-lounge. It was the only time Jack could cuddle and stroke the dog because Billy was also contaminated and as Jack had his gloves on, he felt able to stroke him. Billy didn't care. He loved Jack unconditionally and enjoyed his gloved scratches and cuddles.

Then came a sudden, swift shift from the excessive handwashing ritual not being enough to feel clean, to needing a shower. These could take anywhere from forty-five minutes to an hour and a half, so the avoidant behaviour typical in OCD bred like bacteria on a summer's day. Hours would pass with Jack sitting on my bed, wearing gloves, and watching videos on my laptop to avoid the anxiety-filled shower routine. It was exasperating, especially when it dragged on for eight hours or more. I'd give up nagging him eventually and go about my business.

I tried to explain that avoidance was fruitless because despite hours of avoiding, he *still* felt he had to complete the compulsion anyway, but you cannot reason with OCD. I just wished Jack could see that this was a power struggle between his logical brain and OCD. I wished he could tap into his power and tell that bully and all its bullshit lies to fuck off!

Only a week had passed since Jack's first day at college. He'd been unable to return but was optimistic he could do it once he'd conquered this latest contamination hurdle. The college was very supportive and knew I was waiting for CAMHS. They didn't feel he had missed too much and were confident he would be able to catch up.

Within a day or two, Jack's support worker, Ben, and the new CBT therapist, Abby, came to visit. They listened to Jack describing how he was feeling and the compulsions he was going through and agreed to assess Jack for exposure response prevention therapy (ERP) and get it underway as soon as possible.

Ben encouraged Jack to get himself to college as he felt it would make him feel better about himself. At the time, I remember thinking, "*If only it were that simple, Ben.*" How could Jack go to college and study every day when he spent his days washing his hands and sitting in gloves?

The frustrating thing with OCD is the solution is so beautifully simple: ignore the intrusive thoughts, they are *not* real; feel the fear, ride the anxiety curve, and don't give in to the compulsions. But applying that logic to the illogical OCD part of the brain is not at all simple to someone with the disorder. In fact, it is pure, terror-filled torture.

Ever the optimist, I agreed and tried to encourage Jack to go to college every day whilst staying in regular contact with the college's mental-health support team and his lecturers, who were very supportive and understanding. They hoped as much as I did that as soon as Jack's therapy was underway with CAMHS, he'd be able to get into college and, for the time being, they were exceptionally patient. They sent some work home for him to start and advised that they would let me know if things changed.

Despite my optimism, there remained a little nagging voice in my head making me fear educational history was repeating itself. We'd gone through a similar experience with secondary school, special support school (twice) and online school. Pushing that nagging doubt away, I focused on getting through the days until the first CAMHS ERP assessment.

The assessment was scheduled at the clinic for early October and I was hopeful, but we'd only managed one clinic appointment in three years; all others had been home visits. Jack couldn't cope with the clinical environment and faint hospital smell. As you entered the main door, you walked directly into the reception and waiting area and the one time he went in, it was full of teenagers and their parents, making him feel extremely uncomfortable. It surprised me when he agreed to attend the appointment there, but I went along with it at the time.

When the day arrived, Jack was still fast asleep half an hour before the appointment. I managed to stir him, and the familiar happened.

"I'm not going. I should never have agreed to go there. I hate it," Jack protested.

After some gentle but desperate persuasion, laced with blackmail, he agreed to go, giving me ten minutes to get him there despite it being fifteen minutes away.

There is nothing like a stressful last-minute scramble to get shoes, coats, keys and face masks and get out of the door. The rush almost induced a heart attack but keeping my cool was imperative as Jack's anxiety started peaking a few minutes before we arrived.

Due to the pandemic, we had to call through first and announce we were outside before entering. Abby would then don full PPE gear, and we would get a call back to say it was okay to approach the door. Jack desperately wanted to start this therapy and get better, but the delays in just getting in the building saw him wanting to bolt and run a mile before he even began.

Convincing Jack to approach the door with me, we were let in and instructed to keep our masks on whilst Jack had his temperature taken. I was asked to wait in the car and instantly protested. The only reason I'd been able to convince Jack to come was by reassuring him I'd stay with him. Abby agreed I could stay, and she showed us into a treatment room.

Jack was visibly anxious, twiddling his gloved hands uncomfortably and twitching one leg and tapping his foot furiously on the floor. He couldn't make eye contact with anyone and kept his head down. Abby was adept at putting him at ease, and within five minutes or so, the leg-twitching stopped and the hand-wringing, shortly after.

The entire fifty-minute appointment was swallowed up by painting a picture to the therapist of a day in Jack's life with his OCD. We got as far as his lunchtime and it was clear it was going to take at least two more assessments to finish the picture. Abby said the process couldn't be rushed, and she would be unable to commence appropriate therapy until she had a complete understanding of his OCD. Abby reassured him in time. It could be treated, even cured.

Jack was visibly buoyed from his achievement of actually getting in the clinic, and like me, Abby's words had given him hope for a cure and freedom from this dreadful illness. On the way home, he grinned and asked to go for a drive somewhere. So off we headed, music up full volume, driving to the beach. From there, we detoured on our way home at Jack's request, so he could enjoy the temporary freedom it gave him from his room and compulsions.

Jack remained on a high and spent several hours chatting with Thomas, much to his delight. That night he decided to attempt a shower and managed it in fifteen fantastic short minutes. Jack gained such confidence from that one appointment, and as often was the case in these circumstances, he'd challenge his OCD and win somewhat. But sadly, it was always short-lived.

Jack's college lecturer called me up to check in and see how he was doing. I explained he'd had his first assessment but not started the therapy. The college had started almost four weeks earlier, and he'd not made it back in. His lecturer asked me to tell Jack they weren't giving up on him and didn't want him to defer.

I apologised that he had not done any work at that point, but it felt fruitless trying to explain why. Who on earth would understand how dreadful our days were and how studying now felt like a distant dream? Like Jack, I held onto an unrealistic hope that he'd be fine in a matter of days with a bit of therapy. I passed the message on, and it cheered Jack up no end.

Jack slept through the following two subsequent therapy appointments, despite my best efforts to wake him. It was so stressful as I felt sure CAMHS would tell me off. I'd been warned in the past and told Jack was using sleep as an avoidance tactic but I knew this time was different. Jack *wanted* to get well, but he was caught in a daily cycle of avoidance, shower, eat, sleep and repeat. CAMHS warned me that if he didn't or couldn't engage in therapy in the home or clinic, hospitalisation would be the next and last option.

Abby, however, didn't tell me off. She did the opposite and told me not to worry, and she continued to offer appointments. She accepted the sleep disruption and reassured me she would continue to see Jack. Eventually, Jack made it to his second appointment at the clinic, and he was substantially calmer the second time around.

We'd reached as far as Jack's dinner-time routine before the appointment drew to a close. We agreed a third assessment would be needed for Abby to complete the full picture of twenty-four hours in Jack's life. As we were leaving, I asked her what would happen should we head into another lockdown. It was becoming apparent that we were heading in that direction due to the increased infection rate;

parts of the country were in partial or complete lockdown already.

"Jack's OCD is so severe and life-affecting, he remains a high priority, and I will continue to see him despite any further restrictions," Abby reassured us both.

Finally, for the first time in almost three years of battling with this silent illness, and all the education authorities and health providers along the way, I felt validated. I'd always thought I'd not been taken seriously or listened to about the extent of Jack's illness. Indeed, in that last twelve months, as I'd watched him deteriorate, I felt nobody acknowledged how difficult it was and CAMHS staff had appeased me over waiting lists. In that short sentence from Abby, I felt heard and it was about bloody time. No child should be allowed to deteriorate as Jack had due to a lack of resources. No adult should either, for that matter.

Out of the blue, one day, I received a call from the college whilst Jack slept. The support worker informed me he had been withdrawn from his course. That was that. No negotiation. No discussion and certainly no warning as promised. Angry tears sprang up and my voice shook. "No... no... *no*, I'm not going to accept that! I want to speak to someone in authority," I demanded through sobs.

The support worker apologised and explained that she was just passing on a message. She agreed to get the learning manager to call me later that day.

I waited nervously for three hours for the call and was out walking when the learning manager called. It was immediately apparent from her tone that there was no room for negotiation. "No, I'm sorry, a curriculum decision has been made. As science has so many practical assessments, we feel Jack's missed too much to catch up," she advised unemotionally.

And why would she be emotional? Jack was just another student; a statistic who wasn't attending college. This was her job. But this was *my* son; this was his life. College was the beacon of light and hope for Jack in a dark and monotonous world of OCD. How was I going to break this to him? I'd been down this road three times now.

"I had a call just two weeks ago from his lecturer saying you weren't giving up on him. The mental-health support team promised me this wouldn't happen. You've no idea what this will do to him," I protested, in between sobs.

The place at college had been the ray of hope that led Jack out of his suicidal thoughts. Now what?

"I'm sorry, but the decision has been made, and there's nothing I can do," she offered, with a little more warmth, as my distress had become clear to her.

"I suggest you use this as an example of how not to give false hope to vulnerable students and improve the internal communication between you all," I snapped angrily and ended the conversation.

I fully understood but wasn't happy with how the college had handled it and the lack of notice or negotiation. Nobody had asked how Jack was doing or if he was able to go into college before deciding.

I wanted to scream. Thankfully, my car was parked in its usual spot in a nearby side road and I managed to contain my anger until I reached it. I got in the front and shouted into my coat, "Fuck, fuck, *fuck!! Arghhhhh!*" I slumped in my seat, sobbing in pure rage and disappointment. After a few minutes, I was exhausted but calmer so I got out of the car and headed back home. I was grateful for the brief rain shower to disguise my wet, snotty face.

Turning the corner into my street, the most beautiful full rainbow sat amongst golden-lined cotton wool clouds and a watery blue sky. I gasped as it stopped me in my tracks. It didn't matter about the grey, graffitied buildings with their tired, chipped paint and the dot-to-dot patterns of discarded chewing gum on equally grey pavements. It didn't matter about the piles of cigarette butts or empty bottles. None of them were visible to me anymore. There was the Universe, giving me an incredible gift. It made me cry again, but this time, the tears were of gratitude and joy.

I headed inside, uplifted by the rainbow and thankful to Mother Nature. She kept giving me gentle reminders that her beauty was always present for all to see, despite the bedlam of life below.

I avoided telling Jack for an hour, unsure how to break the news to him and fearful of his reaction. He seemed chirpy, and I didn't have the heart to burst his bubble. "Jack, I've had a call from college..." But before I could finish the sentence, he stopped me.

"I've been kicked out, haven't I?"

"They've had to withdraw you from your course because they feel you've missed so many of the practical experiments, they don't feel you can catch up. As it's graded on these experiments, it wouldn't be fair on you. Don't worry, though. You can reapply next year," I suggested enthusiastically.

It was too late. Jack's shoulders had slumped and his disappointment was visible. His energy dropped, and his self-loathing surfaced. "Leave me alone. I'm useless. I'm giving up. I'm not going back ever," Jack barked.

"I'm so sorry, Jack. I tried my best," I said.

Tears were welling up again, and I didn't want Jack to see me upset. Retreating to the kitchen, I let them silently fall. Remaining calm in front of Jack was imperative, for it did him no favours when he saw me upset.

The news hit Jack hard. "What am I going to tell my friends, Mum?"

Jack had been avoiding telling them he wasn't going. They were all on different courses, and with social distancing, students were staying in their class bubbles, so no one had questioned why they had not seen Jack.

"I'm going to tell them I'm giving up, to focus on getting well," Jack said after some thought.

"Well, that's the truth, Jack. Now you can spend that time getting well. The college will always be there."

A little relief washed over me.

THE BULLY ON HIS SHOULDER

NOVEMBER–DECEMBER 2020

It was a further two weeks and two missed CAMHS appointments before Jack attended his third and final assessment. This time, Abby came to the flat for the appointment instead. She stayed for almost two hours finishing the assessment and had a much clearer picture of Jack's OCD.

Jack went into great detail about his shower routine and the fifteen minutes he would spend washing his hands. By this stage, he was using an entire 500ml bottle of shower gel and about 400ml of hand soap during each shower. It was painful but equally interesting for me to hear his perspective on why he did it. I sat and listened as he explained how he had to catch the water jet from the shower just right on his thumbs to make them feel clean, and other strange and intricate rituals. He had told me about them before, but never really discussed how they made him feel. If it didn't feel right, he'd repeat a ritual over and over until it did. I listened to his description of the counting he did in his head; how he'd pull the skin back on his thumbs to ensure the water was getting underneath the nails; the way his thumb scratching across the back of his hand had to feel. It would take about seven minutes, and his hands were red raw and bleeding where he repeated this action every day in precisely the same spot. I covered my nose and mouth to stifle the cry that was desperately trying to escape.

The handwashing stage marked the end of another few hours of avoidance and the end of the shower ritual, so I hadn't got too emotionally involved in what Jack was doing. To hear it described in such meticulous and painful detail made me empathise with the hellish place he was in.

At the end of the appointment, Abby agreed that Jack's OCD was very complex and would take some time to unpick. Despite the UK entering into another national lockdown, she made special arrangements with her manager, and they agreed that home visits could continue just for Jack. He was the only child she was allowed to visit at home because she felt he needed to be seen consistently. That was both reassuring and a little troubling at the same time.

On her fourth visit, Abby talked a little about how the therapy would work and how slowly she would take it to avoid flooding Jack. She felt that if they went in too hard and hit the most challenging compulsions first, he would flood with anxiety, retreat further into a world of avoidance and therapy would be unsuccessful.

She told Jack to see his OCD as a bully; most importantly, he needed to remember that it was *not* him. Jack found this concept difficult. As far as he was concerned, his brain told him to do these compulsions, and therefore they were part of him. Abby explained the importance of seeing his OCD as separate, thus reinforcing that Jack would eventually overcome his illness. If he saw it as part of him and unchangeable or insurmountable, he could well stay enslaved by this beast.

Just talking about facing a bully that belittled and berated him constantly, made Jack anxious. Abby reassured him we would, all three of us, work together very slowly to unpick the OCD and hopefully send the bully packing for good.

Abby had trained as an autism nurse and seen some crossover behaviours during the assessments that showed Jack could be on the ASD spectrum. She asked me to attend a separate assessment appointment, and we arranged a time to meet.

The following weeks were tedious and changeable with Jack. He continued to avoid the bathroom, more explicitly the arduous shower schedules, which had stretched to fifty-five minutes in length. Jack had quadrupled his washing routines and they now included washing the inside of his nostrils with soap. He would snort water in to clean the soap away over and over, choking as the water hit the back of his throat. Somehow, just setting foot in the bathroom had contaminated the inside of his nostrils.

The bully was very much in charge by this point. It had taken control of Jack and it towered over him menacingly, tormenting him with its warped and twisted commands, day and night. This bully controlled me and my life too.

"Wash your hands 32 times, no wait, 64, no, 128 times," it would instruct him to tell me before I touched his food. It shouted at Jack, and it screamed at me.

I hated his OCD. It was ruling all our lives, and it was robbing Jack of his.

Jack's confidence and self-esteem plummeted. He spent most of his days and nights sitting on my bed wearing gloves to protect himself from an unseen contamination risk. To Jack, the risk was real and all-consuming; staying on my bed for days at a time was more comfortable and safer than facing the shower and all the rituals that followed. He would curl up next to me, and we would end up sleeping top to tail, sharing the duvet and blankets. Jack hated himself for his dependency on me and constantly criticised himself for it.

One Saturday night whilst reading, I sat observing Jack for a moment or two. As was so often the case, he was sitting on my bed, wearing catering gloves, headphones on, listening to music on my laptop.

Earlier that day, after he'd come down from his shower, he paused and turned to me in the kitchen. "Mum, do you know if it weren't for speaking to my friends online, and you, I would have killed myself by now. I don't think I can take another year of this."

"You won't have to, Jack, and things will start to improve. You have to trust this therapy will help you get well."

Watching him sit there, losing himself in the music, made me quietly weep. I could see that all the enabling I'd done, all the poor choices I'd made, all the times I'd encouraged the bully and given it life by helping him with his compulsions, had also saved my son. I'd brought him light and lit his darkness when he couldn't see a way out, and I'd given him hope when he felt hopeless.

I met with Abby alone at the clinic and welcomed the opportunity to speak freely without Jack. We went through the main indicators of autism. Although we both agreed there were some crossover behaviours that Jack displayed, Abby was confident enough to leave the assessment there without pursuing a diagnosis at that point. We agreed to revisit it should he not respond to treatment.

Abby was a mother. She was warm, caring, and professional and instilled hope in me. Trusting her fully, I'd handed her the reins of this nightmare. She reminded me that I was doing an unimaginably difficult job and she didn't know how I held my life together. She explained that Jack's OCD was so severe that it was impairing every aspect of his life, and I'd lost sight of how dreadful things were for us both because we were living it day-in and day-out. Abby's acknowledgement of this and reassurance of her support for Jack and me was refreshing and comforting.

Speaking for a full hour, she gave me time and space to talk. I was angry, and she let me express that anger without judgement. I was frustrated at the lack of resources that left Jack deteriorating on a waiting list for fifteen months; angry that no one listened to me. At least that's how it felt when I kept telling the team things were getting worse. I'd scheduled to go to CAMHS to lodge a formal complaint, but Covid put an abrupt end to that. My appointment was cancelled and I was denied that opportunity by the unprecedented circumstances.

I told Abby how it felt to be pushed down waiting lists, for another child to be prioritised over mine, whilst we survived the days and nights; what it felt like to wait four weeks for a simple callback from the team leader; having to wait fourteen months just to see the doctor; to be told my situation was not enough of a crisis despite the knife he pressed into his neck and pleas from Jack for me to make it all stop; to be denied that help when utterly desperate and crying down the phone; to be told, I was enabling my son's OCD but without any professional support to guide me.

To be left month after month.

"Abby, imagine this. You're a mother. God forbid my son had a life-altering disease like cancer or kidney failure. Can you imagine telling me to go away, manage his illness as best as I can whilst we sit on a fifteen-month waiting list? Can you imagine being told to go on a parenting course to help you be a better parent in the meantime?" My voice wavered as I spoke. "That's what this team did to me. This system has let my son down, and it has let me down too. I've lost my job, my marriage, my family – my life is in pieces."

The fire in my belly roared, and I was grateful for the opportunity at long last to openly express my feelings without fear of judgement. Abby listened, and I had been heard, finally.

We agreed on the next appointment time, and I left, barely making it out onto the pavement before bursting into uncontrollable sobs. I pulled my mask up to disguise the contorted shape of my face as I drifted towards my car, oblivious to the noises I was making. Months of frustration, sadness and anger came to the surface, and I couldn't breathe.

Once in the car, I began retching. My body was releasing all that had been suppressed and pushed deep down for months. I felt relief but overwhelming sadness for Jack too.

It took some time for the crying to stop, to catch my breath and for my body to settle. At that moment, I knew when this was over, I would use this battle to create change somehow, to prevent others from suffering the way he had, the way our whole family had suffered. Something good would come from all this darkness. That was my purpose in all this.

Abby continued to see Jack at home though it was sporadic due to his sleep cycles and her clinic commitments.

We missed three weeks, and in that time, the OCD continued to shapeshift and breed. By early December, he had not been able to muster the motivation to face the shower routine at all for days. Not even the draw of talking to his friends was enough to encourage him. Jack found the hour-long shower routine, particularly the handwashing aspect, which had crept up to about twenty-five minutes, unbearable.

Jack's days and nights were spent entirely on my bed, gloves on, watching videos and drifting into sleep in one long period of avoidance that lasted weeks. It was a complex and infuriating situation for us both; sleep was the only time he had a respite from the intrusive thoughts and subsequent compulsions. Jack was very low during this time and found it hard to stay focused on there being a way forward.

I adjusted to this unusual way of life again. Nothing was ever constant with Jack's OCD as it morphed and changed regularly. It was miserable for us both to share the same small area, restricted by his OCD rules. Jack was critically aware he was in my personal space, and he loathed himself for this intrusion. It became suffocatingly claustrophobic for us both.

In the early hours of one morning after he'd discarded thirty or so gloves, Jack told me to wash my hands sixteen times as I had contaminated his glove box by passing it to him. Walking to the kitchen in an angry, tired protest, I shouted, "*I fucking hate your OCD!* It's 4am, and I'm washing my hands, for what Jack, *for what*?"

I pretended to wash my hands, as it was easier than challenging Jack's OCD at 4am. Angry, frustrated tears splashed onto the sink as I ran the tap.

How the hell could we go on like this?

Sometime after, Jack told me it hurt him when I said I

hated his OCD. To him, it was his brain and therefore part of him, so in effect, I was saying I hated Jack. Of course, I wasn't saying that at all. But I had every right to hate his OCD. So did he. I wanted him to hate it, to get angry and rage at it, because with that hatred was an inner fire. And with fire, he could fight back against OCD, little by little.

A couple of weeks later, Paul had a painful episode of gout in his feet that wouldn't clear up, so the doctor prescribed some anti-inflammatories and painkillers, which he took for two weeks. The tablets irritated his stomach, and he was in some discomfort again.

Paul slipped climbing out of the shower one morning and landed awkwardly on the basin, catching his ribs as he fell. The following day he declined to see me, saying he felt unwell and was in a lot of pain, thinking he had cracked a rib. I left him for three days but then popped in to see him as the pain was intensifying. He could barely get up, and he'd not eaten.

As soon as I saw him, it was apparent Paul was jaundiced again. His face and stomach had blown up and he was clearly in pain, but he refused my suggestion to go back to the hospital that afternoon. He'd barely slept and was convinced that he'd probably overdone the painkillers, irritating his liver again, resulting in jaundice. Paul vowed to flush his system with water that night and promised me he would go to the hospital the following day if he didn't feel any better.

That night he was in excruciating pain all night and didn't sleep. He arrived at the flat in the wintry darkness at

5am and asked me to drive him to the hospital. Paul wasn't one for fuss and wouldn't call an ambulance.

I dropped him at the local A&E – the Covid restrictions didn't permit me to go in with him, so I headed home, back to bed. Paul was admitted immediately, and a catscan and blood tests revealed he had a nasty gall-bladder infection again. The doctors believed he had been passing gallbladder stones, causing the pain. His bile duct was also infected, and his liver was struggling again, attributed to the painkillers and the infection.

Paul spent five days in hospital on morphine and antibiotics whilst they decided if he needed surgery. This time, the infection cleared up, and the specialist decided against surgery.

Paul was discharged, and I hoped this second hospital stay would mark a pivotal point in his recovery and a move into a healthier, sober life. I hoped that this time, he would pay attention to the clear warning signs his body was giving him.

IT'S JUST ANOTHER DAY

CHRISTMAS 2020

Christmas was fast approaching, and any hope I had of any sense of normality over the festive period was fading fast. Jack was with me twenty-four hours a day, sleeping on my bed and avoiding the shower at all costs, spending hours watching TV. Days would slip past, all rolling into one long, tedious blur. I'd accepted it was this way for the most part, but at times, when his OCD scrutinised my every move, I would lose my temper and yell at him.

If I so much as brushed past the bathroom door, went near the toilet or bin, or touched anything in the kitchen, '*it*' would demand I wash my hands: not just once or twice, but 16, 64 or 128 times. (Calling Jack's OCD '*it*' helped depersonalise it and reminded me it was an illness and not something Jack was doing deliberately to infuriate me.)

Of course, I fought hard against it and sometimes refused point-blank to wash my hands such a ridiculous amount of times, but I'd often stand at the kitchen sink pretending to do it, just to get through that episode, angry and frustrated.

If I was making food, '*it*' made me wash my hands

before, during and sometimes again before bringing food to Jack. *It* would listen to my every move and suffocate me. I snuck around in my own flat, trying to go to the toilet without '*it*' knowing, opening the kitchen bin silently so as not to be detected.

I'd watch Jack count and move his hands in mini repetitions backwards and forwards, trying over and over to take the plate of food from me in a way his OCD permitted him to. It would remind me that he had no escape from his OCD; only sleep granted him a break.

It was less than two weeks until Christmas. People were preparing enthusiastically, albeit cautiously, after the latest lockdown had eased. Watching their excitement and seasonal joy made me want to scream at them in the street. I wanted some of that joy, some of that normality. Decorating the Christmas tree didn't bring much joy to anyone, not even me. Christmas Day would be like every other day for us all – contamination fear, avoidance, excessive handwashing, gloves, anxiety, drinking, bingeing and gambling.

Abby called to see how we were, and I took the opportunity to ask if she could come more frequently than once a week. Due to admin weeks and the Christmas holidays, we would get just two therapy sessions in December. Nothing was being accomplished, and Jack was deteriorating, not improving. Unfortunately, due to resources, once a week was all that she could offer. I'd had enough and reached my limit, and Jack was way past his.

In the week leading up to Christmas, his OCD was out of control and becoming even more extreme. Jack felt so completely contaminated, he had resorted to sleeping on the hardwood floor with no cushions and just an old blanket, for fear he'd contaminate anything else. Eventually, the contamination feeling overwhelmed him so much he was unable to touch food or water, so I fed him. It crushed him.

The only saving grace during those two weeks was continuously binge-watching two entire TV series. Jack lost himself in the shows and they temporarily distracted his mind from the intrusive thoughts.

Before dozing off, I'd pull a woolly winter hat down over my eyes to block out the TV light and wedge in earplugs. They were very restless nights. It would be simply unfathomable to anyone that this child could sleep on a cold hard floor, unable to touch the remote control, his body, water bottle or food: anything, in fact. Yet here we sat, day after day, hour after hour, in one tiny room in a living nightmare with no support.

I called Abby a couple of days before Christmas as she was going on leave, desperate for help and crying down the phone. Shouting and swearing, I wanted someone to listen, to help me. She let me yell, and she listened to every word I said, but all she could do was offer me the hope that given time and therapy, Jack should improve. She didn't feel he was at the hospitalisation stage.

I felt numb and alone. It was a further two weeks until our next appointment and it felt so unfair to be left like this. Surely there was something else that CAMHS could do to help us? It seemed not.

Christmas Day arrived, and Jack had finally completed the nightly compulsions by 2.30am. The glove selection process had taken forty-five minutes that morning. I crawled into bed as he settled next to me on the laptop. The bully had allowed him off the floor for one night.

"Merry Christmas, Jack. Would you like to open a present now?" I offered, hopefully.

"I can't even touch my presents, Mum. They're all contaminated from where I slept on the floor by them. Fuck Christmas, *fuck my life*!" he exclaimed.

At almost 3am, I couldn't have agreed more. *Fuck Christmas and fuck OCD!*

I fell asleep and woke at 8am to find him still awake next to me. Jack's mood was dark. It was by far the most depressing and difficult Christmas Day we had faced in three years.

It felt pointless to try and ignite some Christmas joy. I lay there thinking of all the families joyfully opening presents right then and there and felt angry; robbed of a life by circumstance and abandoned to get on with this situation.

Jack was argumentative and upset at the state he was in. He felt utterly powerless and miserable as he'd been unable to step foot in his room, touch his own things or talk to his friends for over three weeks. We lashed out at each other.

"I'm going to walk the dog," I snapped angrily at Jack.

I felt alone and exhausted by this version of life. Paul had retreated into his own seemingly, bottomless depression. Jack was consumed day and night by OCD compulsions, and my only space in the flat was invaded by them. It was all so insidious and suffocating, and I had to get out.

I didn't really want to face the street or people or even muster the energy to tie my hair up from the greasy mess it was, but I had little choice. The dog needed walking and I needed to escape. I grabbed Billy, and hoped it was quiet on the streets. I was in no mood to pretend to anyone that life was alright.

"Merry fucking Christmas, Emily!" I muttered to myself whilst walking away from Jack, slamming the front door behind me.

It was one degree outside, and the wind was sharp and

robbed the wintry sunshine of any warmth. It was the kind of cold that caused your ears to ache and caught your breath when you faced it. Putting my head down to shield against its icy bite, I headed for a nearby construction site, knowing it would be empty.

Turning and facing the fence around the site, I held on to steady myself as the sobs escaped. I walked on a little further and grabbed the lamppost for comfort as the tears fell, not knowing why I was crying. The tears were for me, but they were also for Jack.

By the time I returned home some twenty minutes later, Jack was asleep. Thank goodness. I didn't want to fight with my son anytime, but somehow it felt almost sacrilegious to be bickering on Christmas Day. That was stupid really – it's just another day. Preparing Christmas dinner, crying in between peeling carrots and making stuffing, I held onto the kitchen counter and let out little noises in-between the sobs.

Thomas woke up, and we opened his presents together. It was a little joy, and we both savoured it. I texted my family, whom I never saw. My mother lived in Ireland and the lockdowns ended what little opportunity we had to see each other. I wished them well along with a scattering of friends and pretended to be full of seasonal joy when they texted back. What I really wanted to do was let them see my pain, but why should they need to know? No one would believe the severity of the situation. Like a petulant child feeling sorry for myself, I wanted everyone to know we were struggling. Misery loves company, and I was thoroughly miserable, but of course, I'd never spoil anyone else's day with my self-entitled grumpiness.

'It's just another day' became my catchphrase for Christmas 2020. No one was having a typical Christmas in the UK due to last-minute lockdown restrictions, and it

somehow felt comforting and a relief that I wasn't alone in this unusual situation.

I'd no idea when Jack would wake up and if he'd want any dinner. Thomas was in his room as Jack was asleep in the lounge and Paul was at his place. I plated up a Christmas feast for Thomas, Paul and a neighbour who was spending the day alone. Thomas ate his dinner in his room alone. I sat with my plate balanced on my knee, perched on the second bottom step of the stairs in the December darkness, crying in between mouthfuls. That was a particularly low point for me; a seasonal rock bottom.

I dropped a Christmas dinner to Paul and we sat in his single room without a window, exchanging little gifts. It was a welcome break in some ways but equally, it reminded me that life and circumstance had separated us, and this was the most miserable Christmas I'd ever spent in my lifetime. Paul would later heat his dinner in a communal kitchen of a budget long-stay hotel. How on earth did we end up here?

Jack woke up around 6pm on Christmas night, and I opened his presents for him as he couldn't touch them. The nights he'd spent sleeping on the floor near the Christmas tree in his 'contaminated' state had infected his presents. Jack thanked me for them one by one, and I stacked the gifts in a small pile on the table. Around 8pm, he asked for Christmas dinner, which was a welcome and wonderful surprise.

I fell asleep around 11.30pm as Jack silently watched videos on the laptop. By 1am, he could no longer suppress the need for the toilet and bolted over me to the bathroom. I was half asleep as he returned.

"Can we go out for a walk?" he asked.

"Jack, it's 1am, it's one degree outside, and I'm half asleep," I grumpily replied. I'd no desire to leave the cosy heat and walk the streets at that ridiculous hour on Christmas night.

"Please, Mum, I think it will help me fight the need to shower," he pleaded.

I'd learnt to jump on opportunities that forced Jack to face himself and knew walking helped both his confidence and reduced his compulsions.

"Fine, fine..." I reluctantly agreed. I'd eaten my body weight in shortbread, chocolate, cheese and just about anything else my binge-eating brain allowed me to access under the guise of 'it's Christmas' for the previous four days, so it wouldn't do me any harm. I threw on a coat, hat, and boots and we left.

We didn't meet a soul. And why would we on a freezing December night at 1.30am? But I still enjoyed walking at these odd hours despite the biting cold. Jack was free of his OCD momentarily, and therefore, so was I.

We returned home by 2am. Jack chatted non-stop until 3am about everything and anything. The walk had interrupted his feeling of needing to shower so it was a sacrifice I was prepared to make.

It took forty minutes to apply antibacterial gel and select a pair of gloves. It was almost 4am. My patience was wearing well and truly thin, and I knelt on the floor, resting my head on the arm of a chair, exhausted, dozing until he completed the glove ritual.

Finally, crawling into bed just after 4am, I felt drained. If that's how I felt, can you imagine what was going on in Jack's head? How could I ever explain this nightmare to anyone?

Abby visited Jack on 30 December. Jack had been banished by his brain back to the floor on Boxing Day. Jack sat there, blanket wrapped around him, barely making eye contact; it was apparent that he had deteriorated. Abby listened as Jack said he couldn't fight his battle alone. He said he felt too far gone and needed more help. But Jack knew no one could make him better. The work had to come from within him, and he had no fire left to face the fight.

Abby folded her workbook and said she would go away and talk to the team psychiatrist about what more could be done, perhaps a day-patient unit where he could access regular therapy. It offered us a little light in the unbearable darkness.

SOLITARY CONFINEMENT

JANUARY 2021

NEW YEAR'S Eve came and went uneventfully. Our area had been moved into a more restricted lockdown the day before, so the streets were unusually quiet. Not a single pub, bar or restaurant was open, and it was oddly still outside. I welcomed it. I wouldn't have to listen to people enjoying the festivities. Jack had fallen asleep on the floor around 9.30pm.

When midnight struck, a few people stumbled out of their flats nearby, shouting, "Happy New Year!" in languages I couldn't decipher, though their gesture was universal. They cheered to the backdrop of hundreds of fireworks exploding around the town centre. It was deafening and lasted several minutes. It appeared many people had gathered in their homes and brought in the new year with a private bang.

Jack woke up briefly, muttering at the noise and went back to sleep on the floor.

Thomas appeared and gave me a thumbs up. "Happy New Year, Mum," he whispered optimistically.

I smiled back. "Happy New Year, Thomas." He retreated to the kitchen for food.

Pulling the covers up in the darkness, I thought that there was nothing magical about that clock ticking over to the twelfth hour in our house. There were no celebrations and no joy; no midnight hugs or kisses from my husband. I'd listened to the fireworks and celebrations ten minutes earlier and felt nothing other than jealousy, wanting to feel optimistic and joyful, but instead, feeling hollow and disappointed. Of course, nothing changes with the tick of a clock. I silently scolded myself and fell asleep.

That disappointment bled into New Year's Day. I walked the dog and wandered into an empty car park nearby, sobbing. I felt overwhelmingly sad and continued to cry all day, alone and walking. That was one advantage of wearing a mask and a woolly hat. Only my eyes were visible so that no one could see my mouth curling in sobs. No one was around anyway.

It was cold and dark, and a sinister fog sat heavily in the frigid temperatures. I didn't feel it nor care for the darkness, but was glad of the mist; it was a further disguise for my tears. Sitting at the edge of a car park, surrounded by overfilled commercial bins overflowing with unemptied Christmas rubbish was an ugly and depressing sight.

A new strain of the virus plunged the whole country into a third national lockdown on January 4. As a result, Jack's home visits with CAMHS had to be cancelled and changed to phone appointments until Abby could organise some childcare. She called me a couple of weeks later after she'd met with the psychiatrist. It had been two years since the doctor had visited Jack and nine months since I'd spoken to her. She was one of two psychiatrists who worked for CAMHS. How were two doctors ever going to be able to spread their time across such a large area?

As expected, due to the lockdown, they were not admitting patients to the children's psychiatric ward unless they were at high risk of self-harm and either way, the local unit was full. There were simply no provisions for day patients or daily therapy regardless of a pandemic. The last and only therapy option would be for Jack to be admitted as an in-patient, but even if this were to happen, it would be several weeks away, if not longer. First, the doctor wanted to see Jack herself with Abby and begin the conversations about hospital admission.

I grabbed my keys and ran into the lane at the back of the flats for some privacy, forgetting my coat, so the bitter minus temperatures bit my cheeks instantly. Abby let me cry and sob and rant and soothed me down.

I paced the lane, shouting and crying in the cold, oblivious to who may be listening. At that moment, I didn't care. "Abby, would they leave a child with a broken leg lying on the floor for days without doing something? "I cried. "Just because I'm here killing myself trying to care for this kid, I'm just being left to get on with it. It's not fair, and I need help. It's no life. We just exist in our one room whilst he lays on the floor." I'd lost my grounding and my rational filter, and all my raw emotions came tumbling out.

Abby calmed me, listened to me, and acknowledged every word I said, but we were back in the waiting game with the underlying knowledge that Jack would, at all costs, resist a voluntary hospital admission. He was terrified of the prospect. I'd waited fourteen months for a home visit with a psychiatrist when this journey began and six months for a phone call, and I instantly assumed it would happen all over again.

Abby reassured me it wouldn't be as long this time, and she would have an appointment date for me the following week. I had her word that she was there for us both, and her unwavering support was comforting. It was all I had right then.

We said goodbye, and the reality of the cold hit me. I'd been outside on my phone for twenty minutes without a coat, and my hands were painfully frozen.

By the end of January, Jack was on day thirty-seven of sleeping on the floor. He wasn't washing or dressing, and feelings of contamination overwhelmed him. He suggested I buy him disposable cutlery to enable him to eat. If he used the household cutlery, he felt he would contaminate it so much that it would need to be thrown away. Unable to summon the energy to attempt to rationalise with his brain, I caved in and bought some wooden cutlery. Jack said it made him feel more independent, and I was relieved at no longer having to feed him.

We both resented me feeding him for very different reasons. What started as me simply handing Jack the cutlery soon morphed into it being held and tapped multiple times, with numbers and repetitions being silently counted in his head. If he dropped a fork or spoon and it landed on his blanket, he instantly discarded it as contaminated.

The OCD continued to multiply like some insidious bacteria until it had utterly strangled his will to fight it. Though he didn't recognise it, Jack was deeply depressed, and his world had now shrunk to the lounge floor and one blanket; eating food, watching TV, unable to touch a thing around him. It was no life; it was existing, escaping the misery with television.

Sometimes I'd sit and watch him sleep. My anger and

frustration at him would subside, and I'd feel a pity for him that he wouldn't allow when he was awake. It was the only time he was at peace.

The CAMHS psychiatrist scheduled the appointment for mid-February, which was still two weeks away. In the meantime, I just got through the days and nights, growing to accept the new *status quo*. Jack had been confined to a tiny area, no more than two metres in size, with one cushion on the hard cold floor and a blanket. He was practically living in prison conditions at the instruction of his brain: solitary confinement for twenty-four hours; darkness; meals slid on plates near him, untouched by others for fear of contamination. At least in prison, he'd have had a bed.

Jack drifted in and out of sleep, day and night. He welcomed sleep because it allowed him to escape from intrusive thoughts. He was incredibly lonely and very bored. I'm not sure how he did it; it was peak winter, and the outside temperatures reached the minus range regularly, so the floor was cold and unforgivingly hard. The situation was so abnormal, so unbelievably unacceptable, but it was our reality, and we just survived the best we could.

Abby continued to visit whilst we waited for the medical review. She challenged Jack with the manageable task of getting rid of two rituals a week. Week one was to stop tapping the cutlery before he ate and tapping his water bottle after drinking. Jack managed to reduce both compulsions over the week and eradicate them entirely.

It felt like a small win to me, but it was merely a drop in the deep ocean of compulsions he completed daily. I had to remain optimistic and hopeful, though, for, without optimism, I could slip quickly back into hopelessness.

Abby kept gently introducing the idea of hospital admission. Jack was very resistant; he saw it as a threat. His images of mental-health in-patient units were from films: padded cells and straitjackets, restraints, and electric shock therapy; people pumped with drugs and wailing in terrifying psychotic states. No wonder it wasn't particularly appealing to him. Those images, along with the idea of being separated from me, his home and all familiarity, was overwhelming.

The reality was that we were fast approaching this option if things didn't start to improve, and I thought it was only delayed due to the pandemic restrictions. Sectioning a child under the Mental Health Act was a complex and lengthy process and not one the professionals undertook lightly. It was an absolute last resort for Jack and there was no doubt in my mind he would have to be dragged away kicking and screaming.

SILENCING THE CHATTER

FEBRUARY 2021

One of my best friends was a hypnotherapist in Australia. I would often turn to her online, especially during lockdown when I was particularly vulnerable. She was the only one I'd confide in during all my darkest moments. All the rage I felt, the self-hatred and hopelessness, I would give them to her. It was like entering a virtual confessional box. *Forgive me, for I have sinned.* I would dump everything in a box of text hoping for a cleansing, an absolution. She never judged me, but would cast an objective eye from afar and offer advice and I would feel her love and reassurance. She would always try to gently encourage me to step back, look after myself and regain my strength and power, but I was hellbent on saving three people at the time and couldn't hear a word she was saying.

One technique she suggested to me was daydreaming. I had to choose my moments to practice, either in the bath or just before I fell asleep. It wasn't always easy, especially at night, as I'd often be disturbed by the shouts of the drug addicts who frequented the road nightly, marching with intent for their next fix from a nearby dealer; or the occasional fights that would erupt outside the late-night off-licence and the inevitable sound of bottles smashing. Sometimes, it was the lane gate slamming loudly after the last client left the brothel next door. I'd grown immune to inner-city living and all its often frightening shades of life. It was a far cry from my old, safe suburban life. But these sounds only made me want to escape more from the chaos that surrounded me and create a new life for myself and my family.

Lying in bed, I'd close my eyes and take a few breaths in and out to relax. I'd imagine a different life. I would set a scene and see myself laughing, and I'd envisage myself at a music festival, singing and dancing with Paul. Or I'd be a passenger in a car with the windows down on a warm summer's day, eyes closed, the wind blowing across my face. I saw myself in a new home. I didn't want much materialistically anymore, just a bit of peace and a real bed in my own bedroom. I'd see Billy running around in a safe garden and me growing my own vegetables.

I'd also imagine a world where my children were well and happy. I'd see their faces smiling. I'd imagine their future partners and children. I'd see them settled, working, studying, and healthy. Jack sometimes talked about going to university, so I'd imagine myself at his graduation ceremony, watching him beaming and waving at me proudly. I'd see our blended family back together, all six of us sat round a table once more, laughing, and swapping stories just like we used to.

It came naturally to me, and I could actually feel the joy in the bottom of my stomach and feel excitement and peace spread over my body; it was beautiful. I would literally smile at the sensation. I was experiencing real feelings of joy through deliberate imaginative creation. It gave me a focal point, a place to focus my attention on a new horizon. I guess it was almost a kind of meditation of sorts, but it was very effective and gave me a temporary escape from the self-inflicted purgatory I seemed to have set up camp in.

With confirmed Covid cases in Paul's building, visitors were prohibited; I wasn't allowed to visit him for several months. The lockdown restricted us to only meeting for a walk and standing in deserted shop doorways with the dog to escape the rain and frigid winter temperatures. It wasn't exactly a conducive environment to work on rebuilding a marriage. But in reality, we were nowhere near ready to take that step anyway.

When Paul first began to push me away, I was wounded and so I distanced myself from him. It triggered old feelings of rejection. A little voice in my head told me it was my fault – maybe I wasn't loveable anymore. After all, I no longer cared about my appearance. I was three stones heavier than when he'd met me and was often crying in front of him. Maybe he didn't find me attractive anymore.

Over and over again, Paul would reassure me that it was him not me, but I didn't believe him. I'd feel the knots in my stomach twist at his apparent rejection, clearly prodding at old wounds. They were fragments of my attachment issues from the void my father left in my life all those years ago. I'd walk away from Paul, expressionless until he was out of sight, then I'd permit the pain to surface in waves of grief-filled sobs.

When we first met and indeed, throughout most of our marriage, we had always been very close. Intimacy was an integral part of our marriage. We were both affectionate people, unafraid to express our feelings to each other physically. We held hands, we often hugged throughout the day and never parted from one another without a warm embrace. When we watched TV together, he would gently massage my back or stroke my arms. Paul was sensitive, caring, tactile and did everything he could to make me feel loved and appreciated.

When our connection dissolved, so did any form of affection, and I mourned it for a long time, grieving for the version of the man I'd fallen in love with. I only had memories left of happier times and felt robbed and resentful towards my family's mental illness. It had taken everything from me.

It took a long time, but I was eventually able to silence the chatter in my mind, and that space from Paul's constant chaotic state gave me room to be objective once more. Gradually I realised, as much as I loved this man deeply, I couldn't mend him, stop him drinking, or hush the anxious thoughts in his mind; I couldn't pull him up and out of his depression. That was his job and when I stepped back, he slowly took charge. He had no choice either; for far too long, I'd been sparing his pain and doing everything I could to protect him.

I grew accustomed to being on my own and was so consumed at the time with Jack's OCD, the need for affection gradually faded. But the space from our marriage also taught me another valuable lesson: a relationship is a bonus in life – an enhancement – not a necessity. I needed that space to find my independence, to stand on my own two feet. From the tender age of fifteen, I'd only been single twice, for no more than six months each time. Every other moment had been consumed chasing after or catering to the needs of men – my sons or a couple of men who acted like my sons!

It took a very long time to see why I behaved that way, and the new, empowered version of me would love to go back and shake the old one and tell her to wise up and move on.

PRICELESS MOMENTS

MARCH 2021

As a teenager, I stepped away from the Catholic beliefs indoctrinated into me during my childhood and even now, I can't claim to follow a specific religion. However, I have always believed in there being something greater than me, outside of the realms of what we can see or understand. I also believe in there being something else after this life, though I don't know what, exactly.

I have experienced some unusual and inexplicable occurrences since childhood – sensing, seeing, and feeling things I couldn't understand – but I've accepted that these were part of my life experiences, and they've given me a great deal of comfort throughout my life.

For some time, I kept a framed photo of my dad on my kitchen windowsill. Jack was in my room-cum-lounge twenty-four hours a day, so I was spending more and more time in the kitchen, simply to escape. Sometimes, I'd find myself staring at my dad's picture, and even talking to him at times. Usually it was begging him for help, often in tears, but all he did was smile back.

One day, I looked at that smile in the picture and felt an

overwhelming sense of my father's paternal love and protection all around me. It was a powerful feeling, quite difficult to encapsulate in words, but it was as if I'd been filled with the most incredible sense of love. It reminded me of the feeling I'd felt when the midwife put my sons in my arms, just after giving birth – only stronger if that's even possible to imagine.

I picked up the picture frame and held it to my chest, tightly hugging my invisible father. I closed my eyes and asked out loud, "If you are here, give me a sign please. I need your help right now. I am so lost. *Please* help me."

Within seconds, something tangible touched my wrist firmly, as if it was being held, and I jumped. Opening my eyes, there was nothing or no one there. I laughed nervously. "Wow, Dad, you did it. I felt it, *I felt you*!" I hugged his picture to my chest once more, sobbing. "I'm so sorry... Dad. I'm so sorry I couldn't call you 'Dad'" I cried out, heartbroken that I'd waited so many years to finally whisper that word to him.

I can't rationally explain what happened that day. Still, I know that I felt my dad's presence very much around me, and several times again over a period of weeks afterwards. My sense of there being *something* there, keeping a protective watch over me, listening to my calls for help, gave me a great source of comfort. It seemed the energy of life could carry on in some form or another, and not even death could stop it.

After nine long weeks and two days on my floor, Jack went back into his room.

It had come out of nowhere. Somehow, from some

unseen source, Jack had mustered the courage to stand up to his OCD and its bullying threats. It had taken almost two hours of washing his hands, hair and face to achieve the level of cleanliness his OCD told him he needed.

As he stepped through his door, he sighed at the familiarity. He touched his keyboard and smiled at the contact between the keys and his fingertips as if greeting a long-lost friend. Within minutes he was online and swamped with messages from his shocked friends.

Jack spent nine wonderful hours chatting, laughing and playing games. Staying up all night wrecked his sleep again, but I didn't care – it felt like such a leap forward. I'd also had my first night alone in my own room in over three months, and it felt luxurious.

Jack couldn't sleep in his own bed. That still felt contaminated and overwhelming, so he returned to sleep in my room. But this time he allowed himself to sleep on the bed instead of on the floor.

Most people would say, "Well, he did it, and if he can do it once, he can do it again. No going back now." But it wasn't that simple, despite the glaringly obvious simplicity of daily tasks.

Jack's OCD was so complex. He had to do things slowly, bit by bit. Sometimes he was the tortoise, going along very slowly, and other times he was like the hare, running full-on, feet first, taking great strides when his will and fire built up his confidence enough to hush the OCD.

Abby's visits continued weekly, and she continued to set small weekly goals for him to try and overcome. The medical review came and went. Jack slept through it, unfortunately, due to a challenging night of rituals. It was rescheduled for March, but it was becoming evident from Abby's weekly visits that it would be a pointless paper exercise. The doctor couldn't offer much other than medication, and Jack was still firmly against taking anything. Hospital admission was a distant probability again as Jack was making progress, albeit painfully slow. He was responding to treatment, and the hospital was the last place his clinical team wanted him placed. The psychiatrist cancelled the appointment.

A couple of weeks passed, and Jack could go into his room again after several hours of rituals and cleanliness preparations. The joy I felt laying in the bath that night, listening to his laughter as he spoke to friends online, was priceless. It was just a few hours, but it was progress, nevertheless.

RECLAMATION

MAY 2021

It was apparent that running away to a hotel was neither affordable nor remotely practical over a holiday weekend. In the absence of a tissue, I wiped my face on my sleeve, grabbed my keys and phone, and headed inside. Seeing that dandelion had changed everything. Something had shifted within me and I knew I could no longer share my bedroom with Jack's OCD, nor continue to enable it. I needed to find my own space.

Four years earlier, Paul had temporarily boarded the loft and created a small but comfortable space for his sons to sleep when they stayed with us. It had been nearly eighteen months since either Paul or his sons had stayed at the flat so it was dusty and filled with junk.

Pulling the ladder down, I headed up, a little cautiously. During the first lockdown, rats had decided to take up residence in there, probably in search of food as all the restaurants and takeaways were closed. Thankfully, they had packed their rat bags and long since moved on, but they had left me souvenirs of their trip through several chewed storage boxes. I shuddered.

The loft was no more than five feet in height, with exposed wooden rafters and the floor was interrupted by the bathroom extraction pipe. Paul had whitewashed the walls and laid carpet scraps in a jigsaw to cover the boards. There was a bed too, lying vacant and dusty. I stripped the bedding and bagged up all the rubbish, savagely dumping anything superfluous to my life.

Sifting through the boxes, I came across a familiar bound notebook. It was my journal, begun some three years earlier. I had started writing down my thoughts and experiences with my family's mental illness when it first began, recording my pain and darkest emotions. But halfway through the first lockdown when things deteriorated with Paul, Thomas and Jack, I could no longer allow myself that escape. I simply had no time nor the energy to even write. The journal had been discarded, hidden away in the loft, and the hatch locked down.

Reading through the entries, I ran my fingers across the pages, tracing the slight indents of my words, as if caressing the woman that I was back then, struggling and alone. It was painful to read, and I wanted to go back and soothe her; reassure her that one day she would find her way out from this torment.

I knew in that moment; it was time to write my book. It was time to bring my story out of the shadows.

I threw the bin bags down the hatch onto the landing below, one by one. My space was taking shape; a blank canvas to dress my way, just for me.

I climbed into the storage area at the side of the loft and dragged out a handstitched Kashmiri rug, rolled up and dusty but still full of charm. I had carried this home, alone, all the way from India eight years ago. Someone, somewhere far away, had spent hours, hand-embroidering intricate colourful patterns into this beautiful rug, just for me to roll it up and hide it in a loft. It was criminal really, but no more. My rug was finally being pulled out of the darkness.

I found my handsewn Indian cushions hidden too. Nobody, including me, needs six cushions on their bed, but this was *my* bed, and I would decorate it just as I wanted. They were my cushions and each one held a memory for me of a magical journey of self-discovery many years before.

I plugged in a little lamp, and placed some sweet, scented candles along with a picture of Paul and I, on the side table. He was still in my heart and thoughts every day, despite our separation.

I stood back and admired my new space: a room of my own. I would add to it in time, but for now this would be my sanctuary. I'd staked my claim on this territory and I hadn't asked for anyone's permission either. OCD would not climb up the ladder, alcoholism could not worm its way up the steps, nor self-harm hurt me here. The beast was contained downstairs, and I was at the top of the building, reclaiming my power at long last.

That self-realisation came suddenly and with unexpected force. I'd had to break into a thousand pieces, to experience that final snapping point at the end of three years of hell to rise up and free myself from the invisible bondage that I had found myself in for most of my life. That was the day I turned and faced my family's mental illness and finally said: enough.

HOLDING HOPE

THE TURNING POINT was slow and subtle for Thomas and brought about by several factors.

During the first lockdown, Thomas purchased a new game to play on his computer. This was one gift the pandemic gave to Thomas – between employment furloughs and global lockdown restrictions, there were a far greater number of people at home and online. Connecting online became the new normal for everyone and it led Thomas to join an online gaming community who would meet regularly to play this new game together. The connectivity to other people, albeit digitally, slowly pulled Thomas out of his dark, disconnected world.

The gamers were from all walks of life and many different parts of the world. They would all chat and swap stories with Thomas about their countries, interests and culture and Thomas would join in enthusiastically. People were interested in him, not his academic achievements, and they didn't care about his mental health or lack of confidence; they couldn't see any of that. They just knew Thomas as the English kid who was a great ally in a game, and this little community of sixteen or so people helped him immeasurably without ever realising.

That reconnection with people gave Thomas the confidence to approach his friends again, and soon his group of five friends was back in regular contact. They arranged a few meet-ups during the breaks during and after the national lockdowns. It was fantastic to see Thomas out again, socialising as any nineteen-year-old boy should be.

His need to gamble lessened, but the addiction was still ever-present and reared its head from time to time. It was usually triggered during periods of disconnection, especially during the third lockdown when he was unable to go out or see his friends. Everyone had become fatigued by Covid's disruptive restrictions by then.

Thankfully, Thomas never got hooked on regular gambling sites such as horseracing, football matches, blackjack or slots. Just as well: online skin gambling had already caused more than enough financial damage and heartache to him and me.

Thomas decided to set some personal goals. He bought a notebook and started to scribble down some ideas, including improving his diet, sleep patterns and exercise routines. He would often ask me to join him for a walk, and we would stroll along the beachfront, talking.

As the winter of 2020 turned to spring and the national lockdown eased, we would venture out for early evening walks together. Thomas would notice and comment on the things around us: the billowy clouds, the gorgeous spring flowers in full bloom and sometimes the moon on clear evenings.

"Mum, look at this." He smiled as he pulled down a low branch of a cherry tree for me to admire the blossoms one late afternoon.

When the claws of depression hold you, it's almost impossible to see the beauty of nature around you, let alone be stirred by it. It thrilled me to witness Thomas' awareness of his surroundings emerging once more.

Thomas was often able to find the silver lining in the clouds that sometimes I couldn't see, and he would often remind me of how far we had all come. I enjoyed our walks together, and so did he.

Thomas had his hair cut and ordered some new clothes. When he walked, he held his head up, no longer hiding himself away. Long gone was the teenager who concealed himself behind long hair, a beard, and a hoodie. Slowly, but surely, he was emerging from his darkness. He was less dependent on me to lift him, and although he was still very shy and lacked confidence, he was starting to mature.

The need to gamble diminished, and his ability to manage his emotions improved. He was able to handle the minor incidents that previously would have caused angry outbursts. Thomas had a long way to go to build his self-esteem and improve his self-worth, but even he recognised that he was coming out of the dark place he had been in for the previous three years, and that recognition lifted a weight of burden from me.

Paul still had difficult days. Just because he was sober most of the time didn't mean the cravings for alcohol disappeared. He had times of great stress where he would lapse and drink a bottle of wine or cans of beer, trying to settle the constant chaos in his head.

The underlying emotions were also still stuck deep within him, and Paul needed to find his way to let them go.

They needed to be exorcised instead of suppressed and hushed with alcohol or drugs.

When something pushed his emotional triggers, Paul had to face his feelings head-on instead of drowning them in cheap alcohol. By becoming sober, he had effectively given up both his best friend and worst enemy, but drinking had always been his 'go to' to take the edge off, to feel normal, and he missed that friend dearly at times.

The fact was that he couldn't drink now. If he did, he would become seriously ill. His liver simply wasn't up to being punished with toxic alcohol and cheap fatty foods, especially as he was nudging fifty. Neither of Paul's parents had made it past their early fifties due to health conditions. That in itself should have been enough to encourage him to live a healthy lifestyle, but then amid any kind of addiction, the devil within couldn't care less about such things.

Paul picked up his guitar again from time to time and started to play. He didn't always feel like it and would often have to push himself to, but he was reminded of how much he loved to write music and play when he did. Creativity is often snuffed out by mental illness. When the fire in your belly is all but embers, it's hard to summon the enthusiasm to tap into your creativity.

Glimmers of the man I loved so dearly were returning. Occasionally he would ring the doorbell, and by the time I got to the front door, he would be long gone, but a little bouquet of flowers from the local supermarket sat outside the door. He would buy me simple, practical gifts from time to time, but they were always thoughtful, and it warmed me knowing under all that chaos, hurt and pain was *my* Paul; he still held me in his thoughts.

Paul tried five different antidepressants over eighteen months, and the side effects of each outweighed the benefits. Some people do not respond favourably to antidepressants, and Paul was one of those people. They had given him unbearable insomnia and caused substantial weight gain. The doctor prescribed sleeping tablets, and even they didn't combat his inability to sleep. The lack of sleep exacerbated his anxiety. It was a vicious cycle.

Paul continued to try different antidepressants, but nothing appeared to help lift his mood and he reached another low point. Episodes of drinking and dreadful self-harm resumed. His legs and arms were often scratched and cut by whatever sharp object he could find at the time. Paul experienced days where suicidal thoughts would taunt him too. It was an extremely worrying time for me, despite our separation.

Paul was physically struggling with repetitive painful outbreaks of gout that left him unable to walk or even put on footwear at times. There he was at forty-nine, feeling useless, overweight and unemployed. He was separated from me and estranged from any kind of normal life due to the soul-destroying regime of ongoing lockdowns. He was sitting in a single room of a budget hotel. All things considered, it's no wonder he struggled.

I never gave up on Paul and I never stopped loving him. At times I hated him, or rather his reckless behaviour, but I'd fallen in love with a kind and gentle, loving soul and I never lost sight of that, though at times it was very hard.

In June 2021, after many months of waiting, Paul was seen by a psychiatrist for an assessment. I sat beside him during his appointment, and it was painful to learn the truth behind his years of crippling anxiety, both at work and home; the brain fog, the internal chaos, his feelings of unworthiness and self-loathing that he had been quietly carrying, yet publicly trying to drown.

After some stringent testing, the psychiatrist diagnosed Paul with inattentive attention deficit disorder (ADD) and advised that it was on the severe scale. It had clearly been having a devastating impact on all aspects of his life for many years. The diagnosis went somewhere towards explaining the years of chaotic behaviour and constant path of self-destruction Paul had walked. It also explained why anti-depressants had not really helped him – it was the wrong type of medication.

I felt both sad and relieved at the diagnosis, especially for Paul, as the psychiatrist said that the right medication could reduce up to 90% of his symptoms. Paul had always suspected he may have ADD and I'm disappointed it wasn't investigated earlier by his doctor when Paul enquired – it may have spared us both a lot of heartache.

It would be a further six months before Paul could be seen for the medication referral; the waiting lists had been exasperated by over a year of lockdowns. Despite the wait, it gave us both hope that there was light at the end of his long and dysfunctional tunnel.

Paul began exercising and as he improved his physical fitness and lost weight, his confidence grew; he held more hope for a brighter future. Paul could start to face people; more importantly, he could face himself in the mirror once more. And little by little, the pieces of this broken man started to come back together again.

As the lockdowns finally ended and we headed into summer, Jack continued to challenge his rituals with the little fire he had, and very gradually, things improved. With the small steps forward, though, there were also giant leaps backwards, but we had no option to move forward, one day at a time.

That late May bank holiday, Jack happened to catch sight of raw bacon in the fridge whilst I was cooking, and he realised I had handled it. Instantly his OCD exploded, and he bolted to the lounge, cowering by the window in fear of food poisoning from just *seeing* the bacon. It took thirty-four handwashes and two bleaching episodes of the door handles just to allow me back into my room or anywhere near him. It was this simple incident that would stop him eating any homecooked food again. But it was also the incident that forced me to finally step back from my son's mental illness.

In between those moments were spontaneous little moments of joy that cheered us both up. One night, as Jack had his regular takeaway from a local burger bar, the brown bag it came in was sitting on the floor in my room. Jack hopped up and started playing football with one of Billy's stuffed toys. My room became the pitch, I became the makeshift goalkeeper, and the brown bag became his goal. For twenty minutes, we played football and when he scored a goal with the toy landing in the bag, oh how we roared and clapped and celebrated loudly in fits of laughter. We started to create more and more of these small, uncomplicated moments of joy, giving us space and time to simply be mother and son again.

Anxiety, emetophobia and the arrival of OCD in Jack's life –and the subsequent lack of adequate treatment, along with my enabling – had created a huge and insurmountable wall around his entire existence. With Abby's guidance and support, all I could hope for was that Jack would start to chip away at the mortar that held that wall up. Brick by brick. Piece by piece.

RECONNECTING WITH LIFE

JULY-AUGUST 2021

DURING THE FIRST couple of years of this journey, I isolated myself from everyone, family, friends and work colleagues; I didn't see my family for almost four years. In fact, they still don't know the extent of what I have been going through and never will, unless they pick up a copy of this book one day.

When we were all forced into isolation through lockdowns, it reenforced my desire to hide away. I loved the isolation Covid afforded me, as I lacked the energy or space in my chaotic head, to divulge the sordid details of my life with anyone up until that point. The lockdowns allowed me to take my foot off the brake of life. At times it seemed easier to open up to my friends – I feared their judgment less for some reason – and connecting with my friends digitally became one of the highlights of my day. We were separated both by lockdown restrictions and great distance as my friends were scattered from Australia to Rugby, Devon and beyond. Some days we would chat non-stop, but on others it was just a simple, "Hello, thinking of you." But the reconnection always lifted us.

I made an effort to contact my family once more, and even though we were separated by the Irish Sea, we spoke regularly. I didn't tell my mother about my separation from Paul for fifteen months. Without going into any detail, I kept the narrative to the current story. It was lovely to let my family back into my life, having pushed them away for so long out of needless embarrassment and shame.

One day, quite out of the blue, I received a message from Steve Gunn. He could tell from our conversation that I'd lost my way and needed a little direction to get back on track. Steve agreed to work with me once more, so I spent the next few weeks having Skype sessions with him, working again with the principles of *Ptsen Nhui*. Steve encouraged me to see the effect my imbalance was having on the ones closest to me and reminded me it was not my role to rescue or fix anyone. My sole job was to work daily on restoring and maintaining my own balance in life.

I don't have a garden myself to escape to, so I would make a point of walking every day to find space from the claustrophobic walls of my flat. On those walks, I started to notice the colourful flowers in full bloom again and would stop and, quite literally, smell the roses, breathing deeply and smiling at the faint scent. It reminded me of my childhood, creating perfumes in my garden.

I'm fortunate to live within walking distance of a beach, something I'd overlooked during my darkest days. I started to walk to the beach daily. I'd stand at the cliff top and look out to sea, watching the birds ride the wind currents above me and watch the occasional boat pass by.

Sometimes, I'd close my eyes and listen to the waves below rolling in and out across the sand. I'd observe the wind blustering around my body, and if it were raining, I'd welcome the drops landing on my face. I was reminded of

Jack and his wonderment, that night we had walked in the storm.

I'd hear the faint sounds of children below and watch them running to the water's edge, playfully shrieking as they darted to escape the waves. I'd watch the dogs running and barking, chasing the waves and digging in the sand. Young children and dogs are the perfect teachers of how to enjoy the simple art of just *being* in the moment.

Sadly, it is all too common for someone to stop loving themselves in the process of loving others, especially women. It's something we often slip into over a period of time without realising. I overlooked myself, for years in fact, until I no longer knew what my own interests were.

During recent years, I'd gradually de-prioritised myself to the back of the family queue in a form of misplaced self-sacrifice, becoming self-critical about everything: my looks, my self-worth, my usefulness in society, even questioning my own purpose in life. It is a very destructive path to walk, and it is one I have trodden solidly for three years.

The time had come for that to change. I decided to make myself a top priority again. It's such a simple idea in theory, yet difficult to apply when you have thrown yourself to the bottom of the family pile for so long. It took some getting used to – deliberately setting aside time just for myself, but the rewards for doing so were priceless.

I had started walking every day during the lockdowns, forced to do so because the sanctuary of the swimming pool had been taken away from me, but I continued. Setting myself small personal goals with a step counter on my phone, I began gradually and built up slowly, and as I did, my stamina improved.

I took out a subscription at a local coffee chain and introduced myself to the world of caffeine. It's hardly sex, drugs and rock and roll to drink coffee for the first time at forty-eight years old, but to be honest, it took some time to acquire the taste for it. The first time I tried it, I winced at the bitterness and managed just a quarter of a cup. But eventually, I ended up loving every frothy moment. I'd sit on a bench in the town centre every single morning – me and Billy watching the world go by – spooning great mounds of sweet, chocolate-dusted froth from my cappuccino. With my hot coffee in my hands, I would watch the post-lockdown soap opera unfold in front of me; there was always something to see. It was unadulterated me-time, and it was simply perfect.

I would give notice to the boys that I was taking a bath, which actually meant 'this is *my* time, do not disturb me'. I'd lock the door, light some candles, throw in some bubbles and jump in the most enormous, bubbliest bath you could imagine and soak to my heart's content with no interruptions. Sometimes I'd be there for two heavenly long hours, constantly topping up the warm water until my toes shrivelled like wrinkled prunes.

I'd gingerly rest my phone on the side of the bath and watch a film or documentary. I'd occasionally put on a face mask, and now and then, I'd really push the boat out and shave my legs. Oh boy, I was definitely back in the land of the living when I had the time – and inclination – to shave my legs again!

I returned to moisturising my face twice a day, instead of once in a blue moon. I paid attention to my appearance and even put on makeup again. I ditched the ripped black rags I'd been hiding in and put on my colourful clothes once more.

I'd had at most, five haircuts in three years, but when the hairdressers re-opened following the final lockdown, I had my hair cut, and coloured away the greys, revelling in the unadulterated self-care that I'd denied myself for so long.

It felt both luxurious and comforting for someone to sit me down, wash my hair and brush it for me; someone to take care of me. My hairdresser recently confessed she would purposefully take her time on my hair in order to offer me some much-needed respite and indulge my newly rekindled self-love.

I was surrounded by love and kindness, from my community, friends, work colleagues, neighbours and family, although I'd not allowed anyone to gift that love to me for a long time.

But those days were gone.

I had been able to return to work, albeit on a laptop on my kitchen bench at home. My entire office had moved to home-based work during the first lockdown and has remained that way ever since.

I liked this new normal. Working from home was ideal, as it allowed me to work around caring for Jack full-time. I could sit in my casuals, hair piled on my head, snacks to my left and Billy snoring away in his bed to my right, working away on my laptop and *still* get paid.

More importantly, though, I had returned to something I adore – customer service – and was able to reconnect online to the team whom I loved working with.

During my work hours, I was Emily again – a worker, a respected, conscientious member of a team, offering value and being capable of something other than rescuing people.

All the mental chaos stopped for those few hours. It gave me back a sense of normality.

I'd taken fourteen months of sick leave from work. My bosses had been incredible and supported me throughout. They are two extraordinary women, who just wanted to help me in whatever way they could and keeping my job open was their way. I was, and will always remain grateful, for their compassionate support throughout some of the bleakest years I have experienced.

When the government lifted the final lockdown restrictions in July and the local hotel pool re-opened, I returned to swimming a couple of times a week. I was back to being Mother Mermaid, diving down into the silence. How I'd missed it.

I did not hide my figure this time or cover myself up in embarrassment. I'd accepted this was me, forty-nine years old and actively taking steps to improve my health.

The Weighing Scales of Woe have since been packed away and I have referred myself back to the eating-disorder clinic. It is time for me to get a little support now too.

I have a body full of a warrior woman's scars; memorable reminders of motherhood and a face full of gentle wrinkles to match; one for every frown and two for every fit of laughter.

When I stand in front of that mirror now, I speak softly, and with love and admiration to the woman I see standing before me. I no longer tell her she's weak and useless. I no longer tell her she's overweight and worn. Instead, I remind her how tough things have been for her, and to go easy on herself for seeking comfort in food.

I tell her she is loved, that I see her strength, her bravery, and I remind her that one day soon, she will shine once more.

EPILOGUE

RELIGHTING MY FIRE

Writing this book has been my project, a valuable focal point and a massive part of my healing. There were long periods of time where I stopped writing in my journal because I wasn't sleeping due to Jack's rituals; I had no energy left to even face scribbling my thoughts down. But all the experiences were excruciatingly inscribed in my mind, it was easy to recall them, though agonising to relive them.

Everything changed when I prioritised myself and this book, leaving everyone to their own devices. Sometimes I would sit in the bath and write on my tablet. Other times, I would record thoughts on my phone as I walked the streets with Billy. I was driven by it, and nothing was going to stop me pulling together the threads of the journal and those memories of the previous year.

Writing this book gave me hope and joy. It lit the fire in my belly once more and connecting with my own creativity made that fire roar once again. It also gave me comfort knowing that one day, it could reach another person just like me who might be struggling in the way I did and give them hope and inspiration. They too may see the light at the end of an exceptionally long, dark tunnel.

Recalling the experiences gave me perspective on how far we had all travelled. I could see how my family's journeys with mental illness had risen and dipped over those few years. It showed me how I had spiralled down myself too. But it also showed me I was a fighter. Everything that life had thrown at me, I had survived.

It was truly cathartic.

My focus on this book has set a valuable example to Paul, Thomas, and Jack. I have shown all three men in my life that I can rise above the chaos and adversity I face each day and find success despite it. That is the most powerful lesson I can teach them.

And from that place of focus and balance, the people I love so dearly in my life are naturally responding.

Jack, Paul and Thomas are all slowly starting to take steps towards their own recovery and healing and thinking about their own interests, beyond their mental-health issues.

Shortly before finishing this book, CAMHS offered me an opportunity to be interviewed by a university researching the gap in services for children suffering from OCD and their parents. Parents instigated it, desperate for help that the current mental-health provisions were not equipped to provide. The medical field applied for funding to support the research and gather data, with the view to creating a new structured treatment and support plan.

I willingly agreed. It gave me a platform to speak honestly and openly about Jack's situation and how the lack of adequate resources and professional support had not only impacted our whole family, but also led to me to unwittingly becoming an OCD ally through my enabling. Someone has actually listened to me and will use our dreadful experience to create real and beneficial changes.

Knowing my contribution will lead to actual change in the mental-health services provided to families trying to cope with OCD made me realise that there *had* been a purpose to all this suffering after all. Being involved in the project filled me with a passion and drive I had not experienced for a long, long time.

I waited some time for the elusive happy ending to finish this book. I thought that if Jack was well again, Thomas more settled and Paul and I had reconciled our relationship, I would have the perfect way to wrap up our story. I desperately wanted that and craved the freedom it would give us all. I wanted to draw a line under the last few years and forget they had happened. Once everyone was fixed, life would be perfect once more.

It took four long years to realise the happy ending lay within me. A considerable part of this journey was me learning to let go. I had to stop my one-woman crusade to rescue everyone I encountered in my life, whilst also learning to love myself enough to put myself first. Through this journey, I discovered I *am* lovable and the only person who needed to love me all along, was me.

I learnt to honour the non-negotiable requirement to stay in balance myself and found out the hard way, that my balance, or lack of it, affected those closest to me. I have given myself a really tough time over these last few years, feeling both weak and ashamed – a failure –believing I've messed up at motherhood. Granted, I made mistakes, but the sad reality is that my boys are just two out of a growing number of adolescents with mental-health disorders —two statistics in a sea of hundreds of thousands, perhaps millions globally.

I now recognise that I wasn't weak after all, far from it. In fact, I was remarkably strong, a warrior, but a lost one who'd wandered too far.

I have also had to stop chasing the epitome of a perfect family life. It's not real, and I had been creating an unrealistic image of what I *thought* my life should look like. The more I held on to that ideal, the harder I fell when I couldn't attain it. Life is not one long ride through a sun-filled utopia, and anyone proclaiming it to be, is lying through their social media filters. Life *is* messy and challenging at times, but it's also wonderful and filled with much beauty.

I hid my chaotic family life from everyone around me for several years, ashamed and embarrassed by my own family's instability and dogged by my self-perceived failure. But there was absolutely nothing to be ashamed of. There was no need to cover up my family's mental illness and addiction. Or my own.

I was hiding the very things I was fighting so hard to bring light to. I'd spent the best part of three years fighting to be heard by agencies, begging for their help at times and searching for support. What purpose did it serve, shouting for help whilst hiding, ashamed and shielding my wider family and friends from the reality of mental illness?

Thanks to ongoing public campaigns supported by international celebrities, politicians, and royalty, we are much more comfortable talking about our mental health now. We have access to excellent resources, far more than we ever have. Talking about mental health has been normalised rather than stigmatised. That being said, mental illness remains largely invisible and still hidden by many. But it shouldn't be taboo; it's here, and it's real and it's affecting millions globally.

Struggling with mental illness or addiction can be very isolating and, at times, feel overwhelming. It's so important that anyone struggling in life, for whatever reason, has someone to talk to, whether that's a friend, family member or a support line and be able to access support and healing.

Now, more than ever, it's time to pull mental illness and addiction out of the shadows.

PUSHING THROUGH THE CRACKS

OCTOBER 2021

At the time of writing this afterword, Jack has been sharing my bedroom-cum-lounge for eleven long months, crippled by his OCD. He is still in my room, with brief visits to his own room but sadly, he is still spending his waking hours each day enslaved to his OCD compulsions.

Jack has been unable to eat anything that has been prepared in our kitchen and exists on the same one meal every day from a local takeaway. OCD told him our kitchen was 'contaminated' five months ago, after he spotted raw meat in the fridge.

Jack is on his fourth course of antibiotics for a finger infection that just won't clear up. Ironically, it was caused by wearing gloves twenty-four hours a day in order to protect himself from germs. OCD is *never* rational.

There is no quick fix for this disorder, unfortunately. There are no specialist OCD in-patient units in the UK for children with severe OCD, which is where he probably should be due to the severity of his illness.

Jack has now been placed on a waiting list for EMDR therapy, over two years after it was first suggested by his psychiatrist. I've no idea how long the wait will be this time, but I've been warned it will be months. So, all we can do in the meantime is muddle on, accessing regular therapy from home with Abby, and remain hopeful things will slowly improve in the future.

Jack is much calmer though, and we have forged a close relationship through surviving some desperate and dark times together. He is a fighter; he was from the moment he was conceived, and I *know* he will overcome or at the very least, learn to manage this illness in time. He has a purpose to fulfil in this life. One day, I hope Jack will realise how smart, witty, and incredibly special he really is.

He is *not* his OCD. He is Jack.

Thomas is a little happier in himself and looking forward to emerging from the lockdowns into normal life. He has joined a local gym, something he never had the confidence to do before. After a visit to a homeopathic doctor, he has started on a new medication which is showing really positive results after struggling for three years with IBS symptoms. His trip to Japan is now finally on the horizon.

Things are looking up for Thomas, at last, though he is still a gambling addict, and unfortunately, an element of that addiction may well sit with him for life. Despite his difficulties, he has been an anchor for me and helped me stay focused on a new, more peaceful horizon when I'd often lose sight of things ever improving. Thomas is a gentle, caring soul with the same big brown eyes and mop of thick curls of some twenty years ago.

Mental illness could have driven my sons apart, but it didn't. They could have easily ended up resenting each other, but instead they share an unbreakable brotherly bond that my enduring love helped to create. I am proud to call both of these young men my sons.

Paul is slowly getting his life back together, one day at a time, but he has a long way to go and remains waiting to be prescribed his new medication. I have never stopped loving him and I will continue to do so, from afar, as he heals. Paul is a kind, loving man, but his mental instability and addiction nearly tore us apart, yet love and hope held a light to the darkest corners of our marriage. We remain separated but we still take those walks together most days and are hopefully on a path to rebuilding our life together in the future.

As for me, well, I've just wrapped up writing a book, three long years in the making, with an awful lot of blood, sweat and countless tears. It has been a revelation, and akin to one long, intensive therapy session with myself. It has led me to re discover hidden fragments of my life, revelations that have now shaped me into a woman of strength. This book has taught me to love myself. It has shown me how to heal.

I am happier, more settled and getting on with my life despite the daily challenges. I have accepted that this is the way things are right now, and that acceptance has brought me peace.

My room for one at the top of my world is a haven, a peaceful sanctuary. I'm now enjoying real, uninterrupted sleep for the first time in two years, surrounded by fairy lights and all my favourite things. It's nothing fancy, it's just a storage space in the loft, but it's all mine. The Guilt Monster isn't allowed up here. I've finally sent it packing!

It has been a long and bloody battle. I have spent three years fighting on the frontline, alone, against a war with my family's mental illness and addiction and forty-something years for the penny to drop that these are not my battles after all.

I have laid down my arms and stepped back a little, giving my family the space to do their own healing. I have let the agencies bring in their troops and do their best to help my family. After all, I was never meant to crawl along, bloodying my knees, clearing their way of all obstacles, trying to protect them from life's challenges.

They each have their own path to walk, their own journey to travel in life. Part of their experience in this life is to face those challenges head on, feel fear, discomfort and pain and not run from it – or worse still, be prevented from being exposed to any of it by me.

All I have to do is walk beside them, being myself, and love them just as they are.

ABOUT THE AUTHOR

Emily J. Johnson is a mother, author and advocate for raising awareness and improving access to mental health services. Having spent fifteen years living in Western Australia, Emily returned to the UK in 2010 and now lives on the south coast of England with her two sons and Billy – the family dog.

Real and relatable, Emily continues to live and work around her family's ongoing mental illness whilst splitting her time between part-time work, full-time caring and any-time writing, whenever possible.

A REQUEST FROM THE AUTHOR

If you enjoyed *Pushing Through The Cracks*, please consider leaving a review on your chosen platform. It will help this book reach other people who need it, so that they know they're not alone.

Emily J. Johnson

Printed in Great Britain
by Amazon

77391525R00199